A consumer action guide

MODERN MEDICINE:

WHAT YOU'RE DYING TO KNOW

DR. ALAN R. LINDEMANN
with DIANE HAUGEN and PERSONAL BEST PRESS
ILLUSTRATIONS BY TRYGVE OLSON

Read this Book . . .
And Find Out What YOU Can Do
About Meaningful Health Care Reform

PROLOGUE:
OUR PRIORITIES ARE ALL SCREWED UP

Become politically active and work for health care reform that decreases the capital investment and operating costs of health care providers:

$$\frac{\text{capital investment} + \text{operating expenses}}{\text{number of patients}} = \text{cost of the day}$$

INTRODUCTION:
TAKE BACK YOUR HEALTH CARE SYSTEM

Recognize the ethical, social, and political dimensions of providing basic health care to every person.

CHAPTER 1:
BIG BUSINESS MEDICINE

Reimburse health care providers equally for given procedures, regardless of geographic area.

Everyone should be provided a certain level of basic health care. The "market" works to keep costs down only when the item for sale is something that's nice to own, not something that's a social need everyone must have.

Include in the basic health care services only those technologies considered to provide good outcomes relative to the cost.

Make public the way hospitals arrive at the cost of a day and limit the types of charges they may pass on to consumers.

CHAPTER 2:
MISMANAGED CARE

Remove medical decisions from the managed care folk and put them back in the hands of doctors.

Allow patients's doctors to make decisions about needed additional care—not those whose primary purpose is cutting costs.

Consider limiting administrators to a percent of the hands-on care staff at hospitals and clinics, or cap administrative staff expenses at a certain proportion of the salaries going to those who provide hands-on care.

Medicare's resource-based relative value scale (RBRVS) attempts to diminish payment disparity among doctors, but does not go nearly far enough.

(continued on inside back cover)

Modern Medicine: What You're Dying to Know

A Consumer Action Guide

by

Alan R. Lindemann, M.D.

with Diane Haugen

Illustrated by Trygve Olson

ARL, Inc.
Elgin, North Dakota

Modern Medicine: What You're Dying to Know:
A Consumer Action Guide

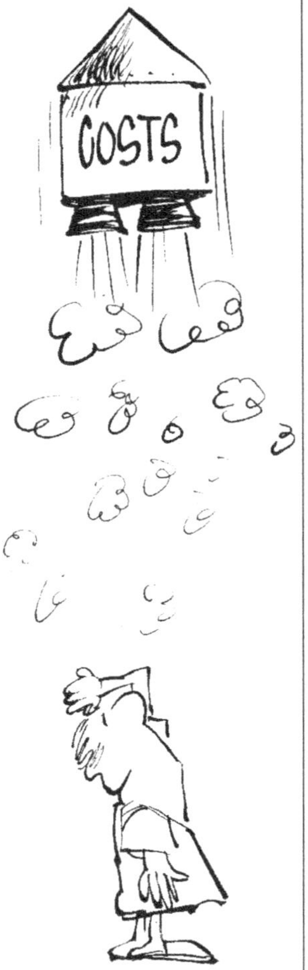

First Edition June 1992

Second Printing January 2020 by ARL, Inc.

ISBN 0-9632244-0-9

Editing, design, and layout by Diane Haugen

Illustrations by Trygve Olson.

Printed and distributed by Knight Printing
16 16th Street South
Fargo, ND 58103

Second printing published by

ARL, Inc.,
P.O. Box 52,
Elgin, ND 58533

Table of Contents

Prologue

Our Priorities Are All Screwed Up

Bulletin Boards

Action Guides

Prologue Summary

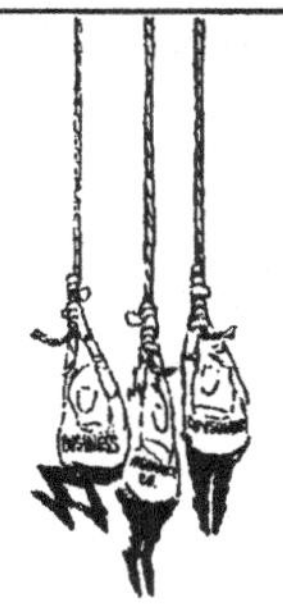

Health Becoming Separated from Care

For all the wonder, grandeur, and lifesaving technology, for all the greatness of medicine and prevention, healing, and super technology today, there is an equally great shadow—a danger that science and technology will hopelessly outstep the humanity of medicine, the caring profession. One day maybe we will cross the point of no return.

We are not there—yet.

Harry A. Wilmer
p. 22

For at least the last 10 years, the problem [*rising health care costs*] has received the attention of government and industry, which have tried a variety of ways to hold down medical costs. They have looked over the doctor's shoulder to make sure hospitalization is needed before authorizing a payment. They have set a fixed reimbursement fee for each procedure. They have instituted or increased co-payments or deductibles, so patients will feel at least some of the cost of the care they are receiving. But nothing seems to have worked.

Sarah Glazer
"The Failure to Contain Medical Costs,"
p. 511

..total spending on health care more than doubled between 1980 and 1990, rising from $230 billion to $606 billion.

Patrick G. Marshall
p. 666

Our Priorities are All Screwed Up

I've been delivering babies for over 15 years, and during that time I've seen my profession change in ways that alarm me. Some people seem disturbed that I've written a book critical of health care. I'm the first to admit that our health care today is in many ways better than ever. But I am critical of what has become the rampaging politicizing of health care. A health care system that has become so glitzy and expensive that many people simply can't afford health care at all. What I call Mercedes medicine.

The Mercedes is a fine, but expensive automobile, and it's not for everyone. Obviously, if there were only Mercedes cars available, there'd be a lot fewer automobiles on our streets. And that's what's rapidly happening in this country with health care. Normally, when consumers buy cars, they take out a loan if they haven't the cash to pay for it. The consumer then makes monthly payments to the bank. There are a lot of similarities between taking out a loan on a car you haven't the cash to pay for and purchasing health insurance. The monthly car payment becomes a monthly premium to the insurance company.

Now, if you feel the monthly payments on the Mercedes will be more than you can afford, you can buy a cheaper car. You know it's not as luxurious or as fine a machine as the Mercedes, but after all, what you need is some kind of basic transportation. We can all fantasize about a new Mercedes, but we're still enough in touch with reality to know that we are indeed fantasizing, and that's OK. We can still go out and buy a Chevy.

With health care, there are some important differences. First of all, car payments generally remain constant over the life of the loan, and the end is in sight, even if it's three or four years down the road. In contrast, health insurance premiums have the nasty habit of going up from year to year, sometimes as much as 30 or 40 percent. And they go on forever. And furthermore, with health care there are no economical alternatives. Mercedes medicine is the only game in town. This leaves consumers in a terrible bind. They've got payments they can't afford on a luxury commodity they don't need, while at the same time they have no basic health care.

What happens next? Consumers begin to complain that their insurance premiums are too high. The insurance company (comparable to the bank holding the car loan) and the hospitals (comparable to the car dealers) tell the consumer to stop using the car so much. Both blame the consumer for the high costs of health insurance premiums because they use the health care services. To make sure that consumers don't use their car more

than the banks or the hospitals think necessary, these organizations set up gatekeepers (the managed care folks, those people who have to approve your health care services before you get them) to prevent consumers from using their cars. Of course, consumers have to pay for all this gatekeeping with higher premiums, while they are told when and where they can drive their luxurious car. And as often as not, the gatekeepers will allow consumers to drive to a Taj Mahal establishment for expensive, luxurious, often unnecessary treatments, while denying consumers a short run to the grocery store for basic necessities. And through all these Machiavellian machinations, the car payments (insurance premiums) keep going up and up.

Does this make any sense? Not to me. But somehow this notion of how to run a health care system has become cast in concrete.

Another commonly suggested cure for our rising health care costs is that we stop using all this expensive technology. Again, the consumers are blamed. But let's look a little more closely at what really happens with medical technology. If carpenters want to buy a new saw, they know that if they really only need this saw two times a year, this new tool is not going to pay for itself. But if the carpenter can send the bill for the saw to consumers, regardless of how often the saw is used, there's really no reason not to buy the specialty saw—or even two or three of them. The results are the same. Consumers pay more the the carpenter's services, even if the new saw remains unused.

If consumers complain that the carpenter charges too much, the carpenter blames the customer—after all, if the carpenter doesn't have all this fancy new equipment, consumers might go to a carpenter who does. Or the carpenter chastises consumers for complaining about the expense because this new saw, after all, is the very best in the world (even if you don't need it). And the carpenter continually reminds consumers about this wonderful, miraculous equipment by advertising. And if consumers still complain, the carpenter says that some day consumers might need this fancy new saw—they might even die without it.

Clearly, the issues surrounding our use of technology are more complex than our analogy, but the similarities are compelling. Blaming technol-

ogy will not solve our problems. The crux of the problem is whether this new technology is used appropriately. Sometimes it is, and oftentimes it is not. And no group of health care providers is alone in misusing it. The lesson here is that there are no easy answers, no single-issue solutions to our health care problems.

The concept of reducing the costs of health care by creating a whole new layer of bureaucracy to take medical decisions out of the hands of doctors—to be made by people who enforce rules without any regard for the patient's individual needs—is so fundamentally wrong that it defies logic. To then blame consumers for abusing such a system is beyond comprehension.

Mad and Glad

This book has been a long time in the making. For over ten years, Dr. Lindemann has seen the need for a book like this. Those of us involved in Personal Best Press have been meeting as a group weekly for over eighteen months to research and discuss the issues, develop our ideas, and create a format that is readable yet outlines for consumers the very complex issues involved in health care reform.

Reform Needed

Health care reform is a political, social, and ethical issue. Our country has no national health care policy, although many states are now in the process of developing state agendas. Yet much of this reform activity is passing consumers by. We hear from state elected representatives that they have been voting on health care issues for years, but never get phone calls or letters from consumers. They hear only from doctors, hospitals, and other health care providers.

At a national level, many elected representatives are holding "town meetings" to discuss health care issues. While these are often well attended, such meetings can only touch the surface of the problem. These meetings often become forums in which consumers ask for help solving individual problems. This type of problem solving is valuable, but cannot substitute for policymaking or progress toward substantive reform of our health care system.

Consumers Need to Study Issues

Consumers need an explanation of how our health care system works, how it got that way, and how it can be changed. And we believe this book meets that need. How do we know? We have had over fifty people from various backgrounds read and react to the book.

As might be expected, many readers have gotten mad. One reader told us the last thing we needed was more angry consumers. Some readers told us they thought they were educated users of our health care system, but still learned a lot from the book.

Turning Anger Into Constructive Problem-Solving

Yes, many of our readers became angry. We believe they have a right to their anger. We also know that one way to diffuse anger is to work constructively toward changing the situation. Other readers, not mentioning their own anger, have commented that Dr. Lindemann seems to be so angry. Well, yes, he is angry, angry that the system often prevents him from providing the quality of care he would like to, yet at the same time holds him entirely responsible for results over which he often has little control.

Is the book one-sided? Yes. Because this is, after all, Dr. Lindemann's book. It presents his perspective, his experience. He doesn't presume to talk for other doctors. But he believes his experiences are neither unique nor unusual, and hence can help illustrate the problems with the practice of medicine almost anywhere in the United States. Dr. Lindemann demonstrates the problems with his narratives, and then discusses the issues, showing consumers how they can both use our present health care system more wisely, and at the same time work toward meaningful reform.

Personal Best Press Associates

We designed this book for readers from many different backgrounds, assuming that various readers would pick and choose from what's here, reading what caught their interest. Our pages are designed to accommodate the browser.
See page 14 for more detailed information on the the layout and design of the text.

Take hospital costs, for example. There are two major components to the cost of running a hospital: the cost of owning and maintaining the physical building (capital investment) and the cost of the people who make it possible to operate the building as a hospital (operating expenses). These costs, which remain relatively constant, are then divided up among the number of patients in the hospital to arrive at how much it costs the hospital to provide the patient a bed.

Utilization review tries to reduce hospital costs by decreasing the number of patients, (by manipulating the denominator of this equation). The high costs of the hospital day, of course, are really buried in the numerator, the capital investments and operating expenses of hospitals.

$$\frac{\textit{capital investment} + \textit{operating expenses}}{\textit{number of patients}} = \textit{cost of the day}$$

It doesn't take a rocket scientist to comprehend that the more patients there are in the hospital, the less it will cost per patient in basic overhead costs. If a hospital has 100 beds and all 100 beds are full, the cost of the day per patient will go down. If some of those beds remain empty, there are fewer people over which to spread the costs.

In U.S. hospitals, the average cost per day is much higher than in other developed countries and the average occupancy rate is about 68 percent, much lower than in these other developed countries. That means that on the average, for every 100 hospital beds, only 68 will have patients in them. The cost of a day in the hospital, then, is higher than it would be if all 100 beds were occupied. Part of the problem with the high cost of a hospital day in this country, then, is because U.S. hospitals are generally only a little more than half full. But what have we done in the past ten years to cut costs? We've tried to decrease the number of patients in the hospital. We haven't looked at the capital investments of hospitals or the kinds of decisions they make about employees.

We know the present system for delivering health care is more expensive than it needs to be and people are often not receiving the health care they need. Attempts to correct the problem haven't made much sense. And that's what this book is about. For years, I've watched obstetrical care become more glitzy, more expensive, and more irrelevant. When I've voiced my concerns from within the system, they've usually fallen on deaf ears. Let me give you an example.

Prologue Summary

Problem:

We offer consumers Mercedes medicine—or none at all.

Issue: Presently, the only way consumers can cut health care costs is to use less health care.

Action: Become politically active and work for health care reform which decreases capital investments and operating expenses of health care providers.

$$\frac{\textit{capital investment} + \textit{operating expenses}}{\textit{number of patients}} = \textit{cost of the day}$$

Hospital rooms with nurses cost about $300 a day. Rooms without nurses (motel rooms, hotel rooms, rooms at the inn) cost about $30 a day. As we practice obstetrics now, women no longer get moved from the labor room to the delivery room to the after-delivery (post-partum) room. Instead, women are put in what are now called birthing beds, beds which cost $9,500 each. These are jack-of-all-trade beds which can do everything needed during the whole birth process as well as afterwards. My question is, why not use the expensive beds for the 6 or 8 hours they are really needed, and let the new mother move to a room with a normal bed as soon as possible after delivery, a room where the nurse doesn't need to come in every hour, a room that is cheap enough that the new mother and her family can stay long enough to learn how to take care of the baby, even get rested up a bit before having to go home, a room with some privacy, possibly even room service.

When one hospital I practice in began plans for remodeling their obstetrical unit, I presented my idea to the head nurse and the marketing person. They didn't like it. I presented the idea to the hospital administrator. He didn't like it either: "Why should I charge $50 a day for a room when I can charge $300 a day."

I do not believe that meaningful, relevant, and humane change of the health care system will come from within. But I have great faith in my fellow caregivers and my patients. With some effort now, we can avoid a lot of trouble later—but time is running out.

Our priorities are all screwed up.

Alan R. Lindemann, M.D.

Our Priorities are All Screwed Up

- *We pay anywhere between $50,000 and $1 million for quadruple artery bypasses (when the patient dies, insurance companies are sometimes billed for the lifetime maximum payment of $1 million for this procedure). We'd rather do this than talk about the benefits of exercise. Benefits in not only preventing our arteries from clogging up, but in reversing the clogging once it starts.* **See Chapter 1.**

- *Our first concern used to be taking care of patients. Patient charts used to help the caregiver monitor patient progress. Now they are used by insurance companies, managed care folks, and lawyers as a weapon.* **See Chapters 2, 3, 4 and 5.**

- *Hospitals used to hire people with differing levels of skills to do various levels of jobs. Now we hire—and pay—highly trained persons and expect them to provide all levels of care. Today we often have more RNs on a floor than we used to, but fewer people actually involved in patient care. As a result, the quality of patient care sometimes goes down.* **See Chapter 4.**

- *Physicians used to be able to call a hospital and talk to the charge nurse and check on the status of all their patients in that department. Now the nurse who answers the phone is seldom the one physicians need to talk to, and physicians have to talk to several different nurses in the same department to check on patients. There is no one person responsible for knowing the status of all the patients on a given department.* **See Chapter 4.**

- *It used to be that if staff performed poorly, creating dangerous situations for patients, physicians could point out the problems and see them corrected. Now it is sometimes more important to be mannerly and not hurt anybody's feelings rather than to be overly concerned with the quality of care provided.* **See Chapters 3 and 5.**

- *It used to be that caregivers were trained for the department where they worked. For example, much of what caregivers need to know in an obstetrical department is gained from actual experience on the floor. A professional degree itself in no way guarantees that caregivers know how to handle a particular problem, know how to use their head, or have any common sense. Now, to save money, business managers keep the number of caregivers to a minimum. If caught too short of help, temporary or short-term substitutes are brought in (often at higher than regular salaries).*

Our Priorities are All Screwed Up

These caregivers may be excellent, but they may also be unfamiliar with the procedures and services in the department, seriously compromising the quality of the care. ***See Chapters 1 and 4.***

- *The health care system used to take care of the serious medical problems that may or may not have resulted from the care provided, care for which there was often no guaranteed outcome. Now we allow the lawyers to set up an adversarial relationship between the doctor and the patient, patients are seldom adequately compensated for problems when they do arise, and incompetent caregivers are free to go on about their business. The lawyers and insurance companies, however, are getting rich off other people's misery.* ***See Chapter 5.***

- *Medical care costs too much in this country. It costs too much because instead of fixing the expensive problems with our health care system, we simply year after year painfully extract a sizeable chunk of additional flesh from the consumers and employers in the form of higher health insurance premiums.* ***See Chapters 1, 3, and 6.***

- *The United States is the only country which allows drug companies to patent medications, even when the government has contributed to the research. As a result, consumers pay two, three, and more times as much for drugs in this country as in other countries. Those unfortunate enough to have rare diseases can pay $2,000 to $3,000 a dose for weekly medications.* ***See Chapter 6.***

- *We spend billions on shutting our old people away in nursing homes, tied in chairs and sedated, keeping them out of sight and out of mind. There is no money to be made in encouraging these people to exercise their minds and bodies so that they could possibly stay out of nursing homes.* ***See Chapter 1 and 6.***

- *We have allowed a sickness industry to develop in place of a health care system because big business makes its money on sickness, not wellness. So we spend billions on treating low-birth weight babies in neonatal intensive care units, when a relatively small amount of money invested in making sure that every pregnant woman in the country had access to prenatal care would prevent from 30 to 50 percent of these premature births. Not to mention dead babies. But the money, for business, is in warehousing premature babies, not preventing premature births.* ***See Chapters 1, 3, and 6.***

Introduction

Take Back Your Health Care System

Chapter Contents

Bulletin Boards

Action Guides

Introduction Summary

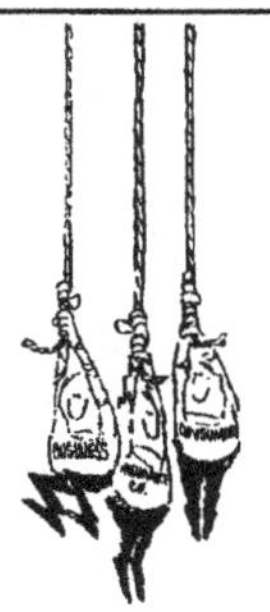

How to Use This Book

Organizing the material for a book on a topic as complex as health care issues presented us with some real challenges. How could we present the information in terms that consumers could understand without simplifying the problems too much? Yet we wanted to provide the kinds of supporting material that would give substance to our discussion without the book looking like a term paper. At the same time, we felt that Dr. Lindemann's narratives were critical to illustrating the problems we were talking about.

We found we had several types of materials to deal with:

- supporting materials,
- suggested actions consumers can take,
- Dr. Lindemann's narratives,
- our discussion of the issues, and
- definitions.

We created a left hand page with a border for the supporting materials and consumer action pages (occasionally these bordered pages will also appear as a two-page spread). We identify the supporting materials pages with a note tacked to a bulletin board. For the most part these bulletin board pages contain direct quotations with the sources clearly identified and complete bibliographic entries listed in the references at the back of the book. In a few instances, the bulletin board material is adapted, or a summary of information from Personal Best Press Associates. Adapted material is clearly labeled as such.

We also use these bordered, left-hand pages for a second type of information—guidelines and steps consumers can take to help solve problems and get needed information. We call these action guides and identify them with the "what you can do" icon.

In Dr. Lindemann's narratives, he is talking directly to readers. He uses the pronoun I and the text is italicized. We put the narratives first in the chapter, followed by the discussion of the topic. In the discussions, we use the pronoun we, meaning Personal Best Press Associates, and the text in normal type.

The narratives and discussions always appear on the right hand page unless there are no bulletin board or actions pages. In these cases, the narratives and discussions are two page spreads. At the end of the discussion sections, we have included a summary of the main ideas in each chapter.

In a book like this, there are often words that need to be defined. These are boxed under an icon of a person searching through a dictionary.

To help readers keep all these varying types of information clear in their minds, we have provided a table of contents for each chapter, clearly labeling the bulletin boards, the action guides, the narratives, the discussions, and summary pages.

Personal Best Press Associates

We had expected our readers to browse through our book, reading what interested them and skipping the rest. We've found more readers than we expected have been reading *all* of the book. They noticed that some of the drawings appear more than once. In working with this material, we found that the drawings often became icons for particular types of problems, so we repeated some of them.

Our Priorities Are All Screwed Up

Many people have written books on what's wrong with health care, but the costs keep going up, and in our opinion, not only the personal attention, but also at times the actual quality of the care itself, keeps going down and down.

Other Health Care Books, Other Audiences

Our book is designed specifically for consumers. Most are not. Occasionally, policy analysts and doctors write books to inform the public about health care, but these sometimes read more like research reports or public policy statements than consumer publications. Alain E. Enthoven's *Health Plan* or Joseph Caliafano's *American's Health Care Revolution: Who Lives? Who Dies? Who Pays?* are good examples.

In other books and articles, professional organizations representing various health care interests such as the American Medical Association (AMA), the American Hospital Association (AHA), and the Health Insurance Association of America (HIAA) also discuss health care and gather and distribute data. The HIAA publishes yearly data on nationwide vital statistics such as infant and maternal mortality rates, the average length of hospital stays in various states, and the average costs of certain hospital procedures. The consumer often does not see this data unless certain statistics catch the eye of journalists with popular magazines or newspapers.

A few books have actually been written to help the consumer make knowledgeable health care decisions. The most well-known is probably *The New Our Bodies, Ourselves* written by the Boston Women's Health Book Collective. Books such as these provide information consumers need to ask intelligent questions and to participate with their caregivers in decisions about their health. We believe consumers need more books like this.

Our Book

In our book, we have noted five problems that are the major contributers to our health care cost increases in the last 30 years. We have devoted a chapter to each of these five topics:

- big business,
- managed care,
- insurance,
- the nursing shortage, and
- liability.

Special Interest Group Politics

Investors in the lucrative 1988 savings and loan [S&L] rescues that were subsidized by the government contributed $2.8 million to presidential and congressional candidates while the deals were being made, according to a study released yesterday....

The 1988 S&L rescue agreements, arranged by the now-defunct Federal Home Loan Bank Board, involved the sale of 220 failed thrifts to 96 investors and financial institutions during that year.

Bush received the largest amount of money, followed closely by Sen. Lloyd Bentsen (D-Tex.), who was chairman of the Senate Finance Committee and a candidate for vice president at the time.

Among the big givers were Barnett Banks of Florida and Georgia, which gave out $377,000; Citicorp, which gave away $401,223; and Ford Motor Co., owner of First Nationwide Financial Corp., which gave $202,458.

"Call it cultural or tradition, [Barnett] really believes in being active politically," said the bank company's chief lobbyist, Marty Farmer." What do we get? I say access."

Susan Schmidt
p. C1, C4

Lobbyists in Minnesota spent a record $4.4 million over the last year to influence lawmakers and other government officials....

The increase shows how well-heeled special interests are gaining presence and influence in government, says Minnesota Common Cause, a watchdog group.

"Money is becoming the primary moving force behind politics in this state," said Common Cause president Jim Ketcham. "Everybody wants to get a piece of the action, and you buy your way in if you've got the money to do it...."

AP, Minneapolis
"Lobbyists in Minn....,"
p. D1

Chapter 1 discusses the problems we are having because we have allowed our health care system, something people need, to be run as if health care were something people had a choice about buying. The provision of health care does not operate according to the classical principles of the economic marketplace.

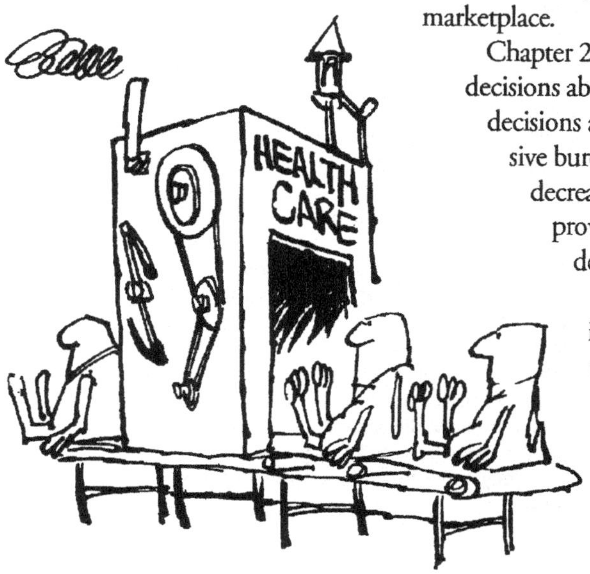

Chapter 2 discusses misguided efforts to manage care by taking decisions about care out of the hands of doctors. Instead, medical decisions are put into the hands of a whole new bevy of expensive bureaucrats. This not only increases costs, but also decreases the quality of patient care because those people providing the hands-on care are replaced by decisionmakers who never see the patient.

Chapter 3 discusses how we have used the insurance industry to ration care, often excluding those who most need it. This denies basic, preventive care to a large group of people who will simply develop more serious, expensive health care problems in the future.

Chapter 4 discusses how the operation of hospitals according to standard business principles requires nurses to take over the duties of aides, orderlies, and ward clerks. The catch word for this practice is primary care nursing. Because nurses working under this system have to provide all kinds of ancillary services once provided by less trained personnel, nurses have less time for nursing tasks and there are fewer people actually providing hands-on care to patients. Many people consider this an abuse of nurses. There are more nurses in hospitals, but there are far fewer employees providing patients with actual hands-on care. The quality of patient care can easily deteriorate under these circumstances. Hospital management, by reorganizing the nursing hierarchy to reduce the numbers of employees, has created what is largely an artificial shortage in nurses.

Chapter 5 discusses how malpractice suits have failed to provide just or fair compensation to victims. Moreover, liability suits fail to prevent harmful health care providers from continuing to practice as usual. Nor does peer

Congressional Paralysis

"Do I think left alone the Congress of the United States is capable of passing a single-payout, Canadian-style national health-care plan which will guarantee health care to all people?" he [Rep. Bernard Sanders, VT] asks. "I think not. I don't think there is the political will and courage in this body to stand up to the insurance companies, the drug companies, the AMA"....

I don't have high hopes that this institution as presently constituted is capable of addressing the real issues. I am in the awkward position of saying publicly that I think we need a lot of new blood in this place, that there are hundreds of members of this body who are not effectively representing working people, elderly people and poor people."....

I want to force this Congress to deal with issues that it otherwise would not want to deal with," he says. "If I can force the debate forward, the debate the American people want to hear, the debate Congress often ignores, then I would have done some important work here."

Lois Romano
p. D1

Instead of statesmanship and enlightenment, Congress has adopted as its hallmarks partisan gridlock and special-interest pandering...

Highway funding is another victim of partisanship and the power of lobbyists. A bill that would restructure highway funding is running into trouble because powerful special interests—the trucking industry, road builders and mass transit advocates—are putting the pressure on Congress. If history is any guide, Congress will cave in to the lobbyists and a meaningful highway bill will be lost.

There are no surprises in all this. The pattern is familiar. Congress—the institution—gets low marks from the public. Meanwhile, individual senators and representatives return to their home states, get high marks, and somehow, distance themselves from the depressing silliness in Congress.

They have raised the flimflam to an art form.

Editorial, The Forum
"Flim Flam is Raised to an Art Form,"
p. A4

review by state medical boards correct these problems. Malpractice litigation fails miserably in providing what is really needed—a quick, efficient way to spot harmful practices, take care of the people who need it, and monitor progress in correcting possibly dangerous situations.

Chapter 6 discusses what consumers can do, in view of the problems with our system, to bring about needed change.

Most approaches to solve our health care problems do not reduce the costs of the health care, they simply ration it by raising prices or reducing availability. Sometimes these approaches appear to work for a while, but soon some other factor is out of control, and the cost of our health care continues to spiral upward. For example, the medicare prospective payment system, a form of managed care, encourages hospitals to discharge patients sooner rather than later by paying a fixed fee for a given procedure, such as an appendectomy or hernia repair. The sooner the patient is discharged, the less of the fixed payment for caring for the patient the hospital actually has to spend providing services to the patient. This approach has significantly reduced patient length of stay in hospitals. On the surface, avoiding spending even one additional day in a hospital, which can cost hundreds of dollars, is an obvious saving. But hospitals and insurance companies have hired so many additional people to manage the care—people who do not actually provide any care to the patient—that consumers have seen no reduction in costs. In fact, they've seen just the opposite.

There are those who say that prospective payment has at least kept medical costs from rising faster than they would have without such a system, but this is merely an attempt to change the subject. Prospective payment leaves totally unaddressed the real problems which drive up the cost of our health care. One of this country's major, major problems is that the cost of a hospital day in the United States is outrageously high—much higher than in any other developed country. Trying to control the length of hospital stay with prospective payment or some other method of decreasing the amount of time spent in the hospital has merely encouraged hospitals to sweep patients out the door before they are ready, in many cases seriously compromising the quality of the care they do receive. The United States has shorter average hospital stays than any other developed country, yet the average cost of hospital care for given conditions is significantly higher here than in other countries.

prospective payment: an advance of payment for health care charges

adapted from HIAA *Source Book 1990*, p. 121

How to Find Your Legislators

If you do not know who your state and national elected representatives are, you need to find out who they are. If you need to locate this information, you can

- often find them listed in the govern ment section of your telephone book,
- ask at your city or county courthouse,
- ask your local League or Woman Voters organization
- check your telephone book for your local Democratic or Republican political parties, or
- check with your local chapter of the Association for the Advancement of Retired People (AARP).

Once you find out who your state and national elected representatives are, contact their offices and ask what they are doing about health care issues.

Most national representatives have specific persons assigned to different issues. Ask your elected representatives which of their staff specializes in health care issues. Keep in touch with these persons and let them know what you think about the various reform measures being voted on.

Perhaps your elected representatives send newsletters to their constituents. Ask to be put on mailing lists. We have talked to elected representatives at the state level who say they've been voting on health care issues for years and have never heard from individual consumers.

Sometimes states, when the legislature is in session, maintain toll-free telephone lines for constituents. Once you have located your elected representatives, ask them if this service is available in your state. Some states, when their legislatures are in session, publish newsletters to report on governmental happenings. If publications like these are available, ask to be put on these mailing lists.

Health care reform is a political issue, and consumers need to become politically active if they are to have any effect on the reform which comes out of the legislative process.

The lesson learned here? Single-issue approaches to the problem of this country's skyrocketing high health care costs do not work. Any improvements in bringing down health care costs will require our understanding and addressing the whole array of problems contributing to this increasingly intolerable situation.

Take Back Your Health Care System

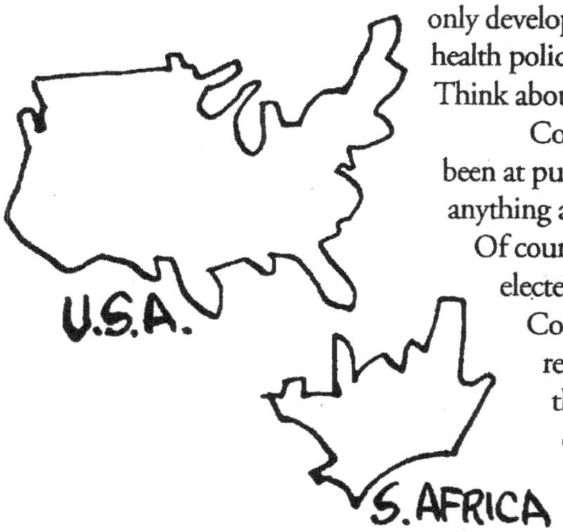

Basic, quality health care is a social need. The United States is the only developed country besides South Africa that does not have a national health policy ensuring all citizens equal access to health care (Rich, p. A17). Think about that.

Consumers need to take back their health care system. We have been at public meetings where elected representatives claim they can't do anything about the rising cost of health care—it's not their department. Of course, this simply isn't true, and consumers need to hold their elected representatives responsible for this kind of evasive behavior. Consumers need to start asking hard questions of their elected representatives, their hospital boards, their insurance companies, their state insurance commissioners, and their state health departments.

What we can do—and this is the key to solving the health care crisis—is recognize that health care is a big business subject to the problems of corporate management, including corporate greed as well as corporate philanthropy.

Health care is a social service, one society has a vested interest in and one that should be provided at a basic level to each and every one of our citizens. Yet policymakers and legislators insist on treating the provision of health care as if it were some sort of optional manufactured household item like a washing machine. And because health care is a social issue, it has become politicized, subject to the whims of a government which allows itself to make decisions based on the lobbying efforts of special interests—often those with the money to pay for the support of their views.

Professional organizations such as the American Medical Association (AMA), the American Hospital Association (AHA), and Health Insurance Association of American (HIAA) are sensitive to criticism of their vested interests. We have rarely seen the American Medical Association, for example, mention the Canadian health

Introduction Summary

PROBLEM:

Consumers are forced to purchase health care as if it were an optional luxury — rather than the necessity it is.

Issue: Basic health care is a social need of every one of our citizens—not something they can do without if they don't have the money.

Action: Recognize the ethical, social, and political dimensions of providing basic health care to every person.

care system in anything but critical terms. In fact, whenever the Canadian system is mentioned, it is usually carefully pointed out that it is a socialistic system, as if that is enough to put it out of mind. Yet the Canadian health care system, at considerably less cost than ours, provides basic health care for every single citizen, while our system leaves over 35 million people with no insurance, and hence, for all practical purposes, with no health care.

We urge consumers to learn about the issues and let their elected representatives know what they, the consumers, want to see in health care reform. Only then will consumer interests be represented. It is no exaggeration to say that the very life of each and every consumer depends upon active consumer involvement in bringing about responsible health care reform.

Chapter 1

Big Business Medicine

Chapter Contents

Narratives

Discussion:

BIG BUSINESS GREED

Chapter 1 Summary

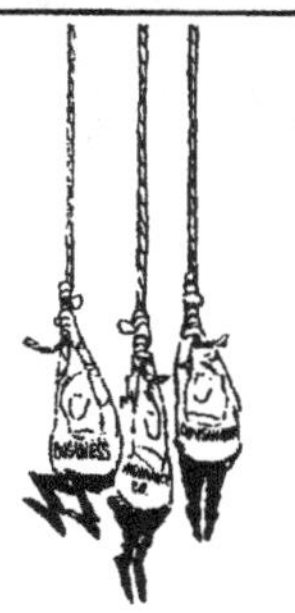

Bulletin Boards

Action Guides

Health Care as Hamburger

"Competition," explains Virginia Hunt, vice president of Shands Hospital in Gainesville, Fla. "requires that people be aggressive. The fact of life is that health care is an industry—like the steel industry and the hamburger industry."

John A. Burns
p. 544.

In 1983, Denver's Presbyterian St. Luke's Hospital had virtually no advertising budget. The next year, it spent $500,000 and the year after that more than $1 million on advertising...

Reacting to Medicare's new prospective payment system and the squeeze it has put on hospital charges. Republic Health Corp. pinpointed surgical procedures that can be "done quickly—often in a few hours, without lots of nurses, tests, meals or general care," and began marketing them to the public "the way hotels offer cut-rate weekends."

John A. Burns
p. 544

The goal of the corporations, then, is to make health care just another consumable service that they provide for a profit.

Stanley Wohl
p. 95

The term *nonprofit*, it should be emphasized, is used very loosely by hospitals, as it is by cemeteries and other profiteering enterprises. The nonprofit organizations that operate the hospitals provide a respectable facade behind which speculators can siphon off enormous profits by controlling such money-making aspects as pharmacies and gift shops

Ruth Mulvey Harmer
pp.136-137

Sorry, Doctor, But It's Too Expensive

In the laparoscopy surgery I often perform, I need to punch a small hole in the abdominal wall and then create an air space inside my patient so I can see what I am looking for. The device for creating the hole is called a trocar, and they come in two forms: reusable or disposable.

While I am not a great proponent of throwaway tools, I find that the disposable trocars have a feature that the reusable ones do not: they have a special protective device which prevents me from cutting too deeply into the abdominal cavity and possibly perforating my patient's bowel in the process. And the nice thing about disposable trocars is that they are always sharp, while the reusable ones often are not. Because these reusable trocars vary widely in sharpness, the surgeons using them are never sure just how much pressure they are going to have to put on the device to make the incision. This may seem like a small concern, but when doctors use an instrument often and never find any two with the same sharpness, they are exposing themselves and their patients to just one more needless variable.

Seven years ago I asked one of the hospitals I operated in to get disposable trocars. The cost, I believe, was about $50. Not a bad price considering the extra protection my patients would receive. I was informed by the hospital central supply that I could not have the disposable trocars because they were too expensive.

Six years ago, I asked for them. We could not get them.

Five years ago, I asked for them. We could not get them.

Four years ago, I asked for them. We could not get them.

Three years ago, I asked for them. We could not get them.

Two years ago, I asked. A year ago, I asked. I had to learn to work with dull instruments, and assume the responsibility of the added risk of working

ter·mi·nol·o·gy

laparoscopy: abdominal exploration by means of a specialized optical system inserted through a tube into a small incision.
adapted from *Taber*, p. L-11

trocar: a sharply pointed surgical instrument enclosed inside a metal tube.
adapted from *Taber*, T-17

insufflate: blow into.
Taber, p. I-33

Are We Beyond Caring?

By most reckoning, the corporate push into medicine was not so much different from what was happening in many other fields in this country in the late 1960s and 1970s. Mom and Pop stores, cottage industries, family farms, and small businesses found themselves facing off against the juggernaut of investment capital, and coming off second best. Fields such as agriculture, horse-farming, book publishing, and entertainment began to fall at this time, more or less under corporate sway.

Stanley Wohl
pp. 48

The economic evolution of health care removes the physician further and further away from the patient's life. What had formerly been a private relationship between two individuals has been reshaped into a major industry, involving some fifty medical specialties and subspecialties and more than seventy ancillary technical occupations. As a result, the physician knows less and less about the patient's life. Yet conditions in the home, job, and community are often extremely important determinants of someone's illness.

Richard Kunnes
p. 88-89

For all the wonder, grandeur, and lifesaving technology, for all the greatness of medicine and prevention, healing, and super technology today, there is an equally great shadow—a danger that science and technology will hopelessly outstep the humanity of medicine, the caring profession. One day maybe we will cross the point of no return.

We are not there—yet.

Harry A. Wilmer
p. 22

with what I considered to be less than optimal equipment. The hospitals, mind you, are not liable if I misjudge how hard I have to push on these variously sharpened trocars to make the incisions, and I had trocars with no protectivetive shields to prevent accidents. The hospital controls the quality of even the simplest of tools I must work with. A central supply or an operating room nurse, trained in how to save a penny here and a penny there makes the decisions as to whether we doctors have the disposable trocars we need—not the doctors who bear the responsibility for doing the work.

Imagine my surprise, then, when not long ago one of the operating room nurses asked me "How would you like a disposable Verres needle?"

"Oh, that sounds fine."

"We can get disposable trocars too."

"Well, it's kind of interesting you're asking me this because I've been asking for them for seven years. Why can I get them now?"

"Well, they weren't available."

"They were too available."

"Well, I didn't know about them."

What had happened to change the hospital policy? I found out the surgeons had asked for disposable trocars. They cost $80 each now, but they're no longer too expensive, it seems, as long as the right doctors request them.

An MRI in Every Back Yard . . .

In the United States, there are 1200 hospitals equipped with MRIs.; in Canada, 12. It can be argued that the United States has a population of 250 million people, and Canada 25 million people. The U.S. is serving ten times the population that Canada is with its 1200 MRI machines.

However, even if you multiply Canada's 12 machines by 10, to make the populations served by the MRI machines in both countries comparable, you are still left with 1200 U.S. machines compared to 120 in Canada.

Summarized from News Clips
"Misleading Statistics,"
p. 449

Means Big Profits

The most efficient and profitable form of industrial or medical practice appears to be the assembly line. It is in this setting where a maximum degree of technology can be applied in the shortest period of time, truly creating an illness industry.

Richard Kunnes
p. 73

The market will put technologies out there that produce the most profit. They may not be the ones that produce the most health. Sometimes those two are the same, but often they're not.

Richard Scheffler in
Patrick G. Marshall,
p. 673

An estimated 30 to 40 percent of health care cost increases are a result of new technological advances and increased use of old technology.

Richard B. Tompkins
"Evaluating Technology's True Value,"
p. 41

According to the Institute of Medicine, "perhaps one-quarter to one-third of medical services may be of little or no benefit to patients."

Patrick G. Marshall
p. 670

Overdosing on Technology

The husband of one of my patients has no high school diploma and no GED diploma, because he believes he cannot do the required math. He works irregularly at various minimum-wage jobs and hence has no opportunity to enroll in any health insurance program. His wife, my patient, also works for minimum wage as a cashier in a convenience store which offers their employees no health insurance benefits (often the case with minimum wage, part-time jobs). Since she has a progressive, hereditary degenerative disease of the connective tissue, she would have difficulty getting health insurance under any circumstances. She and her husband make too much money to be eligible for medicaid, and even if her state offers high-risk health insurance for people ineligible for regular insurance, she could not afford it. This couple is typical of the over 35 million people in this country that have no health insurance.

Since they have no regular doctor and no insurance, like many people in their situation, they rely upon the emergency room for their medical care, and resort to it only when they cannot avoid the problem any longer. Not long ago, the husband had severe abdominal pain and went to the emergency room. He was sent home and told to take Mylanta. Two days later he returned to the emergency room with the same complaint, and was again sent home and told to take Mylanta.

Finally, on the third visit, he was referred to a surgeon. The surgeon perfomed two CAT scans at a cost of $612 each (we find ourselves wondering why two were needed, or even one). The surgeon diagnosed this man's problem as an umbilical hernia, a fairly common and generally non-life-threatening condition. A condition that hardly requires two CAT scans to diagnose. A condition that can very simply and adequately be diagnosed with a manual examination.

This family now has a $6000 medical bill which they have little if any

ter·mi·nol·o·gy

computer-assisted tomography (CAT) scan: creating an image with X-ray techniques that blur surrounding body structures so that a selected level of tissue is highlighted.
(adapted from *Melloni's*, p. 478)

magnetic resonance imaging (MRI): the radio wave energy from a strong magnetic field is absorbed by the center of hydrogen atoms, triggering the release of light particles which can then form a photographic-like image of organs and processes inside the body.
(adapted from *Moseby's*, p. 511)

Ask Your Doctor About Technology

To take back your health care system, consumers need to develop a partnership with their doctors. That means the doctor should explain all the options to consumers and then let the consumer decide what course of action to take. Obviously, doctors will have preferred courses of action, and consumers may decide to pursue the course of action the doctor finds most appropriate.

Some doctors are not comfortable when patients ask for explanations of procedures. Some patients are not comfortable asking for explanations. Ideally, the doctor and consumer would be comfortable enough to discuss treatment options and the outlook for improvement. An informed consumer taking part in decisions about care can then assume part of the responsibility for that care.

Any time your doctor recommends testing of any sort, ask what he or she is looking for. And whether there might be some simpler, less expensive way to find out the needed information. If your doctor recommends an X-ray, ask if there is some other way to find out what information is needed. If your doctor recommends a CAT scan, ask if an X-ray will do. If your doctor recommends an MRI scan, ask what kind of information an MRI will provide that can't be found in some other manner.

If you're not satisfied with the answers you get, ask the doctor to recommend another doctor so you can get a second opinion.

The Best is Not Always Better

Before the development of the CT scan (computer-aided tomography), the lumbar X-ray was used to diagnose lower back troubles. A contrast medium (like a dye) was injected into the area around the spinal cord to make body structures more easily visible.

The CT scan was an improvement over the injected-dye routine because the computer was able to sharpen the areas of concern while deemphasizing the other areas. The CT scan was five times as expensive as the X-ray with injected dye, but it avoids any reaction to the dye which occurs in some of the patients.

CT technology is thus a replacement for dye-injected X-rays. However, it was not long before doctors were ordering a CT scan, followed by an X-ray with injected dye.

We see the same concatenation of diagnostic tools now with the magnetic resonance imaging (MRI) machines. The MRI machine, of course, is much more expensive than any of the other two diagnositc tools. And we are beginning to see physicians ordering an MRI diagnosis, piggybacked onto CT scans and dye-injected X-rays. Because insurance companies will pay for multiple diagnostic tools for a single condition, there is no incentive for the hospitals and doctors not to use these technologies even when they are not needed.

A Radiologic Technologist

hope of ever paying. A large part of that medical bill is not their fault, since the emergency room staff sent the man away without being able to diagnose his problem, but nonetheless felt free to charge him emergency room fees every time he came back. For some reason, he has also been given two CAT scans for a condition that should have been diagnosed without even a single scan.

The surgeon was probably a member of the clinic staff, and hence would be paid by the clinic regardless of whether the clinic got paid. The hospital and clinic, however, are now hounding these people to pay a bill they cannot afford. The collection office has now started calling this woman at work and harassing her about payment of her husband's bill.

What are this family's options? Well, the woman could get herself fired and go on welfare, which she is too proud and honest to do. She and her husband have no way of knowing that they were subjected to a lot of unnecessary charges by the doctor and hospital, and have no means of negotiating the bill down because of the expensive and unnecessary care they received. This family's only apparent alternative is to literally disappear, pull up stakes, and move on to another area and start over.

Consumers have the right to ask collection agencies not to contact them again. You will still get bills, and the bill in question is still your responsibility, but you do not have to put up with harassment by telephone.

About Prescriptions

1. Shop for prescriptions.

Ask several pharmacies what they charge for your medication. For example, in our area, a month's supply of birth control pills cost around $25. If you have a physical every year, the community health department will supply the same month's supply of birth control pills for $8.

You do not need to be on medical assistance to be able to obtain birth control pills from community health.

2. Ask your doctor for inexpensive forms of medications prescribed.

Generic drugs are not always comparable to brand name drugs. Ask you doctor if a generic can be safely substituted for the brand name drug.

Taste, palatability, and convenience play a large role in the cost of drugs. Doctors know that patients will more reliably take a medication twice a day than four times a day, and drug companies charge more for the convenience of fewer dosages. A large, foul tasting tablet can be considerably cheaper than a chewable or even a liquid form of the drug. When your doctor prescribes a drug, ask for the cheapest form of the medication. There may be considerable difference in cost.

3. If you are taking a medication for the first time, get only part of the prescription filled.

If your doctor prescribes a medication, ask if he or she has any samples of the drug. This allows you to try the medication to be sure you don't have an intolerance for it, an unfavorable reaction, or medication that does not help your condition.

If you cannot get samples of drugs from your physician, ask the pharmacist to give you only part of the prescription, such as half, or even a quarter of it if it is very expensive. Sometimes doctors will make the prescription out for a two or three month supply which may cost a hundred dollars or more. You could well take home this medication only to find out you cannot take it.

Pharmacists should not charge extra for giving you only part of a single prescription to try a new drug.

Changing the Leopard's Spots

Drugs come and drugs go. Pharmaceutical companies tend to spend a lot of money advertising their latest creations. However, a new drug or the newest form of an old drug may not be exactly what I need.

I have a standing request of the nurses to call me if any of my patients have a fever of over 100.5° F, indicating infection that needs attention. Depending upon the symptoms, I often order cefoxitin because it is effective against all eight varieties of bacteriodes fragilis, a common infectious agent with women who have delivered babies.

When I got the call from the nurse at 5:00 a.m. indicating one of my patients had a temperature of 102.7° F, I asked that the nurse order cefoxitin. As I made my rounds that morning at 7:00 a.m., I stopped to check on my patient. To my surprise, she had received no medication at all.

I checked with the nurse to see what had happened. I was told that the hospital pharmacy no longer stocked cefoxitin, but instead had replaced it with cefotetan, a newer drug which could be used for similar situations as cefoxitin. The pharmacy had no cefoxitin, so no medication was given my patient. More importantly, I was not informed of the problem. In the end, even though I had no say in the decision to no longer stock cefoxitin in the hospital pharmacy, and indeed was not even informed of this, someone in the hospital made the decision to not treat my patient because the medication I requested was unavailable. What is more, someone in the hospital failed to inform me of the decision to leave my patient untreated. I am the one who bears the entire responsibility—the liability, if you will—for my patient's not getting the medication she needed, even though other people made decisions beyond my control which substantially lessened the quality of care my patient received.

The next day, when I questioned the nurse about why my patient was not given the medication I requested, she explained that those responsible for operating the pharmacy had decided that cefotetan was easier to administer to patients, so would be substituted for cefoxitin. Cefoxitin must be given twice a day or more, sometimes up to four times a day. Cefotetan can be

Doctors No Longer Call the Shots

In 1890, physicians comprised 90 percent of all medical and health care workers. By 1950 they comprised only 20 percent and by 1980 they comprised only 10 percent of that population.... Medical office managers, hospital administratros, government health workers, insurance employees, claims processors, and computer programmers are all careers and professions on the rise.

Stanley Wohl
p. 78-79

In the past, the direct patient-doctor relationship constituted the fundamental element in the health care process, and a large share of the health care dollar was spent essentially for physician and surgeon services. But in recent years a growing proportion of that dollar is being eaten away by ancillary costs—hospital beds, drugs, lab tests, expensive medical equipment, etc. Of $1.00 spent on health, only $0.02 now ends up with the physician.

Stanley Wohl
p. 19

Hospital administration represented 20.2 percent of hospital costs in California in 1987-1988...Extrapolating this figure to the total U.S. hospital expenditures of $194.7 billion in 1987...yielded an estimate of 39.3 billion, or $162 per capita, consumed by hospital administration. In Canada, hospital administration cost $1.27 billion, amounting to 9 percent of total hospital expenditures of $14.14 billion..., or $50 per capita

Woolhandler et al.
p. 1254

Instead of rationalizing the entire system, we allow insurance reviewers to micromanage care and second-guess doctors and nurses. To be sure, there are inappropriate hospital admissions—but checklist reviews are an overly blunt way of restraining the cost. "The present system harasses doctors and patients alike," says Robert Restuccia, director of Health Care for All....

As Judy Feder, former director of the Pepper commission on health care, observes, insurance policies allow for payment based on "medical necessity," a judgment once left to doctors. In the brave new world of managed care, insurance reviewers practice medicine by remote control. But there is a regulatory gap in which nobody systematically reviews the reviewers. If you think your insurance company denied you necessary care, the only thing you can do is sue—and good luck. And, of course, lawsuits only add to the cost of the overall system too.

Robert Kuttner
p. A25

given only once a day, saving bags, tubing, and nurse's time. The cost of the drug per dose, I was told, is about the same.

Drugs, like computers, may not be 100 percent interchangeable. A computer billed as "IBM-compatible" may well be very much like an IBM. But the IBM compatible machine is not an IBM, and there will be times when this can cause problems because the IBM-compatible will not function exactly like an IBM 100 percent of the time. This means that there may be certain procedures, depending upon what the consumer is trying to do with the machine, where the IBM-compatible machine will not do what an IBM machine will do.

I knew from experience that my patients recovered better with cefoxitin than cefotetan. If you read the advertising literature about cefotetan, you will find it is effective against bacteroides fragilis. However, there are several varieties of this bacteria and cefotetan is not effective against all of them. If you check the literature on cefoxitin, you will find that it is effective against all eight varieties of the bacteria.

In its description of the effectiveness of cefotetan, the drug company was telling the truth, but not all of the truth. Sometimes a substitution such as this one might make no difference. However, in this particular situation I had seen the drug I specified make a difference in a number of cases, and now, without my knowledge or input in the decision, a drug I considered important to providing quality care to my patients had disappeared from the pharmacy shelves and I was not told about it. What's worse, my patient simply went untreated and I was not told.

Those running the hospital had decided to no longer stock one drug and substitute another for it because it required less of a nurse's time to administer. A decision was made, driven by the desire to keep labor costs down, which would in many cases result in a poorer quality care for my patients. I had no say in this decision, but bear all the legal responsibility for its consequences.

This is a relatively small incident, but a very good example of the kinds of decisions made for business reasons that are not necessarily in the best interest of the patients.

Median Income No Longer Rising

In... underclass America of mostly blacks, Hispanics and poor whites—millions have inadequate health insurance or none at all. Huge numbers are homeless. The bipartisan Jay Rockefeller Commission affirms that one out of five American children is brought up in poverty. For this part of America, the end of recession, when it comes, will be a statistic without meaning....

In his book, "The Work of Nations," Harvard economist Robert Reich demonstrates that the gap between managers and workers in American is getting wider. In 1960, the salary of chief executive officers at America's 100 largest corporations averaged $190,000 or, after taxes, 12 times a factory worker's pay.

By the end of the Reagan era, however, Reich says, these CEOs averaged $2 million in annual salary, and, given the benefit of tax cuts slanted to the upper brackets, the CEOs' multiple of factory pay skyrocketed to about 70.

Hobart Rowen
p. A15

We had economic growth in the 80s, but corporate and government fiscal policies assured that most of the benefits of the growth accrued to the haves. In 1980, the average corporate chief executive officer received 25 times the compensation of the average worker. In 1990, he or she received 85 times as much as the typical employee.

Meanwhile, Federal Reserve Board Chairman Alan Greenspan admitted to Congress this summer the average American wage earner's real income has been flat, at best, since 1980, and has perhaps declined.

David B. Danbom
p. B5

Median Family Income†

Item	1955	1960	1965	1970	1975	1980	1985	1990
Poverty Level (family of 4)	--	--	--	3,968	5,500	8,414	10,989	12,092††
Poverty Level Income in Constant Dollars	--	--	--	10,198	10,230	10,181	10,220	10,230
National Median Family Income ($)*	4,418	5,620	6,957	9,867	13,719	21,023	27,144	32,448
Median Income in Constant Dollars**	16,479	18,939	22,054	25,358	25,519	25,438	25,244	24,660
CPI Adjustment for Constant Dollars*	3.73	3.37	3.17	2.57	1.86	1.21	.93	.76

* U.S. Bureau of Census and U.S. Department of Labor
** 100 ÷ consumer price index (CPI) = multiplier which converts actual dollars into constant dollars
*** North Dakota Office of the Insurance Commissioner
† dollars have been rounded to nearest whole number
†† for 1988, with constant dollar adjustment factor of .846

Big Business Greed

Health care is big business. That hasn't always been the case, but most consumers haven't yet adjusted their thinking to accommodate this shift in our health care delivery system. Instead of a family doctor who sees to most of our needs, and quite possibly has done so for fifteen or twenty years, we now often see a variety of specialists, many only a few times at most. More than likely none of these specialists have known us very long, so they have no longterm perspective on our health problems.

With all these specialists competing for our attention, we are now subjected to all the trappings of high-powered salesmanship. Our health care dollars are being spent on glitzy public relations, with a pretense of having only our best interest at heart. We are subjected to a tiresome advertising presence, with all the subtlety and honesty of the proverbial used car salesperson.

The American public has long accepted advertisers who sell cars by draping scantily clad women over the shiny fenders of the hottest new models . . . but laser surgery? When we find ourselves driving down the road listening to a sultry voice mouthing voluptuously soothing words about light . . . warmth . . . healing . . . and the wonders of laser surgery at a local clinic, we are repulsed. As if patients choose laser surgery like they do a new washing machine. That we have allowed a medical system like this to evolve, wasting money on sophisticated, professionally produced, expensive advertising instead of reducing our medical and health insurance bills, is obscene.

Increasingly, the middle class can no longer afford health care. We are not suggesting that health care is the only problem for the middle class—only that the cost of health care, like the cost of housing and education, is becoming beyond the reach of the middle America. The economic growth we experienced in the 80s did not benefit the middle class. Instead "corporate and fiscal policies assured that most of the benefits of the growth accrued to the haves" (Danbom, B-5). We need only look at the stagnant median income of U.S. households for the past twenty years to see the credibility of Danbom's observations. For example, in 1980, the average corporate chief executive officer received 25 times the compensation as the employee. By 1990, this officer was receiving 85 times the employee Danbom considers this demise of the middle class as possibly "the most important development of our age" (B-5). Yet during this same ten years, the median family income remained stagnant.

The Myth of the Market in Health Care

The gobbling up of independent health care practices and facilities by corporations is not unique to the health care industry. Many fiercely independent, local

The Market Model

...Because most economists have been preoccupied with the dynamics of short-term, monetary flows in Western industrialized societies, much of the field is irrelevant to issues that arise in long-term global models....

Unfortunately, the limitations inherent in economics as it is most widely practiced today are ones that become very serious in contemplating an end to the expansion phase of the globe's material resources. Assumptions about human goals that served economists well during the period of continuous growth will shed little insight into the behavior of people and institutions during a phase of steady-state behavior in population and capital levels. Techniques like linear regression, which project past behavior into the future, will not provide useful guidance in periods of great discontinuity. *Thus one must be careful in mapping the results of economics on to issues quite remote from those from which they were initially derived* [our emphasis].

Geoffrey S. Holister,
pp. 161-162

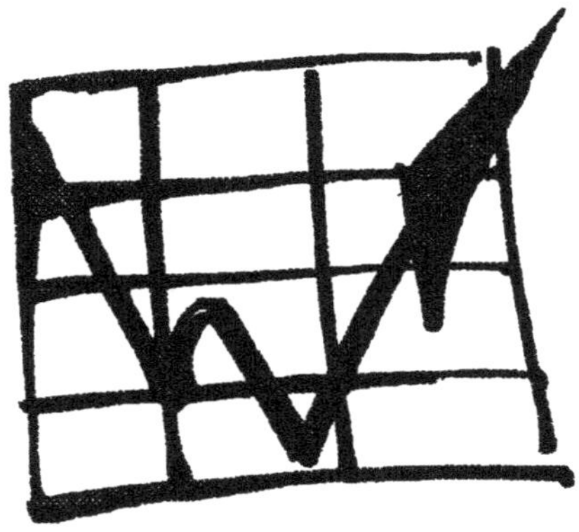

newspapers have been swallowed up by large multimedia corporations. Newspapers can own TV stations and radio stations. Look at the size of the Time-Life company, which now owns a wide variety of enterprises. Structurally, philosophically, and morally, there is no difference between Time-Life and the Hospital Corporation of America or Humana Hospitals.

In a true economic free market model, the manufacturer would have to provide quality as well as competitive price to retain customers. But such a model is, in truth, largely myth. The real world, after all, seldom matches the ideal. In the case of health care, the market model has little correspondence to reality.

Consider the desire for a new washing machine. And note the difference here between the desire for a new washing machine, and the actual need for one. If consumers can't afford a new washing machine, they can continue to make do with their old one, provided their present machine doesn't break down in the mean time. If it does break down, there are alternatives like laundromats or using someone else's machine on a temporary basis. In a real crunch, they could actually wash clothes by hand.

When consumers are ready to actually purchase a washing machine, they can visit several stores, compare features, and choose the machine that best fits their particular use. For some consumers, a large capacity tub is more important than the choice of washing cycles. There are lots of stores offering washing machines and there are lots of models to choose from. The store selling the machine with the desired features for the least amount of money is most likely to make the sale.

Now consider how consumers use health care. First of all, consumers don't merely desire health care, they need it—sometimes immediately. Second, if they're sick, they are in no condition to shop around for the care they need at the best price. In fact, they have no idea what the price will be before they purchase the advice. Oh, there are ads extolling the virtues of this clinic over that one. But there is no real salesperson, someone who can tell the consumer how much the advice is going to cost before purchasing it. Third, they need health care because they need help in figuring out what is wrong

Poor, and Getting Poorer

...Between 1980 and now, low-and middle-income families (the bottom 60 percent of the population) lost between $600 and $800 each, on average, in real after-tax income. Upper-middle-class families gained about $1,700. And the top one-fifth gained about $18,000.

David S. Broder
p. D7

"Among...industrialized countries, the United States has the highest incidence of poverty among the non-elderly and the widest distribution of poverty across all age and family groups," said the report.

"It is also the country in which the poor experience the longest spells of poverty and the only western democracy that has failed to give a significant proportion of its poor a measure of income security," the report said.

Cox News Service
p. A-1

Medical care in this country is like a pay toilet. You take biological necessity and then charge to have it satisfied. Well, let me tell you, there's a lot of people who can't afford the price of admission anymore. And these people are getting mader'n hell at having to crawl under the john door, just to meet their needs. They're tired of wallowing in all that crap. And soon they're going to rip that door off its hinges.

Anonymous remark
in Richard Kunnes,
p. ix

with them and deciding on a treatment. Fourth, not knowing what they need, they can hardly comparison shop. And finally, but most important of all, the care they need may well not be something they can put off until they can afford it.

We don't see any real resemblance here between the market model for manufactured goods and the real world of medical care. We think those voices of reform that are still claiming the market will control health care costs are seriously mistaken. The rise of large corporate hospitals has shown us just exactly what the market does to the provision of health care.

Much of economic theory about the ability of the market to control costs is based on outdated economic models, models based on a manufacturing economy. Health care is not a manufactured product, but those operating our health care system are trying to peddle health care as if they were selling washing machines. We believe that these misappropriately applied marketing techniques have been a major contributor to the shyrocketing health care costs in this country.

Corporate Success Stories

There is no doubt that the corporate managers have turned unprofitable hospitals and clinics into profitable enterprises. There are some impressive success stories. Health East is one such "miracle."

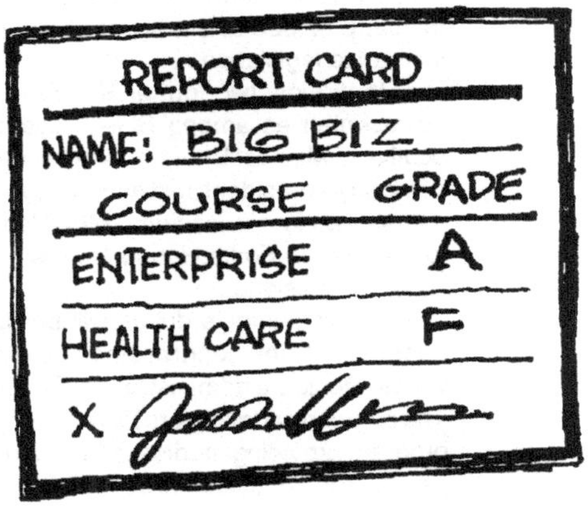

HealthEast

Roger Foussard, chairman of the board of HealthEast, a corporation of four St. Paul hospitals, talked with *Minnesota Medicine* about why the hospitals combined into a multi-hospital system in 1987:

> The four St. Paul hospitals that would become HealthEast found themselves with similar problems in 1987—low utilization and little or no growth potential. Although each one had a strong history of success, and, in most cases, a very strong balance sheet, it became apparent to the hospitals' management, and ultimately to the directors, that there was no real possibility of going it alone in this particular market. Excess capacity and inability to negotiate good managed care contracts brought the hospitals together. (Reece, "A Look at Today's Hospital Board," p. 9)

Corporate Cancer

17 August 1991

Dr. Bruce Carlisle has been named vice president of medical affairs at Blue Cross Blue Shield of North Dakota....His newly created position is effective Sept. 1....He has been on the board of directors at Blue Cross Blue Shield of North Dakota since 1979.

The Forum
"Blue Cross Names Carlisle to New Post,"
p. B5

17 August 1991

State Rep. Rod Larson, R-West Fargo, will join Blue Cross Blue Shield of North Dakota as an assistant vice president for government relations, the company said Friday.

The move virtually assures that Larson, who is chairman of a key House committee, won't be running for re-election. He is finishing his fifth term.

One part of Larson's job will be lobbying the North Dakota Legislature, said Blue Cross spokesman Larry Gauper....

Rod Larson, as chairman of the House Human Services and Veterans Affairs Committee, presided at a number of hearings on insurance legislation....

He will join two former Republican state representatives among Blue Cross' top executives. Michael Unhjem, who becomes the company's president next month, represented Jamestown for six sessions. Mike Hamerlik, a former Grand Forks House member, served for three sessions....

One of Larson's duties will be handling questions from congressmen about Blue Cross' Medicare administration, Gauper said. The company administers Medicare, a federal program providing medical benefits to elderly people, for South Dakota, North Dakota and Wyoming.

The Forum
" Larson Takes Post with Health Insurer,"
pp. A1, A8

24 August 1991

Five employees of Blue Cross Blue Shield of North Dakota have been promoted to vice president in a reorganization of the company's internal operations....

Larry L. Gauper, vice president of communications, said the reorganization will help Blue Cross Blue Shield of North Dakota, which has grown rapidly in recent years, to operate more efficiently.

Blue Cross Blue Shield now has 10 vice presidents: four in external operations, four in internal operations, and two—a general counsel and vice president of medical affairs—who report directly to Unhjem.

The Forum
"Blue Cross Names 5 Vice Presidents,"
p. B3

31 August 1991

John LeDoux, Daryl Peterson and Janine Weideman have been promted to assistant vice president positions with Blue Cross Blue Shield of North Dakota...

LeDoux will be assistant vice president for Medicare systems.. Peterson...will be assistant vice president for information services operations....Weideman... has been named vice president of actuarial and membership services.

The Forum
"Blue Cross Promotes
Three to Assistant Vice President,"
p. B3

7 September 1991

Three men have been promoted to assistant vice president positions at Blue Cross Blue Shield of North Dakota....

Brent Fraase has been named assistant vice president of business systems administration....Marlan Nelson has been named assistnat vice president of private claims....Jim Manly has been named assistant vice president of human resources.

The Forum
"Blue Cross Promotes 3,"
p. B8

The interesting point here is that the hospitals were profitable, but they had a lot of empty beds and the directors could see little chance of the growth. Corporations measure success largely on the basis of growth.

The merger took place in 1987, and HealthEast lost vast amounts of money in 1987, 1988 ($24 million), and 1989 ($35 million). In April of 1989, HealthEast began implementing suggestions made by the Hunter Group consultants, who recommended tighter management of the hospitals, improved managed care contracts to increase revenue, reducing the size of its central corporate staff, reducing expansion into nonhospital businesses, cutting the board from 24 members to 12, and reducing the overall staff by about 10 percent.

By August of 1990, HealthEast showed a profit of about $2.5 million. Working capital was about $3 million in July of 1989, but by July of 1990, it was $30 million.

There is no doubt that the improvement in this corporation's financial health is impressive from a business management standpoint. But what we do not see here is any mention of improving patient care or reducing the cost of providing that care. The changes necessary to make HealthEast profitable were not necessarily the ones that would provide better patient care. Instead, we see an emphasis on increasing profit by negotiating higher rates for providing managed care. We see a 10 percent reduction in staff, which from a business standpoint is always the first place managers look to accomplish quick savings.

It is quite possible that the quality of the patient care decreased, but corporations involved in mergers always claim that they are improving patient care. In truth, we have no reliable means of measuring the quality of health care (Sisk, p. 160-161).

Medlantic

The rise and hard times of a Washington, D.C. area medical conglomerate, Medlantic, illustrates well the problems of running the business of a health care system as if it were a manufacturing industry.

In the early 80s, Medicare and Medicaid paid hospital costs virtually without question, and hospitals amassed a lot of capital to put into subsidiary ventures to increase their profits (hospitals themselves may be non-profit, but often the corporate subsidiaries are not). Medlantic, a non-profit corporation, was created in 1982 by the merger of the Washington Hospital Center (now an 871-bed facility) and Capitol Hill Hospital (with 160 beds). Capitol Hill was a small, inner city hospital

Corporate Compensation

There may be a recession on, corporate profits may be down, but top executives' billfolds continue to bulge....

The biggest paycheck belongs to Jeffrey J. Steiner, chairman of Chantilly-based aerospace conglomerate Fairchild Corp.

In fact, Steiner's whopping $19.3 million in total compensation—$2.4 million in base salary, $4.4 million in incentive bonuses, $13.3 million in cashed-in stock options and $200,000 in other compensation—made him the highest-paid chief executive in the nation....

In a statement, Steiner said: "We at Fairchild believe that compensation should be tied to performance. My salary of $1.6 million [the $1.4 million plus the $200,000] is in line with salaries of other Fortune 500 CEOs....

Many of the critics believe that executive pay is spiraling out of control, that it is too often based on easy-to-reach performance incentive targets and on easy-money stock options that take advantage of what many experts see as artificially inflated stock market prices relative to the overall state of the national economy. More often than not, critics said, executive pay seems to have almost nothing to do with corporate performance....

"The system is bankrupt," charged Ralph Whitworth, president of the United Shareholders Association, a Washington shareholder-advocacy group. "There really is no restraint on these people, and the only things that limits them is their own gall....It's like a bear loose in a honey factory."

Particularly nettlesome, to many observers, is that top executive salaries have soared to an average of 90 to 100 times that of the average worker.

Mark Potts
pp. 1, 20

which, according to reporter Day, had a history of internal bickering among the staff. The Capitol Hill Hospital, by itself, was not a very attractive investment. However, Medlantic, by merging Washington Hospital Center with Capitol Hill, was able to use the Capitol Hill Hospital to greatly boost its assets, and hence qualify to borrow $40 million dollars in tax-free bonds to build a National Rehabilitation Center—"without spending a dime (Day, p. 23)."

Medlantic then used $12.8 million of the $40 million in tax-free bonds to merge with a small group of investors who had just been granted a certificate of need (CON) for a rehabilitation hospital. Since one group in the area already had a CON for a rehabilitation hospital, Medlantic would have been unable to get one too. However, Medlantic was able to "buy" the CON by merging with the group that already had it. The investors were paid $8.8 million for the CON and $4 million for the idea, for a total of $12.8 million. Medlantic paid this $12.8 million from the $40 million in tax-free bonds they had acquired qualified for because of their acquisition of the Capitol Hill Hospital. In theory, CONs are not for sale. In practice, this appears not to always be true.

In 1983, Medlantic had only a handfull of corporate staff. By 1988, they had 137 full time corporate staff plus 150 directors on 10 separate boards. Between mid-1984 and mid-1989, the corporation hospitals earned $91.2, but the corporation itself lost $32 million. How could this be? Medlantic had invested in all kinds of ancillary, money-loosing medical ventures (see sidebar). By fiscal 1990, the corporation was running in the red, losing $9.4 million dollars. Despite these losses, the salary of Medlantic's president skyrocketed. In 1984, his salary was about $150,000. By 1989, considering retirement and other benefits, his salary approached $450,000.

In March of 1991, Medlantic closed the Capitol Hill Hospital because it was not profitable, a hospital that had provided care to inner city poor for over 100 years (Sinclair, D1). Capital Hill Hospital had

A few of Medlantic's ventures are beginning to show small profits after three and four years of losing money: nursing homes, the National Rehabilitation Hospital (built with the $12.4 million certificate of need), and an outpatient surgery center in downtown Washington, D.C.

One of the few consistent moneymakers for Medlantic has been the for-profit parking lot at the Washington Hospital Center.

A few of the money-losing ventures are listed below:

- bought five urgent care centers (walk-in, for-profit clinics) that lost millions. Four of the five have been sold or closed, for a $1.3 million write-off.
- invested $5 million in a free-standing research center which by mid-1989 had lost $4.6 million.
- joined in owning and operating an HMO, losing $3.5 million before pulling out.
- contributed to constructing an unsuccessful office building for doctors, losing $2 million.
- created an education program for doctors (with meetings in Nantucket, Massachusetts, where cottages rent for $2,000 per week during the season), but because of low attendence, lost money.

adapted fromn Day, p. 24

Where Does a 400-Pound Gorilla Sleep?

At the center of America's health-care system are the approximately 6,800 hospitals which every year admit about 40 million patients and provide $170 billion worth of services, more than 40 percent of the nation's total health-care bill. This is big business by anyone's standards.

John W. Wright
p. 547

Corporations can succeed where everyone else has failed because of their financial resources. And unlike the failing HMOs, they can count on added profits from the ancillary services they offer. When an insurance company buys an HMO it can take the up-front subscriber money and invest it at much higher returns than anyone else because of its high-volume business. And no corporation minds losing a million dollars in an HMO when it's making $2 million in increased related services. In short, the corporations could not care less about what system they buy because in the end it is only the profits that count.

Stanley Wohl
p. 46

served its corporate purpose. The actual health care needs of the community were secondary.

Business as Usual in the 1980s

The skyrocketing costs of our health care system today—a system which is increasingly driving the cost of health care beyond the reach of millions of people, and now threatens to bankrupt the businesses supplying health care to their employers—can to a large extent be blamed on the conversion of a service industry to a manufacturing market model. A service industry based on a personal relationship between doctors, nurses, and community hospitals has been swept up into this country's explosion of corporate mergers, where progress is measured by growth, not quality.

The newspapers and magazines are full of stories about community hospitals closing because they can't compete with more profitable, more "businesslike" hospitals. We are pressured to believe that this is O.K. because our great country is built upon the principle of the free market economy. We are led to believe that our health care system is a free market economy. This is, quite simply, a lie.

The Turning Point in Our Health Care System

We believe our health care system is outrageously expensive because those making obscene profits from it would like us to believe that good, basic health care should be provided by corporate giants who measure success by growth and profitability. In reality, the provision of good, basic health care can save millions of dollars by preventing chronic disease, disabilities, and premature births. However, these kinds of health care do not generate large profits, so do not show up on corporate profit and loss sheets—even though they save consumers millions of acute health care dollars later. There is a fundamental conflict here that this country must confront to solve our health care crisis.

> The year 1965 is a watershed year in this story.... Corporate accountants as well as individual doctors quickly realized that Medicare and Medicaid reimbursement schedules were generous in the extreme. The possibility of amassing astronomical profits from running a high-volume, cost-efficient operation was clear from the start. (Wohl, p. 8)

You Need Hospital Care But Have No Insurance

Hospitals must provide emergency medical care to consumers even if the patients have no insurance or the ability to pay for the care. However, if the care is not considered emergency in nature, the hospital has no legal obligation to provide what the patient cannot pay for. Nonetheless, hospitals, if they are to retain their nonprofit status, are required to provide a certain amount of care to people who cannot afford it. And some hospitals, because they have had start-up funding from the government, are required to provide a certain amount of uncompensated care. The problem is how do consumers find out if they are eligible for such care.

If you know you need to be hospitalized and you have no insurance, the first thing you should do is go to the business office of the hospital, tell them your situation, and ask to speak to the person who makes decisions in these cases. Sometimes this person is called the Preadmission Counsellor.

Consumers are sometimes afraid to tell the people in the business office that they cannot pay for needed care because they are afraid their name will be marked and the hospital will refuse to admit them.

Under no circumstances should you admit yourself to a hospital when you cannot pay for the care without first talking with the business office. If the person you first speak to in the business office tells you they can't help you, ask to talk to that person's supervisor. Somewhere in every hospital there is a person who makes the decision about what care will be provided at no charge. You need to find that person and explain your situation.

Once you find that person, you will probably be asked a series of questions along the following lines:

1. Do you have any insurance?
2. If you have no insurance, are you capable of paying for the care your self?
3. If you cannot pay all of the costs of the care, can you at least pay part of the costs?
4. If you have no insurance and have no way of paying for the care, is there someone else in your family who can pay for the care?

The person asking these questions is trying to determine if indeed you really can somehow pay for the care, at least some of it. If you answer no to all of these questions, and convince the preadmissions counsellor that you cannot afford to pay for the required care, even a few dollars a week for a number of years, the counsellor will probably consider you a candidate for free care.

This is a humiliating process, especially for people who have always paid their bills promptly. And it puts pressure on those needing the care to say that they can afford to pay for care that they may well not be able to handle. And finally, it is a process which, because it varies from hospital to hospital, creates a lot of inconsistency in who receives free care and who does not.

We consider this unequal access to needed care a serious problem with our present health care system.

The World's Best Health Care?

Most consumers feel that medical care in the United States is among the best in the world, and rightly so. But there is ample evidence that this health care is more expensive than it needs to be, is unavailable to many people who need it, and is making some corporate owners of health care facilities extremely rich.

A recent study of health care spending (Joint Economic Committee, Congress of the United States, p. 11) in 22 developed countries showed that the average per capita health care expenditure was $848 (in U.S. dollars). In the United States, the average per capita expenditure was $1,776. For years, people accepted the spiralling increases in health care costs because they thought they were paying for better care. This study casts serious doubt on this assumption. Of these 22 nations, only seven had higher infant mortality rates than the United States. Eleven had higher life expectancy rates for men, and eight had higher life expectancy rates for women. Japan has the longest life expectancy rate of the 22 nations studied, and it spends less than half of what we do per year on its citizens.

Every year newspapers bring the latest available statistics on infant mortality to their readers' attention. In 1990, the rate has gone down by the sharpest decline in a ten years—to 9.1 per 1,000 live births. This was trumpeted about with great fanfare. Some reporters did note that worldwide, despite this "sharp" new decline to 9.1, our ranking among other nations continues to fall. In 1985, 18 other nations had lower infant mortality rates than the United States. By 1990, 21 other nations had lower rates than the United States. Many other countries, then, are spending a lot less than we are on health care, but getting better results. Furthermore, in areas of this country noted for poverty and lack of access to health care, the infant mortality rate can run as high as 35 or 36 per 1,000.

Some critics complain that infant mortality rates are really not a very good measure of the quality of health care. Other countries, we were pointedly told by a representative of a health care consulting firm, don't count all of their dead babies

The Politics of Bad Medicine

It has been said that to suppress the truth is to publish a lie. Nowhere is this more meaningful than in research, and nowhere is it more practiced than in the current ban on federal funds for fetal tissue transplantation research.

The suppression of truth in this case is twofold: It is done both to researchers and to sick and disabled people. Under the federal funding ban, researchers are turned away from promising opportunities for cures—not just treatments, but actual cures—of such diseases as diabetes, Parkinson's and Alzheimer's. The path of science is changed by equivocation.

In turn, patients and their families are told that everything possible is being done but that their conditions are "incurable." Their hope is taken away by deliberate omission.

The reason for this policy of suppression is clear. The Bush administration is responding to the most extreme elements of the anti-abortion movement, without ever stopping to consider whether their demands are humane, rational or even moral. Rather than allow transplants to save a life, as happens with organs from cadavers, the administration and its antiabortion allies insist that this tissue be discarded, no matter what good it might do. Don't study it, don't learn from it and above all don't transplant it.

This is bad medicine, and it is dangerous science policy.

Henry A. Waxman
p. A21

Bernadine Healy, NIH [National Institutes of Health] director since last week, testified at hearings before the House Energy and Commerce subcommittee on health and the environment that, personally, she favors lifting the ban [on fetal tissue transplant research]. But as director of the NIH, Healy said she "will abide by the policies, federal regulations or laws that govern this area of public policy."

Sally Squires
"New NIH Chief...,"
p. A5

and the United States, the implication was, does. We maintain that the infant mortality rates in the United States are abysmal compared to those of other developed countries, especially when we also look at per capita spending on health care. Quibbling over a few tenths of a point here and there is no different than trying to pass off the 35 million uninsured in the United States as no real problem because after all, there are *really* only 33 million uninsured. Any way you look at it, other developed countries get a lot better overall results for their health care dollars than the United States does. It's time to find out why.

Special Interest Answers to the Problem

How did we get in this mess? As Dr. Sidney Wolfe, editor of *Health Letter* says: "too many people are making too much money from health care" (August 1988, p. 7).

> All the vested interests in the profits to be gained from health care have their answer to the problem. Sometimes the profiteers simply offer an excuse, like a*fter all, we have all this wonderful technology and it costs money.* Sometimes the profiteers blame the victim. *Americans lead an unhealthy life style, and now they're paying the price.* Or another variation of the same argument, *consumers don't care what it costs to go to the doctor because their insurance company pays the bills.* As if all we have to do is start making people pay for their health care to keep consumers from overusing the system.

Equal Access to Basic Health Care

We already know that when people have to pay for health care, they don't use it—in many cases not because they want a free lunch, but because THEY CANNOT AFFORD IT. People without health insurance do not go to doctors until they absolutely have to, often appearing in emergency rooms for health care that could have been handled by a family physician during regular office hours for a greatly reduced cost.

Lying

Trashing the truth is now so natural, so unremarked in Washington that there were only worldly smirks and shrugs when George Bush began the Thomas saga by saying two things he and everyone else knows are untrue—that Thomas is the person best qualified for the supreme Court, and that his race was irrelevant to his selection. Then, continuing an execrable practice of the Reagan administration, Bush put Thomas into the hands of private-sector lobbyists.

They are "experts" on everything except anything that should matter, such as ideas, constitutional law—stuff like that....

....nothing can still the suspicion that even if the truth does matter for a moment, that moment will be a fleeting aberration in a city becoming increasingly carnivorous as it becomes decreasingly serious about governance.

George F. Will
"How It Came to This,"
p. A23

Are you starting to get the idea that these congressmen—representatives of the common man—don't have a clue about what life is like for the average constituent? The fact is they can't possibly know because they don't live like the rest of us.

We taxpayers spend more than $2.4 billion a year so that Members of Congress can continue to live in the style to which they've become accustomed....

Get a load of the laundry list of perks available to every single Member of Congress: free medical care (doctors, nurses, X-rays, medical technicians, laboratories) on call in the capitol, free pharmacy services in the Capitol, exclusive standby ambulance service on call 24 hours a day. Think about that next time you pay 40 bucks for an office call at the clinic and then another 30 bucks for a prescription drug you paid the 40 bucks to find out you needed in the first place.

Terry DeVine
p. A4

Many who might be able to change the patterns of duplicity in their own lives lack any awareness of the presence of a moral problem in the first place, and thus feel no need to examine their behavior and explore the alternatives carefully. Others are beyond caring.

Still another difference among individuals cuts sharply into the capacity of many to make changes: the difference in the power to carry through a change and in the freedom and security from repercussions should they challenge deeply rooted habits of duplicity. The lack of power and freedom to cope with the consequences of battling deceptive practices reinforces the lack of awareness or concern wherever it exists; it puts great pressure on those least comfortable with deceit.

Sissela Bok
pp. 257-258

Copayments, where the consumer pays part of the doctor or hospital costs, and the insurance company pays the rest, are designed specifically to discourage use. Insurance companies have argued for copayments because consumers with no out-of-pocket expenses go to doctors more often, presumably for no good reason. Copayments work. They keep people out of doctors' offices. But the question is, should we be discouraging people from using basic, preventive health care? We know that certain types of relatively inexpensive preventive care, such as screening for high blood pressure, can identify persons who are likely to have strokes, possilby saving thousands of dollars of future hospital and nursing home costs. We believe that creating barriers to discourage access to this kind of preventive care is not only a waste of consumers's money, but bad health care policy, and viewed from a long-term perspective, unethical.

Copayments have increased over the past ten years as insurance companies and employers have become more and more desperate to control health care costs. The costs of copayments and health insurance can now consume a substantial portion of a family's income. In a recent survey of farm families in Minnesota, their health care costs averaged $1,179—over and above the cost of their health insurance premiums. Almost 20 percent of these families were spending 25 percent of their net income on health insurance and health care. Nearly 10 percent spent 40 percent of their net income on health insurance (Kralewski et al., p. 36, 37).

We may not call this rationing, but it is. Those who can afford health care get it. Those who cannot pay for health care often pay with their lives.

Health Care Rationing

Confronted with the problems of our costly health care system, policymakers and politicians have begun to whisper the word "rationing," as if to soften consumers up to the fact that we just cannot go on providing the best that medicine can offer to every citizen. We suggest the whispering about rationing stop. The health care system this country has allowed to develop has ALWAYS rationed health care—based on who could pay.

To make rationing more palatable, some policymakers have begun talking about "rationalizing" the system. Part of the reason other developed countries can provide health care at a more reasonable cost is

copayment: the amount of the medical bill the consumer is responsible for once the consumer's deductible has been paid (typically insurance covers 80 percent of the bill and the consumer must pay the other 20 percent).
from Robert N. Veres, p. 34-35

We Know What Works—But Don't Provide It

There is no mystery about which programs work, yet they don't cover enough eligible people....We know that prenatal care sharply reduces the number of premature babies. Yet, Hewlett writes that 17 percent of American women of childbearing age don't have medical coverage—up from 12 percent 10 years ago. She cites a government estimate that the cost of caring for dangerously premature babies is $2.4 billion annually. "We are foolishly reckless when we squander $150,000 of public funds on neonatal intensive care rather than spend $400 on preventing the tragedy in the first place.

"The United States is unique in having created this calamitous policy mix. In all other rich nations, pregnant women and newborn children are treated with much more generosity and humanity—which is a large part of the reason why infant mortality rates are so much lower in France, Japan, Sweden and Canada than they are in the United States." And she cites country after country where midwives make home visits to teach mothers about infant care and family planning....

The point is to help parents succeed, so they can help their children succeed. "Neither the right nor the left have wanted to move forward. Instead they have channeled their energy into a variety of ideological confrontations—abortion is a good example—that have served to absorb energy and deflect attention from what is really happening to children in this society."

Judy Mann
"The Abandonned U.S. Child,"
p. B3

The results of a nine-city survey by the federal Centers for Disease Control found that less than half of the 2-year-olds are fully protected against childhood diseases. In the District [of Columbia], which had the second best rate of immunization in the study, only 45 percent of youngsters were fully protected by age 2....

Nationwide, the American Academy of Pediatrics estimates that only seven of every ten 2-year-olds have received their shots. That means the United States ranks 56th worldwide in immunizing minority youngsters against childhood diseases and 17th in protecting all children against these preventable diseases, according to the National Centers for Disease Control.

"That is pretty terrible to be the wealthiest nation in the world and only manage to be in the 17th place among nations for immunizing children," said Martin Smith, chairman of the National Vaccine Advisory Committee at HHS [Health and Human Services]....

An estimated 25,000 cases of measles were reported in 1990, compared to the record low of 1,497 in 1983....The disease has killed 101 children since 1989....

Locally, health departments are reporting a shift. In Charles County, Md., for example, public health officials said that a number of pediatricians are sending patients to the county's immunization clinic, where the cost of all inoculations is just $5 per patient.

Kathy McLaughlin of Waldorf [Maryland] last week brought her son Billy, a seventh grader, to the clinic for a measles booster. She said she saved $93 over a trip to her pediatrician. "I couldn't believe the difference. I'd pay $98 to a pediatrician, and I paid $5 here," she said.

Sally Squires
"U.S. Immunization Campaign Struggles,"
p. 6-7

that they do indeed have a coherent system of health care. U.S. health care costs reached $666 billion in 1990, or 12.2 percent of our gross national product. This is more than any other developed nation spends on health care—and other countries provide basic health care to all their citizens. In Canada, 11 cents out of each dollar is spent on administrative and billing costs: in the United States, 24 cents. If the United States could reduce its administrative costs for health care down to the Canadian level, it could save more than $100 billion a year, "enough to provide health insurance to the entire 33 to 35 million uninsured Americans...." (Rich, "Health Care Paperwork...," p. A1, A16).

Instead of a rational health care system for providing basic preventive health care to every person, we have a balkanized series of health care providers who are out for a bigger and bigger share of the market, and who provide only those services that are profitable. We know that preventive health care is cost-effective, but we also know that as our health care system operates today, it is unprofitable. Few health insurance policies cover preventive health care, doctors are not rewarded for providing it, and many consumers cannot afford it. A rational health care system would make preventive health care accessible to everyone, reward doctors for providing it, and keep costs down by establishing a uniform, consistent payment system.

Big Business and Basic Health Care Incompatible

Big business has had a chance to address the problem of basic health care and has failed. Not, let us emphasize, as a business enterprise. HealthEast demonstrates just how successful corporate management can be. But big business has profoundly failed to provide what our country sorely needs—a health care system that provides equal access for all to basic, preventive health care.

Consumer Groups and Health Care Reform

There are a number of consumer groups which are watching the health care reform proposals. They provide members with up-to-date information about congressional proposals from a consumer perspective.

We believe that consumers must become directly involved in the political process, studying the issues and keeping their elected representatives informed of their opinions. These consumer groups can not only help you keep up with what's going on, but also provide you with a political voice that is part of a larger, organized group.

The organizations listed on this page are interested in health care reform in general and provide a good place for consumers to start in learning about proposed changes in our system. Some produce health care newsletters for consumers. This list by no means includes all consumer organizations interested in health issues. Some groups are monitoring health care reform from a special interest perspective, such as home-births or services for the handicapped. These organizations can be found in reference books in your library, such as the *Encyclopedia of Associations* published by Gale Research.

Call these organizations—or write—and ask what kind of publications they have for consumers. Some will have catalogs of information they publish. Ask for a copy. If they publish a newsletter, ask if they will send you a sample copy.

In addition to these organizations there are numerous national groups such as the League of Women Voters and the American Association of Retired Persons who are monitoring health care reform and have local chapters throughout the country. These organizations can also provide consumers with much valuable information on health care reform efforts. Check your local telephone book for your community's group, or whoever maintains your local community bulletin boards. Depending upon your community, your courthouse, your library, or the continuing education department of your school system might be able to help you locate this kind of information.

Many organizations have persons assigned to monitor legislation of interest to their group. Find out who is monitoring health care issues in organizations you belong to and ask how to reach them to voice your concerns.

Public Citizen
2000 P St., N.W.
Washington, D.C. 20036
202/833-3000

Newsletter: Health Letter

Committee for National Health Insurance
1757 N St., N.W.
Washington, D.C. 20036
202/223-9865

People's Medical Society
462 Walnut St.
Allentown, Pennsylvania 18102
215/770-1670

Center for Medical Consumers
237 Thompson St.
New York, New York 10012
212/674-7105

Health Writers, Inc.
Box 553121
Madison, Wisconsin 53705-9812
608/255-2255

Newsletter: Health Newsletter

Medical Information for Consumers (MEDINC)
9102 Jones Mill Road
Chevy Chase, Maryland 20815
301/897-8144

Newsletter: MEDINC's Consumer Health Reporter

National Health Organization
370 E. 76th St., #9074
New York, New York 10021
212/736-9722

Newsletter: National Health

It's time to stop pretending that the market economy will solve our health care problems. The management which creates successful profit and loss statements cannot at the same time derive its profits and growth from what must be a public good.

In 1985, Dr. Arnold Relman, now editor emeritus of *The New England Journal of Medicine*, said that the purpose of a health care system was to meet the needs of all citizens, regardless of profitability. The single-minded aim of a corporation, Dr. Relman maintained, was to make a profit. To make a profit in health care, the provider must cut back on low-return services regardless of improvement in health, dump the poor and uninsured patients on public hospitals, and skim off the most profitable procedures and affluent patients (Burns, p. 538, 542).

As unattractive as this prediction was, this is precisely what has happened. In the process of allowing a profit-driven system to develop, this country has deprived millions of consumers of necessary and basic health care, greatly increased the cost to those who can still afford health care, and closed many of the needed community hospitals that provide the kinds of services that are necessary, but unprofitable. Reform of our health care system, if it is to be successful, must address the problems caused by allowing a social need to be supplied to consumers as if it were a manufactured commodity.

Chapter 1 Summary

Problem #1:
Big business has taken over our health care delivery system.

Issue: Medicare provided a mechanism for creating relatively consistent, high profits for providing certain types of health care.

Action: Reimburse health care providers equally for given procedures, regardless of geographic area.

Problem #2:
Hospital and clinic costs are skyrocketing.

Issue: Some business people contend that the "market" will control health care costs.

Action: Everyone should be provided a certain level of basic health care. The "market" works to keep costs down only when the item for sale is some thing that's nice to own, not something that's a social need everyone must have.

Chapter 1 Summary

Problem #3:
Many blame new, highly sophisticated technology for driving up medical costs.

Issue: Most basic health care requires very limited amounts of relatively cheap technology.

Action: Include in the basic health care services only those technologies considered to provide good outcomes relative to the cost.

Problem #4:
Shortening hospital length of stay has not decreased costs.

Issue: The cost of a hosptial day is much higher in this country than in any other developed country.

Action: Make public the way hospitals arrive at the cost of a day and limit the types of charges they can pass on to consumers.

Chapter 2

Mismanaged Care

Chapter Contents

Bulletin Boards

Action Guides

Narratives

Discussion:

Strangling the Art of Medicine

Chapter 2 Summary

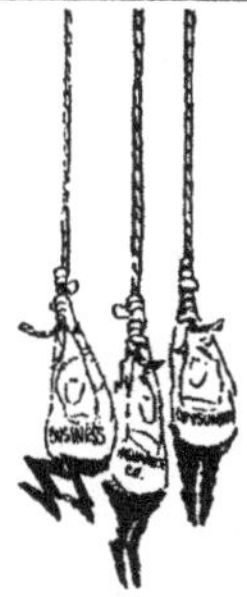

Working Stiff Doctors

I'm aware of some colleagues...who receive salaries or participate in arrangements where the hospital manages the practice and reimburses the physician. The arrangements seem to work well, but I'm wary of the physician's close relationship with the hospital. As physicians, we have to keep the patient's care and welfare in mind. Sometimes hospitals have finances, rather than patient care, as their bottom line. I don't ever want to be in a situation where quality of medical care is just *one* of the most important priorities instead of *the* most important priority. A salary arrangement with the hospital can potentially stretch that principle.

Douglas D. Pflaum
p. 9

The Twin Cities has a mature medical market. A dozen major health care corporations dominate. These corporations are in competitive deadlock. Their stagnant growth forces these large health care organizations to consolidate into still larger corporations....the managed care war is over, and the managers have won.

For physicians like myself, who desire independence and equity and who prefer smaller groups, better opportunities exist elsewhere.

Richard L. Reece
"I Bid You Farewell,"
p. 7

You're Not in Charge Here, Doctor

HMOs are often promoted as the answer to our health care cost problems. To those doctors who find solo practice overwhelming, HMOs certainly offer some attractive advantages. After all, what doctor wouldn't like to be freed from the paperwork of an office, from the hassle of having to deal with personnel problems, or the frustrating task of getting reimbursed for services rendered. What doctor wouldn't like to be able to look forward to some real uninterrupted time off.

A physician friend of mine recently left the area to take a job at an HMO in another city. He was subjected to four weeks of indoctrination, in the same classroom with the new secretaries the HMO hired. Whenever he made a long distance phone call, he had to key in his own personal phone code so that who he called and how much the call cost could be tracked.

During the course of seeing one of his patients, he decided that she should have a copy of her medical history. He gave her the chart when she left and told her she could ask the receptionist to make her a copy. To his surprise, while he was seeing his next patient, the nurse interrupted him to tell him—in front of his patient—that he had no business telling patients they could have copies of their medical records. After all, she told him, "You're not in charge here, Doctor."

My friend is in the process of setting up his own solo practice.

You Don't Have to Leave the Hospital

To protect yourself from inadequate care, you should know that a hospital has no right to discharge you just because you have reached or exceeded the average number of hospital days for your diagnosis-related group. The hospital is obligated to keep you until discharge is safe, and you have the right to appeal all discharge decisions. If a hospital decides that you no longer need inpatient care, it is required to give you a written notice called a notice of noncoverage. This notice does not mean that you must leave the hospital—it means that Medicare will not pay for any more hospital care. If you think the hospital's decision is wrong, you can stay on at your own expense while appealing the decision, and if you win you will be paid back.

If you want to appeal a notice of noncoverage, first find out if your doctor agrees or disagrees that it is safe for you to be discharged. If your doctor agrees with the hospital, you can ask your local Peer Review Organization (PRO) to review the decision....If the PRO reviews the case and agrees with the hospital, you can ask it to reconsider. While the PRO considers your appeal, Medicare will pay for two more days of hospital care, but will not pay for any additional time unless the PRO ultimately rules in your favor.

Even if the PRO rules against you twice, you have a right to appeal further, to an administrative law judge.

Health Letter
"What You Can Do"
p. 11

The American Association of Retired Persons (AARP) publishes a booklet *Medicare's Prospective Payment System: Knowing Your Rights* which explains the appeal process in detail. For copies, request stock #D12330 at the following address:

Knowing Your Rights: AARP Fulfillment
1909 K Street, N.W.
Washington, D.C. 20049

- **even if you are not a Medicare patient, your state PRO may be able to help you solve your health care delivery problems.**
- **to locate your state PRO, see page 69.**

You ARE Going Home, Aren't You?

During my rounds, I stopped by to see one of my patients who had had a hysterectomy the day before.

"How're you doing," I asked.

"Not too bad, I guess. But I still can't eat.

I asked if she had passed any gas yet, since this would be a good indication to me that her digestive system, inhibited by the anesthesia, was now working normally again. She told me no. This wasn't very surprising to me since it is not uncommon for these patients to go until the third day after their operation before passing gas. But this seemingly simple indicator is very important in establishing that the integrity of the GI tract has been preserved.

"Well, I think we'll keep you on the IV today and see how you do overnight."

You can imagine my surprise when I got a call at the office from this patient a few hours later and she said "I feel great. I'm ready to go home."

When I got to the hospital that evening to check her out, she was dressed and anxiously waiting for me to sign the papers that would allow her to go home. It wasn't until six weeks later that I found out what really happened. My patient's daughter is a friend of mine and she called me to tell me that her mother was in no way ready to go home when she did, and she had wondered about it. About six weeks after the surgery, her daughter found out what happened.

The person employed by the hospital to manage patient care had come into my patient's room after I left and told her that the insurance company wouldn't pay her hospital bill after today. My patient had had her

diagnostic-related group (DRG): system that reimburses health care providers fixed amounts for all care given in connection with standard diagnostic categories (*HIAA Source Book*, p. 114).

hysterectomy: removal of the uterus (*Tabor's*, p. H-86).

IV: abbreviation for intravenous, meaning within or into veins (*Tabor's*, pp. I-55, I-42).

Professional Review Organization (PRO): An organization in which practicing physicians assume responsibility for reviewing the propriety and quality of health care services provided under Medicare and Medicaid (*HIAA Source Book*, p. 121)

What a PRO Does. . .

The PRO program, initiated in 1983 to replace the earlier Professional Standards Review Organization, is administered under the Health Care Financing Administration and is responsible for ensuring the quality and appropriateness of care for nearly 32.4 million Medicare recipients in the United States....In addition to several other activities, the PRO program includes the use of procedure-specific explicit criteria in case-by-case prior review to assess the appropriateness of the setting (eg, hospital or outpatient setting) for the proposed care (preadmission review), as well as the necessity for performing specific procedures (preprocedure review)....

Each of the 48 PROs that cover 54 geographic areas are responsible for developing procedure-specific, explicit review criteria in which appropriate indications for use of the procedures are noted. Although PROs may develop preprocedure review criteria in consultation with local or state medical societies, or with input from national or regional specialty societies, currently there are no uniform guidelines for developing either the content or the format of the review criteria....

The estimated 1991 budget for the entire PRO program is $330 million or 0.3% of Medicare expenditures.

Kellie and Kelly
pp. 1265-1266

And How It Does It

First Review

PROs notify physicians regarding preprocedure review criteria prior to their implementation, allowing physicians to make their decisions regarding appropriate use of procedures within the context of the review criteria. The PRO preprocedure review operates at two levels; first, an initial review is generally carried out by nurses, using explicit preprocedure review criteria. For those procedures not found appropriate in the initial level of review, a second level of review is carried out by physician advisors using implicit criteria. Implicit review is based on the reviewing physicians's clinical judgment and on their knowledge of professional standards of care. Explicit review criteria play a critical role in the review process, as they are used to determine which procedure requests will be approved and which ones will be referred for implicit review by physicians.

Kellie and Kelly
p. 1266

Second Review

Prior review findings of the PRO are further verified by a second group known as the SuperPRO working under contract with the Health Care Financing Administration. The SuperPRO retrospectively reviews a random sample of all PRO reviews. A significant difference between PRO and SuperPRO reviews is that SuperPRO review nurses can refer to the second level of physician review those cases labeled as appropriate by the review criteria that, in the nurses's judgment, are suspect with regard to appropriateness. Data for preadmission and preprocedure reviews indicate that SuperPRO nurses referred to the second level of review a total of 2598 of 53,942 cases that fell into this category....Forty-seven percent of those 2598 cases initially labeled as appropriate, however, were subsequently determined by physician reviewers in the second level of review to be inappropriate. These findings from SuperPRO reviews suggest that the explicit review criteria may allow for the mislabeling of inappropriate utilization as appropriate utilization.

Kellie and Kelly
p. 1269

Find Your PRO*

Since the federal government contracts individually with different organizations to administer the PRO program, there is no standard name for the PRO organization in every state. Note that a few of the states have combined organizations.

Get to know your state PRO. Write or call and ask what kinds of consumer information they will provide free. If you are having any kind of problem with hospitals or doctors, check to see if your PRO can help. You, yourself may not be a Medicare consumer, but if your hospitals or doctors treat medicare patients, they are subject to PRO review.

We have given the street address and if there is a P.O. box, we've listed it first. Note that the U.S. Postal System will often return mail as undeliverable if a street address is used when the organization has a P.O. box number.

For street addresses, we have supplied suite numbers when there was room on the address line. If you are unfamiliar with the street address area and plan to visit your PRO, please call for directions.

Alabama
AL Quality Assurance Foundation
236 Goodwin Crest Drive, Suite 300
Birmingham, AL 35209
205/942-0785

Alaska
see Washington State

Arizona
Health Services Advisory Group
P.O. Box 16731, 301 E. Bethany Home
Phoenix, AZ 85014
602/264-6382

Arkansas
Arkansas Foundation for Medical Care
P.O. Box 1508, 809 Garrison Avenue
Forth Smith, AR 72902
501/785-2471

California
California Medical Review, Inc.
1388 Sutter Street, Suite 1100
San Francisco, CA 94109
415/923-2200

Colorado
Colorado Foundation for Medical Care,
6825 East Tennessee Avenue,
Denver, CO 80224
303/321-8642

Connecticut
Connecticut Peer Review Organization
384 Pratt Street
Meriden, CT 06450
203/237-2773

District of Columbia
Delmarva Foundation for Medical Care
341-B North Aurora Street
Easton, MD 21601
301/822-06797

Delaware
see West Virginia

Florida
Professional Foundation for Heatlh Care
2907 Bay to Bay Boulevard, Suite 100
Tampa, FL 33629
813/831-6273

Georgia
Georgia Medical Care Foundation
4 Executive Park Drive, N.E., Suite 1300
Atlanta, GA 30329
404/982-6500

Hawaii
Hawaii Medical Services Association
P.O. Box 860, 808 Keeaumoku Street
Honolulu, HI 96808
808/944-2110

Idaho
see Washington State

Illinois
Crescent Counties Foundation for Medical Care
350 Shuman Boulevard, Suite 240
Naperville, IL 60540
312/876-0652

Indiana
Peerview, Inc.
501 Congressional Boulevard, Suite 200
Carmel, IN 46032
317/573-6888

Iowa
Iowa Found. for Medical Care
3737 Woodland Avenue, Suite 500
West Des Moines, IA 50265
515/233-2900

Kansas
Kansas Foundation for Medical Care
2947 S.W. Wanamaker Drive
Topeka, KS 66614
913/272-2552

Kentucky
Peerview, Inc.
10300 Linn Station Road, Suite 100
Louisville, KY 40223
502/429-0995

Louisiana
Louisiana Health Care Review
9357 Interline Avenue, Suite 200
Baton Rouge, LA 70809

Maine
see Rhode Island

Maryland
see District of Columbia

Massachusetts
Massachusetts Peer Review Organization
300 Bearhill Road
Waltham, MA 02154
617/890-0011

Michigan
Michigan Peer Review Organization
40500 Ann Arbor Road, Suite 200
Plymouth, MI 48170
313/459-0900

Minnesota
Foundation for Heatlh Care Evaluation
One Appletree Square, Suite 700
Minneapolis, MN 55420
612/854-3306

Mississippi
Mississippi Foundation for Medical Care
P.O. Box 4665, 1900 North West Street
Jackson, MS 39216
601/948-8894

Missouri
Missouri Patient CAre Review Foundation
311 Ellis Boulevard, Suite A
Jefferson City, MO 65101
314/634-4441

Montana
Montana-Wyoming Found. for Medical Care
P.O. Box 5117, 21 North Main
Helena, MT 59604
406/443-4020

Nebraska
see Iowa

Nevada
Nevada Physicians Review Organization
4600 Kietzke Lane, Bldg. A, Suite 108
Reno, NV 89502
702/826-1996

New Hampshire
NH Foundation for Medical Care
P.O. Box 578, 110 Locust Street
Dover, NH 03820
603/749-1641

New Jersey
Peer Review Organization of New Jersey
Central Division, Brier Hill Court, Bldg. J
East Brunswick, NJ 08816
201/238-5570

New Mexico
New Mexico Medical Review Assocaition
P.OI Box 9900, 707 Broadway N.E.
Albuquerque, NM 87106
505/842-6236

New York
Empire State Med., Sci. & Educ. Found.
420 Lakeview Road, Box 5434
Lake Success, NY 11042
516/437-8134

North Carolina
Medical Review of North Carolina
P.O. Box 37309, 1011 Schaub Drive,
Raleigh, NC 27627
919/851-2955

North Dakota
North Dakota Health Care Review
900 North Broadway, Suite 212
Minot, ND 58701
701/852-4231

Ohio
Peer Review Systems, Inc.
3700 Corporate Drive, Suite 250
Columbus, OH 43229
614/895-9900

Oklahoma
Oklahoma Foundationf ro Peer Review
5801 Boradway Extension, Suite 400
Oklahoma City, OK 73118
405/840-2891

Oregon
OR Medical Professional Review Org.
1220 Southwest Morrison, Suite 300
Portland, OR 97205
503/243-1151

Pennsylvania
Keystone Peer Review Organization
P.O. Box 618, 645 North 12th Street
Lemoyne, PA 17043
717/975-9600

Puerto Rico
Puerto Rico Foundation for Medical Care
Mercantile Plaza, Suite 605
Hato Ray, PR 00918
809/753-6805

Rhode Island
Health Care Review, Inc.
345 Blackstone Boulevard
Providence, RI 02906
401/331-6661

South Carolina
Metrolina Medical Foundation
3000 Charlottetown Center
Charlotte, NC 28204
704/373-1545

South Dakota
SD Foundation for Medical Care
1323 South Minnesota Avenue
Sioux Falls, SD 57105
605/336-3505

Tennessee
Mid-South Foundation for Medical Care
6401 Poplar Avenue, Suite 400
Memphis, TN 38119
901/682-0381

Utah
Utah Professional Standard Review Org.
540 East Fifth South Street, Suite 200
Salt Lake City, UT 84102
801/532-7545

Vermont
See New Hampshire

Virgin Islands
Virgin Islands Medical Institute
P.O. Box 1556, Christiansted
St. Croix, U.S. Virgin Islands 00820
809/778-6470

Virginia
Medical Society of Virginia Review Org.
P.O. Box 6569, 1904 Byrd Avenue
Richmond, VA 23230
804/289-5320

Washington
Professional Review Org. for WA
2150 North 107th Street, Suite 200
Seattle, WA 98133
206/364-9700

Washington, D.C.
see District of Columbia

West Virginia
West Virginia Medical Institute
3421 Chesterfield Avenue, S.E.
Charleston, WV 25304
304/925-0461

Wisconsin
Wisconsin Peer Review Organization
2001 West Beltline Highway
Madison, WI 53713
608/274-1940

Wyoming
see Montana

*state listings from Charles Inlander and Charles MacKay, pp. 297-300.

Aggressive Cost Cutting by Any Other Name

...on March 23, I opened a certified letter from the Metropolitan Life Insurance Co. to discover that in 30 days it would cut her [my wife's] nursing to four hours a day.

No reason was given....

My lawyer tells me if Naomi dies as a result of a cutback the company may well be liable for civil and criminal action.

And if Naomi dies she will be the victim of what is called managed care.

At its most benign it can reduce unnecessary hospital stays and improve patient care by trading home care for hospital days, for example.

In fact, it enables Metropolitan Life to overrule physicians' judgments.

The term is a euphemism for aggressive cost-cutting....

It corrupts the medical and nursing professions: insurers pay M.D.'s and R.N.'s with Orwellian titles such as "utilization reviewer," to reduce services.

For medical professionals who are supposedly committed to preserving life, this should be an ethical problem....

The company declines to release the guidelines it uses to overrule doctors, perhaps because they mix medical and financial criteria and are arbitrary, leaving the carrier with discretion to decide "on a case-by-case basis."

Despite great efforts by the union and myself, Metropolitan has never defined the evaluation process and the Governor's Office of Employee Relations has supported it in its refusal.

Jesse Lemisch
p. A4.

Quality assurance [QA] companies operate by previewing every hospital admission, every proposed surgical procedure, and every medical treatment plan for each of the company's employees.

They assign an arbitrary length of stay for each diagnosis for every hospital admission. They review all diagnostic procedures for "medical necessity," both in the hospital and in the physician's office. They review all bills from the hospital. Physician and laboratory bills are reviewed for medical necessity and range of fees.

They do these reviews for all employees and their covered family members without regard to the insurance company holding the health care contract for the company. The QA company for which I did part-time consulting calculated that it saved its clients $28 million in 1987. That money was diverted from patient care to administrative costs, QA company fees, and to some savings for the company.

Farrell S. Stiegler
p. 505

hysterectomy the second day she was in the hospital and her insurance would pay for only three days in the hospital for this procedure. As a result, on her third hospital day, my patient was only second-day postoperative—and I felt I needed to watch her for another day.

Now I knew that most insurance companies will only allow three days in the hospital for a hysterectomy, with the patient entering the hospital the day of the surgery. However, in this lady's case, there was a good chance that I might have to remove an ovary, and this might require that I actually cut into the bowel, depending upon the condition of the ovary. Whenever a doctor believes that it is necessary to cut into a bowel, it is customary to admit a patient a day before the operation for a 24-hour bowel cleansing procedure that includes antibiotic treatment. This information was, of course, on the patient's chart.

The hospital's managed care person had not considered it important to question me about my patient's care or ask me why I thought my patient should be hospitalized an additional day. Or whether there were any extenuating circumstances she should know about. Or even, apparently, to read my patient's chart.

She simply terrorized my patient into leaving the hospital.

Pit Bull Economics

This rapid and persisting increase in health care expenditures has led to activities designed to control costs by discouraging inappropriate and unnecessary utilization of medical and surgical services. Among these activities are programs that are designed to review and approve the appropriateness or necessity of medical or surgical procedures before they are provided, as well as the most appropriate site for performing the procedures. As noted in a 1989 Institute of Medicine study of the role of utilization management in controlling health care costs... such prior review programs are now common among health care insurers, employers, and other groups who are responsible for organizing, managing, and paying for medical and surgical services, including the federal government in its responsibilities for the Medicare program.

Kellie and Kelly
p. 1265

Blue Cross and Blue Shield of MN
P.O. Box 64560
St. Paul, MN 55164

June 24, 1991

Dear Physician:

This letter is intended to be a reminder that as a participating provider with Blue Cross and Blue Shield of Minnesota (BCBSM) you are obligated to comply with the provisions of your participating provider agreement. One of those key provisions is that a participating provider will assume financial liability for the performance of medically unnecessary services or services which are deemed by BCBSM to be experimental/investigative. This liability will exist unless the participating provider has obtained from the patient, prior to the performance of these services, written approval that the patient understands and takes financial responsibility for these services. If the advance approval has been obtained in writing, the patient may be billed for such services.

In addition, I would like to remind you of your obligations under the participating provider agreement with BCBSM which stipulates that you are to refer to other participating BCBSM providers when a referral is necessary. If you refer to a non-participating BCBSM provider you must, in writing, provide notification to the patient that the provider being referred to is non-participating with BCBSM. Once again, that notification must be prior to the referral occurring. Your failure to comply with this provision will mean that you will be held responsible for the additional out-of-pocket financial liability incurred by the patient.

Again, this is a reminder in the interest of our subscribers. We ask for your cooperation. If you have any questions, please contact your Health Services Consultant.

Sincerely,

John Doe
Vice President
Provider Relations

Catch-22 for Doctors

Before the days of rigorously managed care, patients who had had strokes, heart attacks, or blood clots and were put on blood thinners (usually coumadin), sometimes had to be hospitalized while the proper dosage was determined. Or sometimes they started reacting differently to the usual dosage and needed to be watched until we could regulate their medication. Insurance usually covered this type of hospitalization.

A doctor friend and I were comparing managed care notes not too long ago. He had an elderly patient who needed her coumadin regulated, and he knew she had no one to stay with her at home. The hospital insisted

that she couldn't stay until the medication was properly controlled. He believed that she needed to stay in the hospital because he was familiar with her home situation and knew that she had no one to stay with her in case there were problems.

"The hospital wanted her out?" I asked.

"Yes. I suppose they didn't think Medicare would pay for it. She really had no one to take care of her and she certainly wasn't in any shape to take care of herself."

This doctor had many years of experience caring for this type of

ter•mi•nol•o•gy

Professional Review Organization (PRO): An organization in which practicing physicians assume responsibility for reviewing the propriety and quality of health care services provided under Medicare and Medicaid (*HIAA Source Book*, p. 121)

Substituting Checklists for Medicine

A system of appropriate medical standards, guidelines, and hard-and-fast rules that can be used by physicians in caring for their patients—referred to by many physicians as "cookbook medicine"—continues to be devastatingly controversial, providing a bonanza for litigators, a conundrum when patients do not fit the standards, a bureaucrat's paradise, and the last stand for free physicians....But those who are devising these aids for physicians are responding to a real problem—the need to sort out and apply more rigorous analysis to the combinations of conflicting technology, changing technology, halfway technology, and unempirical technology in modern medical practice....Standards, then, are not some rigid laws to be followed blindly forever; they are a starting point—data elements and recommendations that respond continually to what is learned from application and subsequent research.

Paul M. Ellwood,
p. 1553

To: Dr. Alan Lindemann
From: Utilization Management Subcommittee
Date: 7-6-90
Re: Admission of Joanna Doe (MR#3604892) on 6-18-90 discharged on 6-22-90 with diagnosis/procedure reiomyoma /THH & B80

THIS MEMO RESULTED FROM RECENT REVIEW OF HOSPITAL RECORDS

1.___Could have been a Short Term Stay admission rather than a regular admission.
2.___Hospital admission necessity questioned.
3.___Apparent unnecessary preoperative day noted.
4._X_Intensity of services or severity of illness criteria not met for continued hospital stay.
5.___Chart review indicates that a late afternoon discharge would have been feasible.

UPON RECEIPT OF YOUR RESPONSE, THE UTILIZATION MANAGEMENT COMMITTEE WILL REVIEW THIS CASE. PLEASE SUBMIT ANY ADDITIONAL INFORMATION YOU FEEL WOULD CLARIFY THE CARE DELIVERED. IF NO RESPONSE IS RECEIVED, THIS WILL BE CONSIDERED AN INFRACTION OF THE UTILIZATION MANAGEMENT POLICIES AND PROCEDURES, AS APPROVED BY THE MEDICAL STAFF EXECUTIVE COMMITTEE.

COMMENTS: [none]

patient and was well qualified to make a decision about whether she should go home or remain hospitalized.

"So what did you do?"

"I sent her home—but I wrote on her chart that the PRO had told the hospital to send her home."

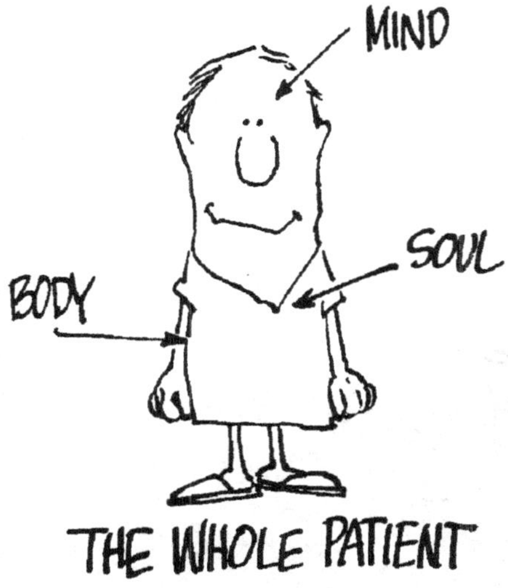

"And?" I asked, dreading what I would hear.

"She had to be readmitted later because her blood was too thin. Somehow she had gotten over-coumadinized."

"So you were right, after all?"

"Yes. But then the PRO decided that because the patient had been sent home too soon, the second hospitalization shouldn't be covered."

All I could manage to that bit of news was "Huh?"

My colleague continued his unbelievable story: "The PRO refused to pay for her second hospitalization."

"You've got to be kidding!"

"Nope. What's more, the PRO also decided that since I had sent the patient home too soon, I should also be chastized."

"Chastized?. You didn't send her home, the PRO did!"

"Well, yes. But for some reason, the PRO considered the care I provided below standard. For disciplinary purposes, they will be reviewing all of my charts for the next three months."

"But that's the kind of thing they do if they think you've provided inadequate care," I groaned.

"Precisely."

"Oh, I see..." I couldn't keep the sarcasm from my voice, "they're harassing you because you told the truth and disagreed with their decision."

"What do you think?"

"I think its high time the managed care folk pay the piper when they call the tune."

Misusing Statistics to Deny Care

This 17-year old heroin and cocaine-dependent patient clearly needs in-house rehabilitation for at least 3 to 4 weeks....the utilization reviewer cites a reference, beginning with "and you can see we cannot justify any longer paying for inpatient treatment because the science simply does not support it." The cited reference was a comparison of inpatient vs outpatient detoxification...demonstrating that for mild alcohol withdrawal, individuals could generally be treated as outpatients. Few reasonable readers would dispute the central findings of the article, but they are irrelevant for most patients we see in our population, and irrelevant when deciding whether a patient needs inpatient or outpatient rehabilitation. Defeated, I put the phone down and am flooded with worries for the patient. What if he uses again? What if he overdoses? My ruminations proceed to concerns about the reputation of our hospital, my reputation, and the ever-present specter of malpractice. Anxiety turns to anger. The literature I read on outpatient vs inpatient chemical dependency excludes my patients before the studies begin: the patients who are medically unstable, who have multiple psychiatric diagnoses as well as chemical dependency, and who are from unstable homes involving spouse abuse, incest, and other horrors. My patients' chemical dependencies are multiple and their dosages are twice to three times that of the subjects in the controlled trials; of course those patients in the studies do equally well in outpatient rehabilitation programs.

Outpatient rehabilitation for chemical dependency is often a big lie. Few insurance policies actually pay for such programs, and quality programs are few and far between. Too few offer full-day treatment programs. Day programs come and go because they cannot make a profit.

Robert Malcolm
p. 90

The Chart Becomes the Patient

In theory, charts are a record of a patient's illness. In practice, the evolution of managed care has turned the chart into a weapon. This is a subtle point, but a very important one, and has had a profound effect upon how medicine is practiced.

For example, in my Chapter 4 narrative about my patient who nearly bled to death because the attending obstetrical nurse couldn't find the pitocin (see page 141), the chart would merely record when bleeding started and when it was stopped, with no indication of the reason for the lengthy interval between the two. In fact, I have actually seen nurses take the time to write on a patient's chart that she was hemorrhaging before bothering to try to stop the flow of blood. To my mind, the patient's well being deserves to come first, not the chart.

The medical chart, once a log of a patient's vital signs, was a friend of those providing care. But now, the chart has been misappropriated by the managed care folks to make decisions which cannot be made on the basis of vital signs alone. There is data in the patient's chart, but the doctor or nurse's art is not recorded there. Yet every day thousands of managed care decisions are made based upon this type of data alone, something we know from the research in artificial intelligence cannot be done (see discussion in this chapter). I am not against managed care, but rather the misuse of data, particularly patient charts, to assess the practice of the art of medicine.

Recently I received the letter on page 39 questioning the care I provided for one of my patients. My patient was a 54-year old woman who had been bleeding heavily for a long time. She had been anemic for two years, had several D&Cs, pelvic pain, a fever, and a white blood count of 18,000 and a fever of 102 to 103, indicating a high degree of infection (a white blood count of 7,000 to 11,000 is normal). Furthermore, her religious beliefs prevented her from being given blood if her condition deteriorated to a point where I considered it in her best interests to be tranfused. In addition, my patient was very much overweight, diabetic, and had high blood pressure. And a history of breast cancer.

Because she lived 90 miles from where I was going to perform her hysterectomy, my patient had her preoperative testing in a hospital close to her home. As I looked at her preoperative tests just before the surgery, I noticed that her EKG had been abnormal and it was noted that she had previously

ter·mi·nol·o·gy

chart: A simple form or sheet of paper for recording course of a patent's illness. Includes records of temperature, pulse, respiratory rate, blood pressure, urinary and fecal output, and doctors' and nurses' notes.

Taber's, p. C-46

charting: the making of a tabulated record of the progress of a disease; a clinical record.

Record information about the patient and his treatment that may be gathered only by the attending nurse. The doctor needs detailed information which the nurse may contribute through her observation of and contact with the patient. These notes containing details of patient's reactions and progress, aid the doctor in making his diagnosis. The nurse's responsibility for supplying this information is very great. Verbal reports are not sufficient; they take time and make mistakes possible.*

Taber's, p. C-46

*** A detailed description of the types of data collected follows, including information about general records such as blood pressure and diet, dressings, fluids, medications, personal care, symptoms, treatments, sudden changes in patient's conditions, and physical and mental symptoms..**

Advocating for Patients

Any time a consumer becomes a patient in a hospital, it is helpful to have someone there who can monitor what goes on and help the patient consider decisions about his or her care.

We do not say this because we think hospitals are awful places. Rather, with the fragmentation of care, with specialists of all kinds often involved in a patient's care, it is very difficult for the patient to keep track of what is going on, much less family members. It is not unusual for patients to have several doctors involved in their care, and often no one doctor will take the overall responsibility of managing that care. Patients wind up having to listen to all the doctors—with every possibility that not all of them will agree on a given course of treatment.

Certainly patients need to know their treatment options so they can make prudent decisions about their care. But patients also need a doctor who is willing to take the primary responsibility for their care, to be there when the patient needs to talk things over, to help sort through the options. Specialists often find this a difficult role, and primary care physicians, because they are usually not the person supervising the specialty care, often defer to the specialist. Many primary care physicians, after all, do not really know their patients that well. In this situation, the patient is left in the lurch.

And that's why patients need an advocate. Usually a family member can function in this capacity, especially if the patient is recovering well. If there is no one in the family to serve in this capacity, and the patient is willing, try to involve a friend. Whether your advocate is a family member or a friend, you will need to notify your doctor and the nursing staff that you want your designated advocate to be kept informed of your progress.

Nurses can be very helpful. They are authorized to read a patient's chart and relay information to family members or patient advocates. In addition, they are often willing to comment on how well a patient is doing such as whether the person's appetite has improved or whether the person seems stronger today than yesterday.

Larger hospitals have social workers to help a family assess what kind of care a patient will need upon leaving the hospital and help the patient and family arrange for that care. Sometimtes they can even locate doctors when no one else seems able to track them down. And social workers can be very helpful in finding out just when a patient will probably be released from the hospital.

- **When you are hospitalized, keep a journal of what health care providers come to see you, what they say, and any medications they order for you.**
- **If you're too ill to write, ask those who come in to write the information for you. If you're too sick to ask questions and write them down, have a family member or friend provide this service.**
- **If you have a question, write it down and keep asking the question until you get an answer. Write the answer in your journal.**

suffered a heart attack. In fact, all of her relatives had died from heart attacks.

I do not believe that it takes an extraordinary amount of reasoning to be able to come to the conclusion that perhaps this woman really did need an extra day in the hospital. She lived 90 miles from the hospital and had no one to stay with her if she did go home, not to mention the many serious health risks her chart outlined. In this case, the person doing the utilization review had adequate information from the patient's chart to determine I had good reason for exceeding the three-day guideline for utilization. Sometimes I wonder if these people even look at the charts. In this case, the guideline was being administered as a rule and the system of review did not require the person requesting the information to exercise any responsbility in the decision.

If the persons reviewing the records are incapable of exercising a professional judgement about the appropriateness of the care—and more importantly, not held responsible for that decision—they should not be reviewing the work of professionals. THE PRACTICE OF ALLOWING THOSE DOING UTILIZATION REVIEW TO QUESTION CARE WITHOUT ANY RESPONSBILITY FOR THE INTEGRITY OF THEIR QUESTIONING INVITES ABUSE OF THE SYSTEM. *It is often said that consumers who do not have to pay for their health care abuse the system by overusing it. The same criticism can be raised against a utilization review system which requires no responsible decision-making from its reviewers.*

Unnecessary and unjustifiable questioning of medical practice does little to improve the quality of the care provided. It does, however, greatly increase the costs of everyone's medical care by creating many more salaries that need to be paid, salaries which contribute nothing to the care of the consumer, but much to the increase of the cost of the consumer's health care.

Don't Be Mislead by Numbers

- **what is the point of the numbers?**

In the narrative (opposite page) about junk statistics, the person supplying the information gives no reason for the numbers. Anyone presenting statistical information needs to tell you the point of the numbers. Are they considered good or bad?

- **where did the numbers come from?**

Anyone supplying statistics should give you information about how the data was collected. There are two reasons for this.

First, many studies are paid for by companies who have a vested interest in a particular result. How the numbers are interpreted can be skewed by who pays for the collection of the data. Consumers can't stop this, but they should be aware that this situation exists.

Secondly, legitimate researchers are not afraid to tell you how they collected their data—their methodology, in research parlance. Consumers don't have to be statisticians to know that asking people their opinions about something and then collecting it into a table and attaching some meaning to the results doesn't signify much. Consumers should question whether what researchers are measuring is indeed measureable by whatever yardstick the data gatherers use.

- **are units of measurement clearly labeled?**

The graph in the sidebar on the opposite page doesn't provide the reader with any information about the units of measure. The title of the memo is used as a label for the numbers running up the left side of the grid. We don't know what was used to create the ratios. My physician number is tossed in somewhere near the vicinity of one of the bars and appears to be a unit of measurement for the row.

- **are important normal values clearly identified?**

Before statistics can have any meaning, consumers need to know what the important baselines are, like what is normal for the numbers being presented. The cover letter mentions that 1.0 is the norm, while the 2.0 mentioned in this same letter doesn't even appear on the graph.

Junk Mail Statistics

I received the memo in the sidebar on this page from one of the hospitals to which I admit my patients. I get lots of letters like these. Most physicians do. Under the guise of quality assurance, many hospitals now staff whole offices to shower their physicians with useless statistics like these.

To: **All Physicians**
From : **Utilization Management Committee**

Enclosed is a graph depicting comparative data on the average length of stay for the patients you have admitted during the months of October-December 1989. The graphs are compiled by clinic medical staff departments. Your bar graph is labeled with your number.

The ratio of los to std (y axis) was calculated by dividing the average length of stay of all your patients admitted by the national norm for the same groupings of patients. In other words, the data is controlled for the types of patients you have treated. The comparison is made with a similar group of patients. A ration of 1.0 would indicate that, on the average, the length of stay of your patients is equal to the national average. A ration of 2.0 would indicate that the length of stay of your group of patients is twice as long as the national average.

This type of graph is forwarded to you every month reflecting the most recent three months data. It is for your information solely. If you have any questions, don't hesitate to call.

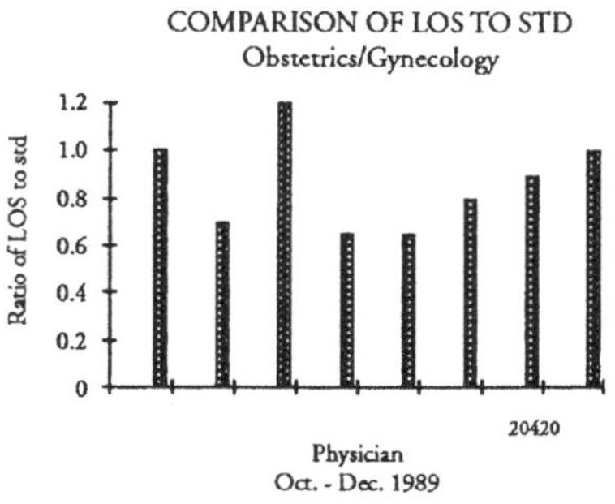

Please don't misunderstand me. I would welcome useful information about what my patients think about the care I provide. Do they feel that I really care about them as people? Do my patients on Medicaid or Medicare feel that I provide them with the same quality of care as my patients with private insurance? Was I there when they needed me? Did I take the time to explain the care I was offerring them? Were they encouraged by me to participate in the decisions about their care?

This memo reflects no concern whatsoever about the quality of the care my patients receive. In fact, the purpose of the information is left unstated. Probably because there is no clearly identifiable point to be made, except perhaps a veiled threat that I'd better watch out that my patient length of stay isn't longer than that of my associates.

This letter is a good example of much of what passes for managed care.

Like our cultural prejudice about science and hard facts discussed in "Art vs. Science" in this chapter, many people tend to accept statistics as fact, as if the mere existence of an attractively displayed array of numbers somehow gives those numbers magical significance. This is a mistake. Consumers do not need to be mathematical whizes to ask some basic questions about statistics.

Websters (p. 856) defines statistics as "a branch of mathematics dealing with the collection, analysis, interpretation, and presentation of masses of numerical data."

First of all, notice that the numbers in and of themselves are not the issue, but rather the analysis and interpretation of those masses of data. The numbers do not scream a point by their mere existence. Actually, what this definition does not make clear is that statistical information does not present facts, per se, but

Statistics and the American Cancer Society

It's always been said that its easy to lie with statistics. But that makes it look like the statistics are at fault, when the culprits are really the people using the numbers to deceive. Sometimes people or groups distort statistics because, after all, their intention is good. This is the worst kind of lie.

> The American Cancer Society, which announced in January 1991 that women's odds of getting breast cancer had risen to 1 in 9, admitted that the number is "more of a metaphor than a hard figure, but says it is used for good ends—to persuade women to examine their own breasts and to get regular mammograms....
>
> But 1 in 9 is the cumulative probability that any woman will develop breast cancer sometime between birth and age 110....
>
> Because the cancer is most common in older women, she said, it is uninformative to calculate risk without talking about age. Even women in their 80s do not face a 1-in-9 risk of getting it in the next year. For women under age 50, she said, the risk is closer to 1 in 1000.
>
> New York Times
> "Some Say Risks...,"
> p. 12A

Every woman must make a decision whether to risk exposure to radiation and have a mammogram, or to avoid the risk of exposure to radiation and possibly miss early detection of breast cancer. But every woman has a right to accurate information upon which to base that decision.

The American Cancer Society has betrayed that trust.

Risk of Breast Cancer Rises to 1 in 9 American Women

About 30 percent of the 44,000 annual deaths from breast cancer could have been prevented had the tumors been detected early and treated appropriately, Samuel Broder, director of the National Cancer Institute, told a group of representatives of 100 major American corporations recently.

Bernard Fisher, director of the National Adjuvant Breast and Bowel Project, the nation's largest group of clinical trials of breast cancer treatments, told the group that despite intensive efforts to publicize the value of mammography and the importance of breast self-examination, only half of the breast cancers diagnosed last year were discovered in the earliest states, when patients have the best prognosis and can be treated with minimal discomfort and disfigurement and for the lowest cost....

According to new figures from the American Cancer Society, the lifetime risk of breast cancer has risen to one in nine American women, from one in 10. The society estimates that in 1991 the disease will strike 175,000 women, making it the second leading cause of cancer death after lung cancer.

Sandy Rovner
p. 5

We cannot overemphasize the need for consumers to look behind the statistics that are bandied about so blithely by many of the people involved in health care.

probabilities. Consumers, particularly consumers who do not regard themselves as mathematicians, tend to equate statistical numbers with facts. Statistical numbers reflect the PROBABILITY *of something occurring.*

The person providing me with this data has told me nothing about where the numbers used for comparison came from. In fact, I have no way of knowing what is actually being compared here since I am only told that the length of stay for "all my patients" are being compared to some "national norm for the same groupings of patients." Where did these national norm numbers come from? National norm for what? For that matter, what is a national norm? Without this information, this graph, regardless of how nice it looks, is meaningless.

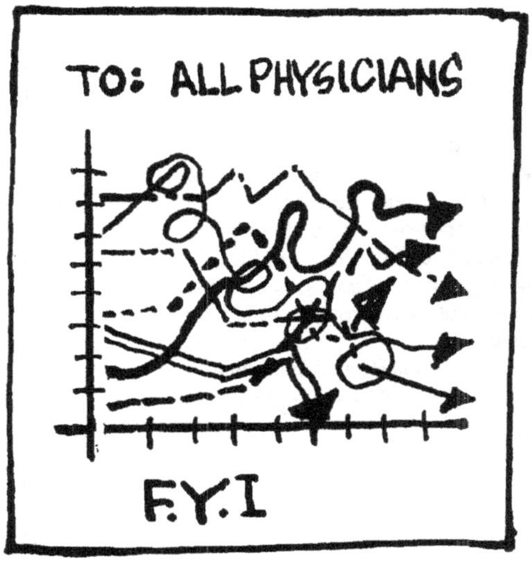

Secondly, anyone presenting statistics should tell the point of the numbers. Statistics provide support for a point—they can't anonimously stand in for the point being made. This may seem like splitting hairs, but think about this for a minute. Two different people could look at the same graph and come to two very different conclusions about the numbers presented. Note that the writer of this memo fails to tell me what the point of the graph is, only that it is "for your information solely." I could look at it and conclude that, gee whiz, all of my colleagues are showing patient length-of-stays that are apparently quite normal. What I don't know is whether the person who sent me this memo considers the patient length-of-stays shown here good or bad. If the writer of this memo has no real point to make, why waste my time?

Statistics can provide valuable additional information about an issue, and medical practice is no exception. But they cannot substitute for the issue or be the issue and they have no value out of context, that is, without a purpose.

Mind Over Matter

AI [artificial intelligence] researchers started out thinking that they could reproduce all of cognition through a 100 percent top-down approach: functions calling subfunctions calling subsubfunctions and so on, until it all bottomed out in some primitives. Thus intelligence was thought to be hierarchically decomposable, with high-level cognition at the top driving low-level cognition at the bottom.

Douglas Hofstadter
Metamagical Themas,
p. 653

The brain itself does not "manipulate symbols"; the brain is the medium in which the symbols are floating and in which they trigger each other. There is no central manipulator, no central program.

Douglas Hofstadter
Metamagical Themas,
p. 648

There is in AI [artificial intelligence] today a tendency ...toward developing programs that can do such things as medical diagnosis, geological consultation (for oil prospecting)....Yet there is no program that has common sense; no program that learns things that it has not been explicitly taught how to learn; no program that can recover gracefully from its own errors. The "artificial expertise" programs that do exist are rigid, brittle, inflexible. Like chess programs, they may serve a useful intellectual or even practical purpose, but despite much fanfare, they are not shedding much light on human intelligence. Mostly they are being developed simply because various agencies or industries fund them.

Douglas Hofstadter
Metamagical Themas,
p. 636

Decisions fall out as the holographic correlations are performed. One doesn't have to think things through one-two-three-four—a step at a time. One takes the whole constellation of a situation, correlates it, and out of that correlation emerges the correct response. and one can execute numerous correlations simultaneously.

Karl Pribram in Goleman's
"Holographic Memory,"
p. 80

...we have written programs that can do wonderfully well at what people have to work very hard at doing consciously (*e.g.*, doing integrals, playing chess, medical diagnosis, etc.)—but we have yet to write a program that remotely approaches our ability to do what we do without thinking or training—things like understanding a conversation partner with an accent at a loud cocktail party with music blaring in the background, while at the same time overhearing wisps of conversations in the far corner of the room.

Douglas Hofstadter
Metamagical Themas,
p. 640

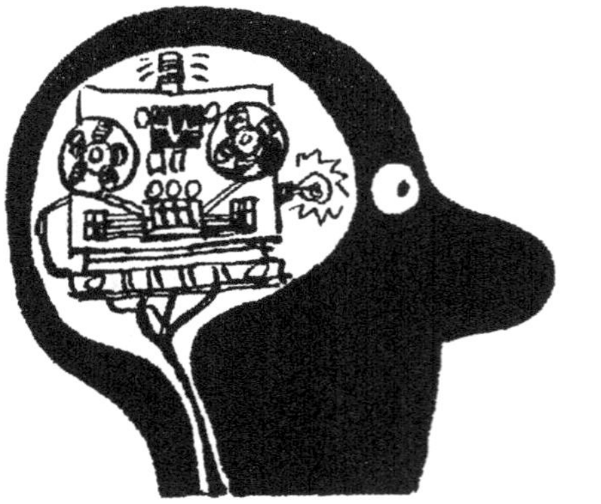

Strangling the Art of Medicine

The concept of managed care has developed out of efforts to monitor—and hence control—skyrocketing health care costs. The problem with any attempt to "manage" care is how to judge the appropriateness and the quality of the care provided. Rules developed for "managing" care are concerned first and foremost with keeping costs down. Unfortunately, in practice, the rules for keeping the costs of care down have often also been used for measuring the quality of that care as well. This creates serious problems.

In theory, restricting health care services should bring down health care costs. Cut out an extra day in the hospital and the bill goes down. Prevent unneeded surgeries and the bill goes down. Replace aides, orderlies, and licensed practical nurses with registered nurses who can do all the jobs done by these people, and hospitals can employ fewer people and hence lower their total outlay for employee salaries. The lower costs created by these methods are real, but of course, our health care costs have continued their spiral upward. In practice, what we've done is decrease access to health care services, thereby cutting costs, but at the same time created additional levels of bureaucracy to soak up any savings.

So the concept of managed care is seriously flawed in that it doesn't really save money. But there is a second, more serious problem with managed care. The guidelines for lowering costs can—and have been—mistakenly assumed to also yield better quality care. In truth, researchers are still working on ways to validly assess the quality of medical care (see Sisk). Individuals, for any number of reasons, respond differently to the same treatment. Circumstances will create different outcomes even if the treatment is the same.

In this chapter we will be looking at why we believe "managed care" has often become "mismanaged care" and how what should be guidelines for allowable costs have developed into rigid rules. To understand the problems created by such practices, it is helpful to look at the differences between art and science, our culture's preconceived notions about science, and what researchers have discovered about expert behavior.

Art vs. Science

The practice of medicine is usually considered to be a blend of art and science and philosophers have argued about the differences between these two approaches to knowledge since ancient times. Our culture tends to assume that science is based upon verifiable, unchanging fact. But a lot of these facts have become a little less clearcut as we make more and more discoveries about our universe. For example, not many years ago light was believed to be a wave, but we now know it

The Demise of the Art of Medicine

The practice of medicine is a delicate balance between art and science. Clinical skills and scientific knowledge are essential, but the art of medicine lies in personal skills—a caring relationship with patients, an ability to communicate clearly, a flash of intuition that leads to diagnosis. Our challenge as physicians is to maintain that balance in the face of increasing deprofessionalization....But the physician's autonomy is being gradually diminished by economic pressures from health care administration, megacorporations, the licensure of paraprofessionals, and malpractice litigation. The mystique of the healer is being eroded by forces that make health care more impersonal.

Robert D. Christensen
p. 599

The American approach to financing health care has gone awry. From physicians to patients, from The Heritage Foundation to the AFL-CIO, there is agreement that the system needs reform....Many advocate adjustments of familiar regimens: larger doses of employment-based insurance and greater infusions of public funds to expand Medicaid or to subsidize risk pools for the uninsured....Because such measures do not confront the interdependent problems of rising costs and declining access, they cannot ensure health services to all at a cost the nation can afford. A lasting remedy requires basic restructuring of the way we pay for care.

Grumbach et al.
p. 2549

This is the second year of our quality control campaign. It has filled our mailboxes with memos, protocols, and surveys, packed charts with extra forms and colorful stickers, occupied parts of many of our weekly educational meetings and entire hours of several. Once we listened to a lawyer—a plaintiff's lawyer!—recount all the malpractice horrors he'd won.

These efforts have produced some "quality." But mostly they've produced extra charting and paperwork and an increase in the already high level of resentment pervasive among family physicians.

Mike Oppenheim
p. 507

can at times behave as if it's a wave and at other times as if it's a particle (*The Economist*, p. 289). These kinds of discoveries are playing havoc with our preconceived notions about the "facts" of science.

Recently, researchers (Bazerman, Bruffee, Kuhn) have begun to document that science is a social construction, not a collection of unchanging rules which scientists "discover," much in the manner of a miner panning gold, hoping to discover some preformed, finite, tangible gold nugget.

> This assumption, briefly put, is that "hard" knowledge in mathematics and the sciences is arrived at by mechanistic accumulation of facts objectively verified by testing in relation to fixed laws and previously established facts. The twentieth century has challenged this view, arguing instead . . . that what is known is a matter of probability rather than certainty, influenced by the observer's frame of reference and instruments and symbol systems. On the subject of scientific knowledge, as we have seen, Thomas Kuhn is among those who argue that knowledge is constructed by means of ongoing argument, and eventually, acceptance by a consensus of a community of thinkers (LeFevre, p. 136).

We can think of few areas in which this confusion of art and science is more evident than in the practice of medicine. We are developing wondrous machines to help us diagnose and treat disease. Organ transplants, laser surgery, and the treating of birth defects in unborn babies, for example, are only a few of the modern, technological "miracles" medicine can now perform on a regular basis. The problem with wondrous technology is that it is all too easy to credit the cold, hard technology with the science of medicine, and come to regard the doctors as merely the technicians who operate the machines. This is a human, but very grave error.

Medicine is truly as much an art—in truth, we believe even more so—than a science. Technology is an ADJUNCT to the art of medicine. It cannot substitute for it. For example, the monitor to detect contractions in a pregnant woman cannot tell the doctor whether those same contractions are long enough and often enough to thin the wall of the cervix so the baby's head can descend and the cervix dilate, indicating the woman is in active labor. Science—the monitor to detect the contractions—provides "hard" evidence that there is the presence of contractions. However, it is the doctor who must determine if the contractions are actually productive. From the

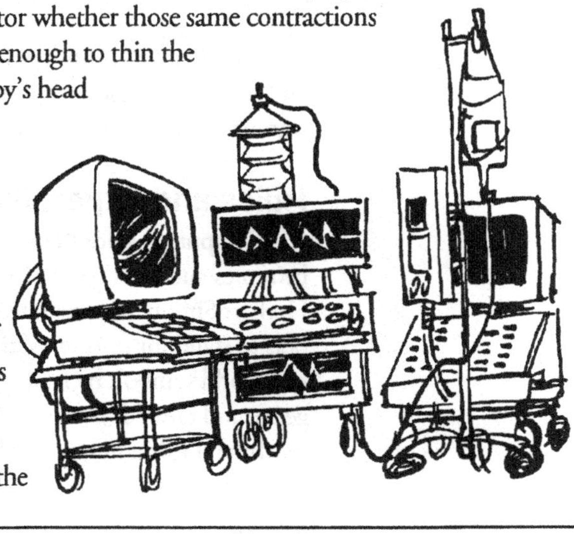

ter·mi·nol·o·gy

disciplinary matrix: "To describe the myriad shared features that define the accepted science of a period, Kuhn used the term *paradigm*, but changed its meaning from a model or exemplar used to conceive of phenomena to the entire complex of shared habits rarely raised to the level of explicit rules....Kuhn has since proposed the alternative terms *disciplinary matrix* (to indicate that what a discipline shares is more complex and something other than adherence to a particular theory...and *exemplar* (to indicate concrete problem-solutions that determine tacit preferences).

Bazerman
p. 161

doctor's many *similar-but-not-identical* past experiences, the doctor gains the expertise to quickly assess a given situation and come up with a solution—practicing the art of medicine. As Jencks (p. 2679) reminds us, more and more researchers "emphasize that the scientific base for many decisions that physicians must make is quite limited—a reality that physicians have long described as the 'art of medicine.'"

The art of medicine, then, those certain kinds of knowledge derived from a doctor's many, many observations of similar situations, is often not reducible to rules. Guidelines, yes: rules, no. Nowhere is the confusion between guidelines (sometimes called heuristics) and rules better illustrated than in the tension between medicine and managed care.

> Practicing physicians know that some characteristics of sick patients can't be measured. We handle individual cases with specific nuances. Yet our practices are evaluated by algorithm-wielding nurses on case management phones and by...standards that attempt to generalize and quantify medicine. (Charles Meyer, p. 451)

Rules have a legitimate purpose in any endeavor, but attempts to formulate rules from situations which can and ought to have variable outcomes can be disastrous.

> Heuristic procedures should not be confused with rule-governed procedures. A rule-governed procedure specifies a finite series of steps that can be carried out in mechanical fashion without the use of intuition or special ability and that infallibly results in a correct answer....If we all follow the same rules, we all get the same result. (Young et al., p. 120).

To gain a better understanding of this conflict, the interplay of art and science and how people use rules, it is necessary to take a look at what researchers have learned about expert behavior.

Rules and Expert Systems

Computers, since their inception, have been used to manipulate data that can be represented as a series of *yes* or *no* responses. Then, in1963, Allen Newell and Herbert Simon demonstrated that computers could be programmed to use symbols to stand for features of the real world, with computer programs linking these real-world symbols by rules. This discovery launched the field of artificial intelligence and created the powerful analogy of the mind as an information-processing machine (Hofstadter, p. 653).

Simon, in developing his information-processing model of intelligence, began studying how people solve problems, and he discovered that rules play an important part in this process. The early chess games for the computer were developed largely in response to these studies of human problem solving. This led to the hope that we could create "expert systems" by creating massive lists of interrelated rules. A doctor, for example, could feed a computer a list of patient symptoms, and the computer would generate a list of the possible causes with an associated list of possible treatments. Many of the "ask a nurse" type of services use computers to guide those answering the phones. Researchers developing these systems thought that all they had to do was interview experts and find out what rules they used to solve their problems (or, as the case may be, to make their diagnoses).

The researchers were in for a shock. While some types of human intelligence are rule based, some are not. Humans are able to form and process images in a way that cannot be captured by operations on symbolic descriptions. The differences between how novices and experts solve problems is not a matter of the expert having learned more rules. True, experts do know more rules than novices, but more importantly, experts also use the rules they know in a different manner. Novices generally use rules very consciously. Experts, on the other hand, often use rules without even being aware of what they are doing. More importantly, experts make decisions by comparing past experiences, and these experiences are not reducible to rules. In fact, expert behavior is characterized by the ability to sort through and use a vast number of unique experiences which bear no names and defy complete verbal description.

> The capacity of experts to store in memory tens of thousands of typical situations and rapidly and effortlessly to see the present situation as similar to one of these, apparently without resorting to time-consuming feature detection and matching, suggests that the brain does not work like a heuristically programmed digital computer applying rules to bits of information. Rather it suggests, as some neurophysiologists already believe, that the brain, at times at least, works holographically, superimposing the records of whole situations and measuring their similarity. (Dreyfus and Dreyfus, p. 327)

Hofstadter believes that Simon and those who hope to produce a model of the human mind based upon an information-processing analogy, where they will simply build a bigger and bigger machine which can process more and more bits of

data, are doomed to failure (Hofstadter, p. 647-648). He maintains that this approach is merely to imitate logic and deduction at the expense of the kinds of thinking processes that people are not even aware of. A classic example of this different kind of thinking is illustrated by the problem of trying to teach a computer to recognize the difference between a letter A and a letter B.

> Take the letter A. Hofstadter has hundreds of them on his office wall in a poster cataloguing a variety of typefaces. They are all different, but they are all A's How to recognize letters in any of the many shapes they can take was one of the classic early problems of artificial intelligence. But it was largely abandoned in favor of programs that could read a narrow range of specially designed characters, like the numerals on bank checks. The computer program has not yet been written that can tell any recognizable A from any B.

The insights provided by the study of artificial intelligence are beginning to shed some light on the differences between art and science and the limits of rules. There is a place in medicine for guidelines. There is a place in medicine for expert systems. But until the focus of those using these systems become guidelines for appropriate practices rather than rules to ration health care and cut costs, consumers are likely to have neither appropriate medical care nor reasonable costs (Reece, "A New Breed...,"p. 387).

Guidelines vs. Rules

Managed care takes many forms. When your doctor is required to have your surgery preauthrorized, or you are required to go to another doctor to get a second opinion about the necessity of surgery, the insurance company is "managing" your care. In practice, the guidelines for determining that the care you receive falls within normal ranges too easily become rules. Regardless of the circumstances surrounding the preauthorized surgery, a patient is allowed only so many days in the hospital for that given procedure. Any deviation from this "rule" often results in all kinds of needless, time-consuming unpleasantries for everyone involved. In theory, the doctor explains the need for any additional days without any implied threat that the care being provided is somehow substandard because the hospital stay is not within the specified allowable days. In practice, managed care deteriorates into the kinds of problems illustrated in this chapter's narratives. In these situations, the quality of care is apparently not the issue, but rather, saving money.

In another form of managed care, some hospitals employ for-profit "quality assurance companies" to review patient records with the express purpose of discovering any possible cost reimbursable by the insurance company which might have been overlooked. If these persons find an omitted charge, they submit a claim for it and the company keeps a percentage of the claim as payment for their services. Such companies, for example, might find that a hospital charges $3,000 for a hip replacement operation, but could charge $10,000 if the accounting department filled out reimbursement forms differently. Again, quality of care is not the issue. Making money is.

Quality of Care Difficult to Measure

Consumers need to know that there is a difference between managing health care to keep the costs down, and measuring the quality of that care. As noted earlier, researchers are finding that the quality of health care is difficult to measure because it involves more than just checking for a given set of symptoms and ticking off whether or not they are present or absent (Sisk, p. 30).

At the same time, there is compelling evidence that the quality of this country's health care is less than it should be, with a significant portion of our medical care deemed inappropriate, and in some cases even causing death. In a Rand study (Reece, "A New Breed...," pp. 387-388), it was concluded that 17 to 32 percent of the major procedures provided to the Medicare population were inappropriate. A study by the Office of Technology Assessment (Sisk, 1988) reports that up to one third of hospital deaths and hospital-acquired infections may be preventable (p. 12).

THE MEASURING OF HEALTH CARE

Yet this same study (Sisk, p. 30) indicates that many of the traditional measures of quality are really poor indicators of good care. For example, sometimes the disciplinary actions of state medical boards are used to assess quality. However, single instances of discipline used without considering other measures does not reliably indicate quality (see Chapter 5). In other cases, the number of hospital deaths for a given procedure is used as an indicator of the quality of care. Again, this can be an unreliable indication since some hospitals treat poorer and often sicker patients than others, so the mortality statistics from one hospital to another may not be comparable.

Increasingly, the quality of health care is being measured by comparing "outcomes," that is, how much a given treatment improves the patient's condition. With our present health care system, doctors and hospitals are often reimbursed—sometimes at great cost—for treatments that provide little real improvement in a patient's health, if any at all. Little improvement in our health care crisis will be realized until we as a nation develop a rational health care policy about what kinds of health care services produce worthwhile results for the costs involved, and what kinds of health care services cost horendous amounts of money but provide virtually no improvement in status in a patient's health. Let us emphasize that doctors should be making these kinds of decisions, in concert with consumers. The state of Oregon has begun this process. It can be done. But let us emphasize that these are not the kinds of decisions that managed care folk should be making by reading patient charts, nor are they the kinds of decisions that only "experts" can make.

A North Dakota nursing home group says $680,729 was spent during the 1989-91 biennium to identify one resident found inappropriate for nursing care under a Medicaid screening program it calls wasteful....

The screening program is to identify patients who need specialized care for mental illness or mental retardation, and is meant to prevent "dumping" residents in nursing homes where they would not receive adequate care.

State figures indicate $510,729 was spent during the 1989-91 biennium for eight nurses to screen residents for mental illness or mental retardation. Another $170,000 was paid to a consulting firm for evaluations during the period.

Approximately 6,900 nursing home residents were evaluated in 1990 and only 353, or 5 percent, were identified with a mental illness, according to a report by the association. Of the 353, 36 were recommended for specialized services, only one of whom was required to leave a nursing home.

"Our argument is it's such a waste of federal and state dollars," said Shelly Warner, executive director of the North Dakota Long Term Care Association...."

Patrick Springer
"N.D. Care Group...,"
p. A1

The Failure of Managed Care

We believe that a large part of the failure of "managed" care to control costs can be blamed on a system of oversight which tends to formulate guidelines, and then inappropriately enforce those guidelines as rules, often inconsistently. To operate, such a system requires a large number of people looking over the shoulders of those actually providing the care, setting up an adversarial relationship between the professionals providing the care and the reviewers. Furthermore, a large proportion of the savings created by identifying unwarranted care is offset by the costs of the armies of people required to do the reviews.

We are not saying that there should be no oversight, but rather that the system of oversight which has evolved in our health care system is costly, relatively ineffective, and based on a very serious misconception about the realm of the art of medicine.

Researchers attempting to measure the quality of health care seem to realize that there are dimensions to the issue of the quality of health care which cannot be reduced to inflexible rules. Many of those organizations charged with "managing" health care have not yet reached this level of understanding.

Managed care as it is generally practiced today has created an enormous amount of wasteful procedures which take health care workers away from their primary job—caring for people—and create vast amounts of jobs for people no longer involved in the actual hands-on care of consumers, people whose job it is to look at the medical charts and make decisions from a paper trail without any real concern, much less understanding, for the human beings represented by the medical charts. Little wonder that there is a high level of frustration among health care providers who would prefer to treat the patient, not the chart. Little wonder that health care providers feel that the rules are usurping their ability to make professional decisions, decisions they have spent years preparing to make, and decisions that their years of practical experience qualify them to make in a way for which no rulebook can substitute . Decisions that often are not amenable to any explicit rules.

Little wonder that managed care has done so little to improve the quality of our health care, and so much to increase its cost.

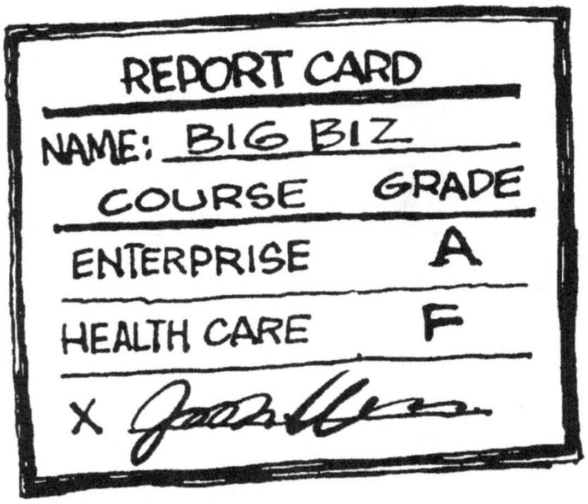

Chapter 2 Summary

PROBLEM #1:

Medical decisions have been taken out of the hands of doctors.

Issue:

Medicine is an art as much as a science, and only doctors who are treating patients should be making the medical determinations about patient care.

Action:

Remove medical decisions from the managed care folk and put them back in the hands of doctors.

PROBLEM #2:

All patient problems are forced to conform to rigid patterns of expected progress, with no mechanism for easily and efficiently dealing with exceptions.

Issue:

Doctors should not have to waste so much of their time arranging for and justifying needed patient care.

Action:

Allow patients's doctors to make decisions about needed additional care—not those whose primary purpose is cutting costs.

PROBLEM #3:

With managed care, we measure the quality of care by reading paper reports rather than observing the actual practice of medicine.

Issue:

The army of managed care folk who evaluate patient care by reading paper actually costs more than any savings generated by limiting health care usage.

Action:

Consider limiting administrators to a percent of the hands-on care staff at hospitals and clinics, or cap administrative staff expenses at a certain proportion of the salaries going to those who provide hands-on care.

PROBLEM #4:

There is a tremendous disparity between what various types of doctors are paid.

Issue:

Some doctors earn millions of dollars a year performing surgeries that add relatively little to the consumer's quality of life, while doctors supplying basic primary care to the poor often cannot make enough money to pay their medical school debts.

Action:

Medicare's resource-based relative value scale (RBRVS) attempts to diminish payment disparity among doctors, but does not go nearly far enough.

Chapter 3

Rationing Health Care the Insurance Way

Chapter Contents

Narratives

Discussion:

Yes, The U.S. Rations Health Care

Chapter 3 Summary

Bulletin Boards

Action Guides

Unnecessary Advertising

In autum 1988, the Honorable Richard D. Lamm, former governor of Colordao, wrote: "We have too many hospital beds, possibly too many doctors, and too often they are not where they are most needed. On a typical day in the Untied States, there are at least 200,000 empty hospital beds...."

Therein lies a major factor in American's enormous health care expenditures. How did the Reagan Administration and Congress respond to the problem? On January 1, 1987, the Health Planning and Resource Development Act was repealed, ending its 40-year existence....the administration was not pleased with its regulatory functions, nor were some of the powerful forces in the health care facilities industry. It was repealed without a replacement.

Because of the increase in total beds and the increase in those unoccupied, the hospitals of America have changed dramatically the way they operate, to the consternation of some patients and many physicians. Advertising now seems mandatory. All sorts of new services are being offered. Women's clinics, senior citizens' services, wellness clinics and fitness centers, and joint ventures with physicians are examples. These, too, increase costs, but they also attract patients who help fill empty beds.

Davies and Felder
p. 75

We heard the following ad purred over our local radio airwaves every day, several times a day, for several weeks. These sultry messages were supplemented by a number of billboards displaying the much-touted rose without the thorns:

> "think of light...warm, pure, and natural...then think of the laser.... Medicine has harnessed the power and purity of light for your good health....In the hands of skillful surgeons, the laser offers a new kind of healing....precise, quick, gentle...a step ahead...like the rose without a thorn."

We can't help but wonder if the consumers, given a choice, wouldn't have rather had the clinic charge less for their laser surgery, and in turn, pay lower health insurance premiums, than listening to the syrupy sound of medicine being marketed like a washing machine.

Personal Best Press Associates

Gilding the Lily Big Time

Over the last ten years I have seen millions and millions of dollars spent on unnecessary remodeling.

Seven years ago a local hospital paid $7,500 EACH for replacement beds on the obstetrical floor. This hospital has just now completed another major remodeling of its obstetrical floor in keeping with the "home-away-from-home" birthing place so fashionable now in maternity care.

We no longer have that dreary hospital atmosphere where babies are born on obstetrical floors that look just like the floors in which sick people are

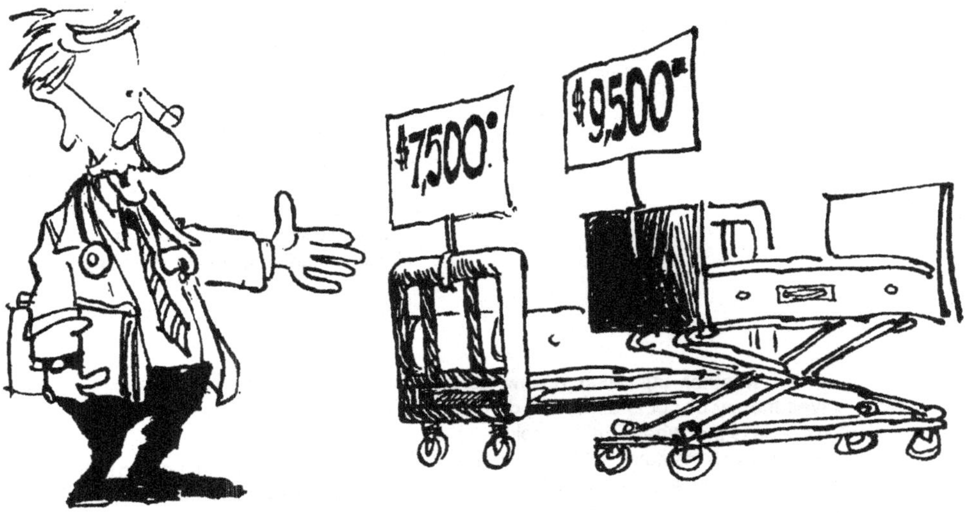

treated. Instead, as the expensive, four-color insert in the local newspaper said of the new premises, we have "private bedroom suites" which "are an experience in themselves." For the life of me, I can't figure out why the hospital should provide my patients with palatial accommodations when the insurance company is only interested in getting them in and out of the place as fast as possible. A clean, quiet room is all we really need. But many hospitals seem intent on making childbirth a luxury hotel experience: "The spacious, homey suites include custom bedspreads, window dressings, wallcoverings and artwork. Most suites feature a private whirlpool and a view...." Including room service: "Before you depart, we treat new parents to an intimate dinner in your [sic] room."

Administrative Waste

The United States health care system, wasting vast amounts on paperwork, spends up to 24 cents out of every dollar on administrative and billing costs....

By comparison...11 cents out of each dollar is spent on such costs in Canada. If the United States could push its paperwork burden down to the Canadian level, it would save more than $100 billion a year, enough to provide health insurance to the entire 33 to 35 million uninsured Americans with something left over, according to the study's authors, Steffie Woolhandler and David Himmelstein of the Harvard Medical School.

Spencer Rich
"Health Care Paperwork,"
p. A1

U.S. health care costs hit $666 billion in 1990, or 12.2 percent of the gross national product—the highest percentage of any developed nation....

"In 1991, health bureaucracy will consume between $633 and $769 for each man, woman and child," Dr. Steffie Woolhandler, a professor at Harvard Medical School and co-author of the study, said at a May press conference. "Implementing a national health program could save $459 to $540 per person on paper pushing alone...."

Blue Cross/Blue Shield of Massachusetts insures 2.7 million subscribers and employs 6,682 people—more than are employed by the entire Canadian national health program to administer coverage for more than 26 million residents, she said.

Woolhandler, who pointed out that the Untied States spends $1,000 more per capita on health care than Canada, said the study favors going to "Canadian levels of efficiency, not Canadian levels of spending."

News Upfront
"Health Care Wasteland."
p. 5

But whether utilization review actually saves money or not is difficult to determine. Custer says that when EBRI [Employee Benefits Research Institute] looked at claims data for the Houston Area Health Care Coalition from 1985 through 1987, it found that utilization review significantly reduced charges for hospital services, but that it significantly increased outpatient charges..."It's effective in controlling for hospital services, but some care is shifted elsewhere that's not under review. We found, in fact, that total costs may go up with utilization review because of the increase in outpatient charges."

Patrick G. Marshall
p. 671

"Our health care financing system is wasteful, inequitable and obsolete," said Dr. Kevin Grumbach of the Institute for Health Policy Studies at the University of California, San Francisco. "We can no longer afford not to have national health insurance...."

Unlike the United States, which has nearly 1,500 private health insurers, Canadians have a single insurer: each provincial government.

Carla Atkinson
"A National Health Plan,"
p. 20

- **we can no longer afford our present level of inefficiency**
- **we need a national health policy that provides for one method of reimbursement**

I suspect that new parents just might prefer to pay a little less for their health care and forego the private dinner and the whirlpool. With non-profit hospitals, the costs of capital improvements (including remodeling or acquiring shopping mall space as an investment) is considered part of the operational expenses and can be passed on to the consumer in the form of higher premium rates. There is no control, absolutely none, over what a non-profit hospital decides to spend on remodeling. They simply pass the costs on to the insurance company paying the bills, and ultimately you, the consumer, see a big jump in your premium rates.

When they remodeled this maternity floor, transforming it into a luxury spa, they also replaced the beds for which they spent $7,500 each just seven years ago with beds that cost $9,500. When I asked why we had to replace the relatively new beds, I was told that these beds go down further than the $7,500 ones so patients can get into them easier. And they go up higher than the others, so nurses don't have to bend over and hurt their backs.

Will my patients get better care from the $9,500 bed than from the $7,500. Of course not. Will my patients be warmer? Drier? No way. Will my patients have a lower infection rate from these changes? Absolutely not. Will we have fewer cesarean section deliveries at this hospital because of these changes? Pathetically, no.

But what we will have is higher insurance rates next year because the state legislatures who set up the regulations about what kinds of costs can be passed on to the consumer in the form of higher health insurance rates make no attempt to control this kind of glitzy, unnecessary remodeling. If the state legislatures allow these kinds of "improvements" to be factored into the formula for figuring out the rate increases for health insurance, the state insurance commissioners have no recourse but to allow the increases in health insurance rates, even if they believe them unjustifiable. And hospitals will continue to waste millions of dollars on these kind of changes that do not increase the quality of health care delivered a single iota.

Insurance Company Hype . . .

Minnesota Blue Cross's new newsletter, *CQI: Communicating Quality Initiatives*, is a good example of the type of stuff many managed care folk busy themselves with. They tell us

> CQI (Continuous Quality Improvement) or TQM (Total Quality Management) and other similar names represent an increasingly popular concept. CQI offers a set of tools aimed at transforming our approach to our work. Its goal is to greatly improve the quality and outcome of our daily work, while saving money by reducing waste and increasing efficiency (Solberg, p. 2)

And what are these marvelous new "tools"?

- understanding the needs and expectations of patients,
- understanding and continually improving the processes involved in patient care,
- using multi-disciplinary teams who meet regularly to study and improve processes,
- collecting, analyzing, and displaying data as the basis for all improvement plans,
- using cyclic or closed-loop steps until a process has improved to the desired level of performance, and
- training of all personnel, both in CQI techniques and in relation to their usual work (Solberg, p. 2).

Is there anything really new here? Pathetically, no—just some fancy new terminology for what good doctors and hospitals have always done. But all this hoopla about the process has certainly added lots of additional costs to your health care bill. How?

Outside consulting groups will be needed to conduct surveys and hold focus groups. Focus groups is the fancy term for jam sessions. Get a few people together to let their true feelings hang out about pressing issues like whether or not you as a patient really groove on being able to have a choice between oatmeal or cornflakes. Someone trained in psychobabble takes careful notes on how you feel so someone trained in pseudostatistics can run all kinds of number exercises on data that is too skimpy and too variable to have any significance whatsoever. For years we simply asked patients what they wanted or needed, which was plenty good enough—*if you bothered to listen to what they had to say.*

There will be official studies of the process of how to make patients feel more comfortable and to get better faster. Most doctors have always cared a great deal about the comfort and well-being of their patients. They don't suddenly need a new set of "tools" or to study the "process."

Where's the patient in all this concern for process. Chances are, sacrificed to a well-oiled process.

And Insurance Company Reality

The same organization that babbles on about Communicating Quality Initiatives sent Dr. Lindemann the letter in the sidebar on this page, a letter which is unable to tell in plain English why it thinks Dr. Lindemann's patient did not need an acute level of care (see the narrative "The Chart Becomes the Patient," on page 77). Even though Dr. Lindemann was the only one who saw the patient, and the only one who has *all* of the data, if you will, to make a judgement about the appropriateness of the patient's additional hospital day.

Medicine is an art, not a science. Those who would substitute bureaucratic process for the art of medicine have little understanding of quality care, much less art or medicine.

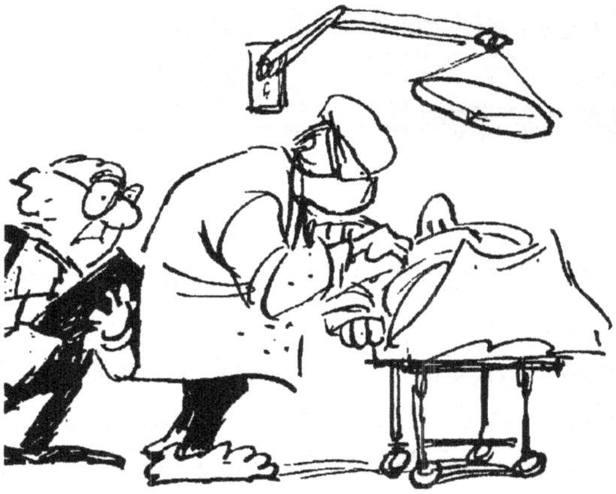

Dear Dr. Lindemann:

The available medical evidence relating to this admission has been carefully evaluated. Such review includes assessment of the documented physical and medical condition of the patient in relation to the services provided. Where possible, attempts are made to obtain information directly from you, the attending physician.

Based on the above, our Utilization Review staff considers that hospitalization from January 17 to January 18, 1990 was not medically necessary at the acute level of care.

Thus, two days (s) have been ascribed to you as the attending physician under the Hold Harmless program while payment is being made by the Plan since your Hold Harmless days were 0.0 percent and 0.0 percent respectively during the last two quarters.

Should your Hold Harmless days exceed one percent of the total hospital days you furnish our members during two consecutive calendar quarters, the Plan would deny claims payment as a service benefit for any days determined non-medically necessary and identified as Hold Harmless during the succeeding quarter. This notification does not imply that medical care was unnecessary, but that it could have been safely and prudently given at a lesser or alternative level of care.

Should you have pertinent information to support necessity for stay at the acute level of care, please send the same to us in writing so that we may consider. Your continued careful attention to the level of care appropriate to a particular clinical situation is much appreciated.

Sincerely,

Medical Director, Managed Benefits

Simon Legree is Alive and Well

A lot of the cost of our health insurance goes to administer the policies—up to 24 cents of every dollar we pay in premiums. In Canada, with only one insurer, between 8 and 11 cents is spent on administration and billing. This may not appear like much, until you consider that the difference between what the U.S. pays for administering health insurance and Canada pays would provide health care to the 35 million people in the United States that have no coverage.

How does the United States spend so much on administrative costs? Let me give you an example.

I recently referred one of my patients to a psychologist. She was a member of an HMO, so her insurer required a letter of referral to cover the cost of seeing him. I sent the letter of referral to the HMO the day before he saw her. I had a copy in my files.

First, the HMO complained that I did not send the letter of referral on the correct day. It should have been dated 15 days before her visit to the psychologist. My patient, however, needed immediate care. She couldn't wait 15 days for treatment.

Four months later, my office manager asked the HMO why they hadn't paid the psychologist's $800 bill. Sshe was told the HMO did not have a copy of the referral letter and therefore would not pay the bill. My office manager sent them another copy of the letter. Still they did not pay the *bill. When she called again, they claimed they had no such letter. She sent them a second, and a third copy. The psychologist also sent them a copy. Still they insisted they had no letter of referral.*

Whenever my office manager calls the HMO, she speaks to a different person. She is never able to talk to the same person twice. But the story is always the same. Without a letter of referral, they cannot preauthorize the treatment. It certainly appears to us that the HMO is simply trying to avoid paying the costs of this patient's care.

My patient's HMO has evidently told her the problem is not theirs, but mine. The last time my office manager talked to her, the patient said "Look, honey, it's your mistake. You fix it or I'm going to the insurance commissioner."

By now my office manager has spent four hours trying to help the psychologist get reimbursed for $800. If this were a rare occurrence, it would not be so frustrating. But this kind of stonewalling happens all the time. It seems a shame we can charge $1400 for an MRI without any trouble, yet we have to go through so much to get relevent care which avoids lots of problems later.

And that's one of the reasons insurance companies spend so much of your health care premium on administration—and one of the reasons doctors have to spend so much money getting reimbursed by insurance companies.

Live Flies Preferred

In one clinic I worked, I had a lot of problems with flies. For two years I complained to the clinic administration and nothing happened. Since I was performing what were supposed to be sterile procedures in these rooms, the presence of numerous flies was more than just an annoyance. It was downright dangerous.

I had those pesticide strips put up in all my rooms, but still I had flies buzzing around. I finally went out and bought a fly swatter for each room. I asked my staff to help me swat the flies, and most of them cooperated, although some complained that fly-swatting was not in their job description. One particularly memorable day I swatted 90 flies—I was distraught enough to count the corpses.

I didn't really need a Communicating Quality Initiatives program or a managed care consultant holding focus groups with my patients or staff to know that the flies were really downright annoying and something ought to be done about them. In a well-run clinic, this kind of situation would never have been tolerated.

A few days after I stocked all my rooms with flyswatters, I got a letter from the clinic administration informing me that they didn't want me swatting flies any more. I continued to swat flies anyway. So a few days later, somebody in a suit and tie came in and confiscated all the flyswatters and gave me a verbal warning not to get any more. Apparently the clinic management preferred live flies to dead flies.

Right On, RBRVS!

Doctors of some medical specialties often make many hundreds of thousands of dollars more per year than doctors who have in many cases had equally specialized training but who provide primary care—the first-stop care. Consumers tend to assume that specialists make more money because they have more training. This is not always true.

A friend of mine told me that when he first got out of medical school, he was working full time in a clinic for a salary of $36,000 a year. Only later did he find out that the radiologist who came by the clinic on his lunch hour three days a week also earned $36,000 a year.

There have been lots of efforts to keep the cost of health care, and most have simply made the problem worse. The new resource-based relative value scale (RBRVS) reimbursement procedures initiated by Medicare is a step in the direction of lessening the disparity between what specialists like radiologists earn as opposed to primary care physicians. But it doesn't go far enough.

Since Medicare, Hospital Fees Increase Faster than Doctors Fees

Observations:

- From 1950-1965, physician and hospital costs were nearly equal.
- In 1965, with the introduc tion of Medicare and Medic aid, hospital costs began to surge ahead of physician costs.
- By 1990, hospital costs were two times the costs of physician care—with hospital costs ($182.3 billion) now consuming what we spend on physicians, drugs, and health insurance combined ($179 billion).
- Hospital costs have increased ten times more than physician costs.

Costs of Medical Care (in billions of dollars)*										
Item	**1950**	**1955**	**1960**	**1965**	**1970**	**1975**	**1980**	**1985**	**1988**	**Increase†**
Hospital	2.1	3.4	5.6	8.9	19.7	40.1	82.0	140.2	182.3	86+
Physicians	2.6	3.8	5.8	8.5	14.0	23.5	42.0	73.5	105.0	40+
Drugs	2.2	3.0	4.7	6.4	10.0	14.9	23.5	36.0	44.7	20+
Health Insurance	.3	.6	.8	1.3	2.1	3.2	6.9	21.6	29.3	97+
Total**	8.8	13.4	20.6	31.6	55.0	96.9	185.7	327.5	443.0	50+
Purchasing Power of Those Dollars										
CPI Adjustment***	4.15	3.73	3.37	3.17	2.57	1.86	1.21	.92	.85	**Increase†**
Hospital	8.7	12.7	18.9	28.2	50.6	74.6	99.2	129.0	155.0	18+
Physicians	10.8	14.2	19.6	27.0	36.0	43.7	50.8	67.6	89.3	8+
Drugs	9.1	11.2	15.8	20.3	25.7	27.7	28.4	33.1	38.0	4+
Health Insurance	1.3	2.2	2.7	4.1	5.4	6.0	8.4	19.9	25.0	19+
Total	36.5	50.0	69.4	100.1	141.4	180.2	224.7	301.3	376.6	10+

* data in top half of table from Health Insurance Association of America. Source Book 1990, p. 61
** total costs are higher than the sum of these three because they include additional medical costs.
*** 100 + consumer price index CPI) = multiplier which converts actual dollars into dollars constant dollars, based on (1982-1984 = 100).
† 1986 dollars + 1950 dollars

Yes, the U.S. Rations Health Care

Let's not kid ourselves. The United States rations health care—based on who can pay for it. There is an illusion that we provide the finest health care in the world to everyone one of our citizens. We do—to those who can afford health insurance. To the over 35 million citizens who have no insurance, even the simplest of preventive health care is prohibitively expensive.

We've talked a lot about the kinds of things people blame these increased costs on. Oftentimes they blame doctors for charging too much. But the table on the opposite page clearly shows that hospital costs have increased twice as fast as physician fees over the past 25 years.

Medicaid and Medicare: The Turning Point

This table shows that we spent about the same on physician costs as hospital costs from 1950-1965, but after 1965, these two costs diverged markedly. What happened? Well, for one thing, in 1965, the United States Congress passed legislation establishing Medicare and Medicaid. Savvy corporate accountants recognized the generous payment schedule for Medicare as a wonderful opportunity to make princely profits.

> The United States had no investor-owned hospitals before the onset of Medicare and Medicaid in 1965. Within five years, there were 207, controlled by 29 corporations. During the 1970s, for-profit hospitals chains grew faster than the computer industry...Most of their early growth came from the acquisition of independent proprietary hospitals. More recently, in this decade, the chains have purchased an increasing share of not-for-profit or public hospitals. From 1980 to 1984, investor-owned enterprises in the United States increased their number of hospitals from 982 to 1,171, and their share of all U.S. hospitals from 16.2 percent to 20 percent.
>
> Today, four large investor-owned enterprises—Hospital Corporation of American, Humana Inc., National Medical Enterprises Inc. and American Medical International Inc.—own or manage 53 percent of the investor-owned hospitals and 75 percent of the beds. Their 1985 profits came to more than $11 billion. (Burns, p. 537).

The Uninsured Get Sicker and Die Sooner

An estimated 2,300 children were denied health care in Minnesota last year because they lacked insurance, according to the Children's Defense Fund of Minnesota.

About one-third of those children were denied care for serious or potentially serious conditions, such as asthma, pneumonia and kidney infections, the organization said....

An additional 13,000 children put off seeking care, almost all of them because of the costs....In more than half of those cases, the child's illness grew worse, and an estimated 4,000 of those children reported missing school because of their illnesses.

AP, St. Paul
"2300 Children Denied Health Care,"
p. A10

The death rate for hospital patients without medical insurance is as high as three times the rate for similar insured patients, according to a report published in the January 16 *Journal of the American Medical Association*....Results also suggest that doctors are less likely to order expensive procedures for uninsured patients.

Summarized from News Clips
"Uninsured Hospital Patients,"
p. 45

Newborn infants whose parents lack health insurance get less medical care than newborns covered by private insurance or Medicaid, according to a recent study of infants at public and private hospitals in California....

It concluded that uninsured infants received services costing 28 percent less than infants with insurance, and were discharged 2 1/2 days sooner.

Los Angeles Daily News
"Study: Uninsured Newborns Get Less Care,"
p. A9

For two decades, the District's infant mortality rate has been among the worst in the nation. It is now the third worst, only slightly better than New Haven, Conn., and Detroit. The District's most recently reported infant mortality rate was 23.1 deaths per 1,000 births. Even more dismal, the rate in Ward 8, where Greater Southeast is located, was 31.4 deaths per 1,000...

More than one-third of the 2,100 women who delivered at Greater Southeast last year, for example, had received no prenatal care or had only one to two doctor visits late in their pregnancies.

Consequently, 10 percent of Greater Southeast's newborns ended up in the Neonatal Intensive Care Unit because of problems directly related to prematurity. Of the infants who survived, most remained in the unit for three to six weeks at a cost of $500 a day—in contrast to the typical two-to three-day hospital stay at a daily cost of $300 for a healthy newborn. The heavy financial burden of caring for these premature infants is shouldered by the hospital and by D.C. taxpayers and is mirrored in at least six other city hospitals.

The solution to this situation is not just more Medicaid coverage for these pregnant women or increased payments to obstetricians.....

But these problems are not insoluble. With some innovative thinking, Mississippi, for example, did the seemingly impossible—it lowered its infant mortality rate for black babies from 54.4 per thousand in 1965 to 16.1 in 1988....

In 1986 that state lowered Medicaid eligibility requirements, resulting in a 33 percent increase in the number of covered women and children....

Raymond W. Turner
p. B8

For-profit hospitals, Burns tells us, are not new. In the 1920s, 40 percent of the hospitals in the United States were small, independently owned institutions, often created and operated by physicians (sometimes called proprietary hospitals). Today, investors often own these hospitals and run them as corporate enterprises for the express purpose of making money (Burns, p. 536).

Therein lies the difference. A very important difference. (See Chapter 1).

The Fundamental Issue: Access to Basic Health Care

Who are the over 35-million uninsured? The unemployed, you assume? Nope. Almost 55 percent of those who could not afford insurance are employed adults. Ten million are children. Only about 18 percent of the uninsured are non-working adults (Carlson, p. 8).

What's happened, then, that people can no longer afford health insurance? Well, for one thing, while the cost of health care has skyrocketed, the median family income in the United States has stalled, and even dropped slightly in the past year. This stagnation is in sharp contrast to what has happened to the incomes of this country's wealthiest families:

> The income gap between the rich and poor widened in the 1980s, with average incomes increasing 122 percent after taxes for the top 1 percent of households but falling 10 percent for the bottom fifth....
>
> For the top 1 percent... income measured in today's dollars rose from an average of $203,000 per household in 1977 to $451,000 in 1988....in the 1950s and 1960s "income disparities narrowed in the United States. In the early 1970s, disparities began to grow. This trend then accelerated in the 1980s" (Rich, "Rich Got Richer," p. A4).

So while the cost of health care has gone up year after year, the median family income has remained about the same, or decreased. That means that the cost of health care has taken a bigger and bigger bite out of the family paycheck. In the Minneapolis-St. Paul area, the average household spent $1,458 on health care in 1987, an increase of almost 12 percent in two years (News Clips, "Twin Cities Health Care Costs"). In a survey of Minnesota farm families, 18 percent spent at least 25 percent of their net income on health insurance and health care. Nearly 10 percent were found to be spending 40 percent of their net income on health insurance (Kralewski et al., p. 37). This at a time when farmers are getting less and less for their crops. And the median income was stagnant.

The growing ranks of the uninsured are not the poor and out-of-work. The growing ranks of the uninsured are middle class working Americans.

There are those who claim that there aren't 37 million persons without health insurance in the United States. There's really only 33 million. We think it's silly

Cost Shifting

Currently, an estimated 340,000 to 400,000 Minnesotans are uninsured, and they will leave behind about $120 million in bad debts and charity care for physicians and hospitals in 1990....

Currently, the cost of caring for the uninsured and underinsured is passed on to the patients who pay....A Chicago benefits consulting firm estimated that 29.5 percent of the 1989 increases in employer premiums were due to this so-called cost-shifting.

Harvey Meyer
pp.27; 28

Every Medicare recipient in this country pays the same amount for Part B Medicare, yet the return they get through reimbursements varies by as much as 300 percent. It happens that two of the three lowest Medicare districts (out of 240) in the country are in Minnesota. Unfortunately, people across the nation don't understand that disparity, and, naturally, the people who benefit from it don't want it to change.

"Face to Face"
Paul S. Sanders,
p. 14

Hospitals in the District [of Columbia] provided about $212 million in uncompensated patient care for uninsured persons in 1989, up 20 percent from the $176 million provided in 1988 and up 35 percent from the $157 million provided in 1987....

In the past, hospitals have charged paying patients more to offset the cost of caring for nonpaying patients, Jessamy said. But hospitals are reluctant to continue that practice, choosing instead to cut services to save money.

Molly Sinclair
p. E3

to quibble about whether there may be a few more or a few less million people without health insurance, as if only 33 million uninsured persons is in some way less morally reprehensible than 37 million. Let's talk about whether it is tolerable that ANY U.S. citizen is denied access to basic health care. Because that's the real issue here.

We know that people who do not have health insurance die more often than those who have access to adequate health care through insurance: "The death rate for hospital patients without medical insurance is as high as three times the rate for similar insured patients" (News Clips, "Uninsured Hospital Patients," p. 45). People without health insurance do not get preventive care, do not go to the doctor until they absolutely have to. When they do finally wind up in hospitals, they are often sicker, and hence die more often than insured patients who have had medical attention when they needed it.

The issue is not whether we have only 33 million uninsured instead of 37 million. The fundamental issue is do we as a nation support access to basic health care for every single person in this country. Our position is yes, we should.

The Status Quo: Cost Shifting

The cost of providing medical care to those without health insurance is presently shifted onto the shoulders of the insured. How? The rates hospitals are allowed to charge are reviewed every year and increases determined by various state-set formulas, usually administered through the state insurance commissioner's office. Care provided by hospitals to the uninsured is factored into the operating expenses of the hospital, and hence ends up as premium increases. This situation is not new. Indeed, the whole purpose of insurance, per se, is to spread the risk of something as evenly as possible among a given group of people. As the costs of providing medical care escalates and the dollar amount of uncompensated care increases, we wind up spreading higher and higher costs amongst fewer and fewer people.

It is often argued that this country simply cannot afford to provide equal access to health care for everyone. Actually, the uninsured are already part of our health care system because the cost of providing their care is included in the premium charges of those who are fortunate enough to be able to afford insurance. Hence, the argument that we can't afford to provide all that free care is misleading. We're already providing that care, although the mechanism to pay for it is hidden. Providing equal access to a basic level of health care for every person would simply bring the true cost of health care out into the open where it can be examined publicly.

It's Not the Length of the Stay, But the Cost of the Day

Average Cost Per Patient

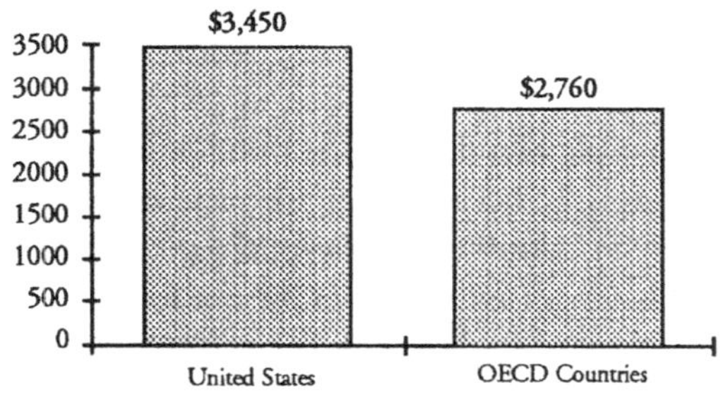

The average cost per patient in the United States is only $700 more than in other developed countries. Is there a problem here? After all, we're getting all this advanced technology for our $700.

Look Again!

Average Length of Stay

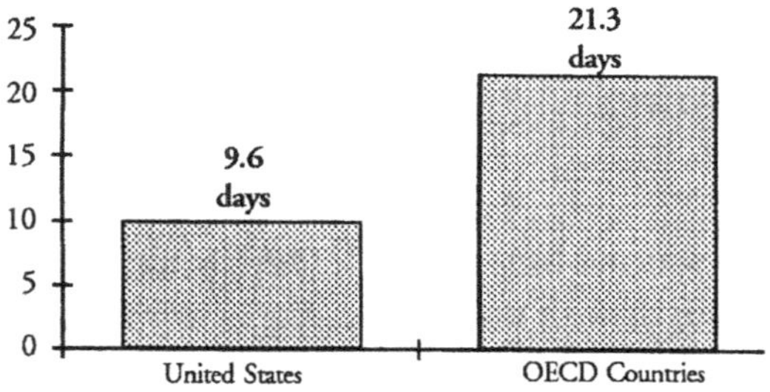

Average Cost Per Day

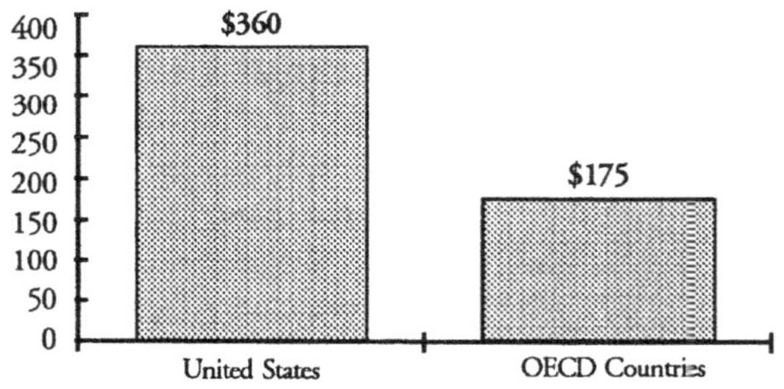

U.S. consumers are spending an average of **ten fewer days** in the hospital for an average cost of almost **$200 more per day** than other developed countries.

Source: Joint Economic Committee, Subcommittee on Education and Health, p. 27.

Organization for Economic Cooperation and Development (OECD): Group of nearly all industrialized countries, including Australia, Austria, Belgium, Iceland, Ireland, Italy, Japan, Luxembourg, Netherlands, New Zealand, Norway, Portugal, Spain, Sweden, Switzerland, Turkey, United Kingdom, United States, and Yugoslavia (associate member).

The World Almanac, p. 781

> Each year Minnesotans pay roughly $450 million for the health care of the uninsured and the underinsured through existing government programs, uncompensated care by doctors and hospitals (which is passed to insured Minnesotans in higher fees) and in high, unpredictable out-of-pocket payments by the uninsured....
>
> The argument that we should wait to insure the uninsured until we lower health care costs is not new: It was first raised in health care policy debates in 1933. Since then it has been repeatedly demonstrated that the easiest way to cut costs in health care is to cut people out. Reducing access by making more people uninsured, by raising deductibles and co-payments, or by refusing to insure people with medical conditions, is a far easier approach to cutting costs than effectively managing health care or administrative costs. (Quam, editorial page).

Many of the community hospitals which are closing at alarming rates are having financial difficulty for the very reason that they provide a preponderance of the care for the poor and uninsured. These hospitals cannot compete with privately owned institutions which generally confine themselves to treating primarily insured patients, often times specializing in procedures which are elective and turn the greatest profit (Burns, p. 542).

National Health Insurance Proposals

Many groups—political, professional, or both—have come forward with their solutions to our crisis. Senator George Mitchell's plan (S 1227), requires all employers to provide health insurance for their employees and families or pay a penalty in the form of a percentage of their payroll. The money collected from the payroll penalties would help pay for AmeriCare, health insurance for those who have no access to insurance through their employer. Employers could require their employees to pay no more than 20 percent of the premiums. Dubbed the "play or pay" plan, Senator Mitchell's AmeriCare would have a deductible of $250 for an individual and $500 for a family, requires a 20 percent copayment, and puts a $3,000 maximum on out-of-pocket medical expenses per year (Association of Health Insurance Agents, p. 1).

The American Medical Association (AMA) has proposed a similar program, calling it Health Access America. The AMA's plan (The AMA Proposal...) has a basic deductible of $350 per individual and $750 per family, with out-of-pocket expenses limited to $1,500 per individual and $3,000 per family.

There are two problems with these proposals. First, the median income of the United States household in 1990 was $29,943 (AP, New York, p. B3). Add 20

Premiums Keep Going Up Despite Profits . . .

After raising premiums an average of almost 20 percent, Minnesota's HMOs collect more than $29 million in 1989. HMO officials said the increase was needed to build reserve funds to make up for heavy losses in the mid-1980s. This year's average premium increase is again expected to approach 20 percent.

News Clips
"Record HMO Profits,"
May 1990, p. 49

Minnesota's health maintenance organizations saw record profits totaling more than $57 million in 1990, up from $27.5 million in 1989. The state has required HMOs to build up reserves equal to a month's operating costs by 1991, and some have already met the requirement....

HMO officials said premiums are rising 20 percent to 15 percent this year....

News Clips
"HMOs See Record Profits,"
May 1991, p. 43

Minnesota's 11 health maintenance organizations continued to rebound financially by posting 1990 profits of about $57.1 million, up from $27.5 million in 1989.

Premium increases, which averaged more than 20 percent for each of the last three years, dropped into the low teens last year, said George Halvorson, chairman of the Minnesota Council of HMOs.

The rate of premium increases probably will continue to decline for two more years, Halvorson said Friday....

But while rate increases fluctuate, actual premiums will continue to increase because the practice of medicine continues to change rapidly, he said....

Physicians Health Plan, the state's largest HMO, reported profits of $16.2 million on revenues of $374 million. The plan's membership grew by 44,148, to 378,826.

AP, St. Paul
"Minnesota HMOs Continue Rebound..."
p. A10

Socking It to Consumers and Employers

...the cost of health care has become a national disgrace. Pick any gauge—the $4 Tylenol tablets, the $50,000 operations, the $2 billion total spent on health care *each day.* For middle Americans, those numbers aren't just outrageous—they're impossible. Which might explain why 35 million people are without health insurance of any kind.

It will happen because business owners are getting frustrated at having to shell out higher and higher insurance premiums for their employees. In 1965, companies paid 17 percent of the nation's health-care bill, or $38.2 billion. By 1989, they were paying almost 30 percent of the bill, or $583.5 billion. In case anyone doesn't know, there's nothing in the Constitution that requires a business to offer free—or nearly free—insurance. A lot of business owners are figuring that out pretty fast.

Mark Lacter
p. A4

...American employers who spent an average $3,217 per worker for health care lat year, up 17.1 percent from 1989.

Victor Cohn
"HMOs and Other Managed Care,"
p. 22

The Federal Employees Health Benefits Program provides insurance for about 9 million federal employees, dependents and retirees. Employees can choose from more than 20 fee-for-service options and 400 health maintenance organizations (HMOs) offering various levels of coverage at varying premiums.....

On average, employees pay a health insurance premium of $71.16 a month, according to the Office of Personnel Management (OPM). The government's average premium payment per employee is $201.72 a month.

Dana Priest
p. A15

The annual health-cost survey by A. Foster Higgins & Co., a benefits consulting firm, gives an indication of how those costs are mounting.

In 1988, the cost of employer medical plans was $2,160 per worker. In 1989, it jumped to $2,600. In 1990, it leaped to $3,161. If the trend continues, said Foster Higgins' John Erb, the figure will exeed $22,000 by the year 2000.

AP, New York
"Health Care: Old Problem...,"
p. B3

percent of $3,161 ($632) to the $3,000 out-of-pocket cap on medical expenses, and you have a household with a median income of $29,943 spending $3,800 a year on health care—nearly 13 percent of their *gross* income. Furthermore, in 1990, according to a study by A. Foster Higgins and Co., employer medical plans cost companies $3,161 per employee. These plans, then, merely sock it to the employer and the employee. Neither of these plans or the ones like them address the real problem with our medical care—it is simply more expensive than it should be.

Second, none of these plans deal with one of the major actual causes of our exorbitantly expensive health care: THE UNREGULATED COST OF A HOSPITAL DAY.

The state of Minnesota, with great fanfare, has passed a health care program to cover the state's uninsured. Called HealthRight (see our bulletin board, pp. 124-125 for details), it has been over a year in the making. Last year the Governor of Minnesota vetoed the bill because there was no funding mechanism provided. This year, by taxing cigarettes, hospitals, and health insurance companies, the bill was passed, with great fanfare as a tremendous bipartisan success. Of course, to keep costs down and accomplish final passage, coverage was cut to the bone. There are 375,000 persons in Minnesota who have no insurance. It is estimated that 158,000 will sign up for HealthRight by 1997 (Sandok, p. B1).

This bill fails to address the causes of our overly expensive heatlh care system. It merely taxes the providers. The politicians claim that it will help reduce costs, but there has never been any real analysis, at least publicly, of how this is to be accomplished. Only some general hand-waving in the direction of strengthening certificate of need regulatory powers, and establishing various health care committees to study costs.

The Minnesota legislature railroaded it's bill to passage. Those drafting the bill held a few town meetings to listen to consumers. In our area, an hour was scheduled to hear 250 attendees. On several occasions we at Personal Best Press presented information about our research to the drafters of the bill. None of the sponsors bothered to acknowledge that they received the information, much less address the issues we raised. After passage of the bill, one legislator acknowledged receipt of our letter, ignored the issues we raised, and told us the bill was a step in the right direction.

Unable to get any response from the drafters of the bill before it was passed, we tried to reach our local elected representatives. Only one responded, and that was to tell us—without even looking at our research—that we had no business criticiz-

Price-Gouging Takes Many Forms

Radiology laboratories have been examining body parts with fluorescent dyes for many years. Some of the dyes can cause temporary stains if they get on the skin. And sometimes people can have a bad reaction to the dyes, alhtough the antidote is always available in the room the testing is done.

The intravenous pylorgram is a typical procedure of this type. Fluorescent dye is injected into the patient so the pylorus can be examined. Traditionally, ionic dyes are used, and while there are sometimes reactions, there is very little risk if the doctor has taken a good medical history and if certain metabolic tests are normal.

Recently, a nonionic dye has become available which does not so readily stain the skin and which is supposed to provide less chance of a bad reaction. The cost for the older, ionic form of dye is $13.50, but the cost for the newer, nonionic form is $135. Medicare sill not pay for the expensive dye.

Radiology technicians would prefer to use the expensive form of the dye because there is less risk, although there is certainly not ten times less risk. Or, they want the doctor nearby if they use the cheaper, nonionic form of dye. But what to do if Medicare will not pay for the expensive form.

It has been discovered that while Medicare will not pay for the expensive dye if it is taken off the shelf in the radiology department, Medicare *will* pay for it if it is ordered from the pharmacy.

This is a very good example of the misuse of technology. The vastly cheaper form of the dye presents very little risk to the patient if a doctor has done his or her homework. But the radiology technicians prefer the expensive form, and have found a way to get around Medicare nonpayment, at great cost to the patient—and ultimately, the consumer.

A Radiologist Technician

Since the government put similar controls [prospective payment] on payments for in-hospital care in 1983, doctors have shifted many services to hospitals' outpatient clinics, which are not covered by the controls.

From 1985 to 1990, Medicare spending for outpatient services grew three times as fast as spending for patients admitted to hospitals....

Medicare payments for hospital outpatient care jumped to $8.4 billion in 1990 from $3.9 billion in 1985, an increase of 17 percent a year, or three times the rate of increase for inpatient services....

Medicare classifies inpatients in 490 "diagnosis-related groups" and pays a flat amount for each patient, depending on the diagnosis. The new plan would extend this concept to outpatients, bundling medical tests and services into 297 "ambulatory-patient groups."

New York Times
"Plan to Trim Medicare Costs...,"
p. A6

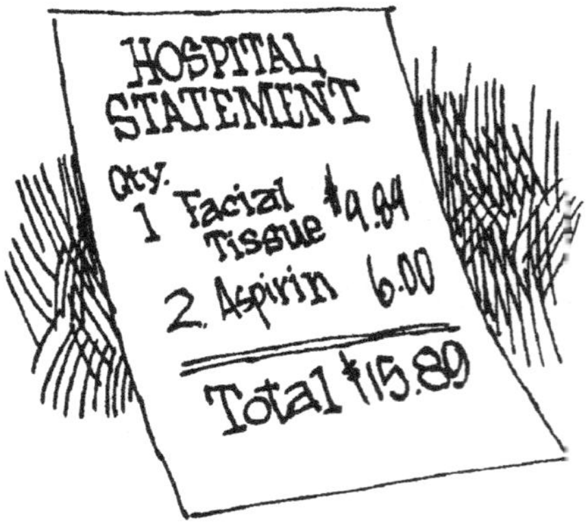

ing a bill that a bipartisan committee had worked on so hard and so diligently.

With passage of this bill, the state politicians grandiosely claimed that they wanted Minnesota to be known as the first state to respond to the people's demand for health care reform (they seem unaware that the state of Hawaii already has a plan in place that covers all but about 5 percent of its citizens.)

We think the consumers in Minnesota should tell their elected representatives loudly and clearly that this bill is a fraud—it does not reform our overly expensive health care system, it merely taxes consumers and providers even more, shifting costs in the same manner as insurance does. And it still leaves more than half of the state's uninsured with no coverage.

Until consumers become politically active and demand responsible legislation from their elected representatives, we will continue to see political posturing rather than substantive, meaningly reform in our health care system.

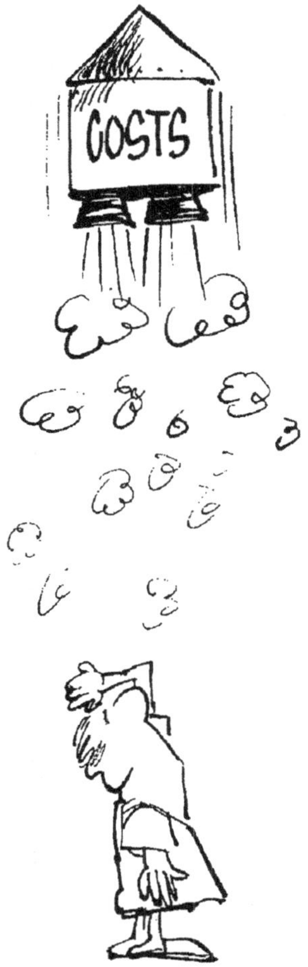

It's Not the Length of the Stay, But the Cost of the Day

There is no control—absolutely none—on the costs that hospitals pass on to consumers in the form of higher insurance premiums. Both Senator Mitchell's and the AMA's proposal leave the cost of hospital care untouched. So does Minnesota's HealthRight. It's time to face the facts. Until we control the cost of a hospital day, reform will consist of no more than taking the increasing costs out of the hide of consumers or their employers. And prospective care and utilization review in no way addresses the real problem—on the average, a day in a U.S. hospital costs twice as much as it does in OECD countries (Joint Economic Committee, p. 27).

Health care reform, to be effective, must address the causes of the high costs, not simply paper over the results.

We believe that trying to reduce the cost of hospital care by shortening the length of stay is a dangerously misguided effort. Dangerous, because the welfare of the patient—the quality of care—is secondary to forcing the patient to fit the desired pattern of utilization. The length of stay is not the culprit in our runaway hospital costs. Its the cost of the day itself.

Every developed country in the world except South Africa provides basic health care to each and every one of its citizens. And they do it for far less than the

The Minnesota Medical Association Whines . . .

Physicians across the nation are outraged by the proposed Medicare payment system scheduled to begin January 1, 1991. We trusted assurances from Congress and the Physician Payment Review Commission (PPRC) that Medicare payment reform would be budget neutral, but instead, the proposed rules would reduce overall physician payments by 16 percent!....

The staggering 16 percent reduction results from three factors included in the proposed rules for payment reform:

• First, HCFA [Health Care Financing Administration] applies a "behavioral offset," in which initial payment levels are reduced by 3 percent to offset anticipated volume increases. HFCA has made the unfounded assumption that for every $1 cut in Medicare fees, physicians will increase the volume of their services by enough to recapture 50 cents.

• Second, HCFA proposes a 2 percent payment reduction to adjust for the "asymmetry" of the 1992 transition process. During the transition, payments due to increase under the new system would begin before any payment reductions. The intent of this asymmetrical transition is to speed pay increases to primary care providers and to lessen the negative impact on physicians with reduced payments. HCFA's proposed 2 percent overall payment reduction is intended to offset this acceleration in Medicare expenditures.

• Third, these two adjustments would be applied only to the RBRVS [resource-based relative value scale] conversion factor. However, until 1996 the proposed payments would be a blend of RBRVS and historical payments—two-thirds historical and one-third RBRVS in 1992. Applying the adjustments only to the conversion factor causes a "tripling effect"; a 1 percent adjustment to overall payments requires a 3 percent reduction in the conversion factor because it represents only one-third of the total Medicare payment. This causes many projected payment levels to be considerably lower than those in HCFA's 1990 "Model Fee Schedule," as well as those in previous impact simulations.

HCFA's proposals are clearly unjust. The promised budget-neutral Medicare reform would instead result in substantially decreased Medicare payments. Additionally, no data support HCFA's assumptions about the need for behavioral offset.

Richard B. Tompkins
"Payment Reform...,"
p. 35

And Business Administrators Cut Basic Services

Beginning January 1 [1992], Medicare is radically altering its payment scale for doctors' services. Payments for many specialists will be reduced, while payments for many primary care doctors will increase....

Fargo Clinic's early forecast is for medicare revenues to decrease $3 million to $3.5 million in 1992, Pitts [Rhyn Pitts, senior associate administrator] said....

"To be honest with you there's no way to improve the revenues," Pitts said. "I think it's fair to say it will have to come out of the expense side....."

"We're not that far down the pike yet," Pitts said of the possibility of layoffs at Fargo Clinic.

Patrick Springer
"New Medicare System...,"
pp. D1, D12.

Fargo Clinic disclosed a major cost cutting plan Wednesday that includes closing its Breckenridge, Minn., office, laying off 66 employees and trimming hours for another 133 staff members.

The moves are intended to save about $3 million this year—the amount the clinic expects to lose from major changes in Medicare's payment scale for doctors....

Meanwhile, Fargo Clinic predicts lean years ahead as pressures mount to curb spiraling health care costs. Officials Wednesday acknowledged other satellite clinics in rural areas might close in the future....

Clinic administrators said the cutbacks will enable the clinic to avoid raising its general fees this year....

There are 1,747 Fargo Clinic employees, including 267 physicians, in 15 to 20 major locations in North Dakota and northwestern Minnesota....

Patrick Springer
"Fargo Clinic...,"
p. A1, A18

RBRVS has begun the painful process of narrowing what is sometimes a very inequitable gap between reimbursements for differing kinds of physician's services.

This clinic's response typifies the market approach to the provision of health care. The clinic, rather than allow RBRVS to equilize payments to varying kinds of physicians, and adjust their administrative costs accordingly, chose to close a satellite clinic which provided the very services for which RBRVS has provided more equitable reimbursement. The clinic could then continue to maintain the core of specialists at the central site who are the target of lowered reimbursements.

As we have said many times in this book, health care decisions based on profits, or "the market," will almost always result in the disappearance of the kinds of health care services we need—and the preservation of the kinds of health care services that are most profitable.

United States spends on the health care of those who are fortunate enough to be able to afford health care, or the insurance to pay for that care. The average cost of care for each hospitalized patient in the United States is $700 dollars more than it is in the countries making up the Organization for Economic Cooperation and Development (OECD). See page 114 of this chapter.

The additional cost may not seem too out of line, considering we are talking about several thousand dollars. But when we also look at the average length of hospital stay in the United States compared with the average in the OECD countries, these numbers become particularly telling. In the United States, then, the average length of stay in a hospital is about ten days, but in the OECD countries, about 21 days. THE OECD COUNTRIES, ON THE AVERAGE, ARE KEEPING PATIENTS IN THE HOSPITALS TWICE AS LONG AS WE ARE, YET THEIR HOSPITALS ARE STILL CHARGING ON THE AVERAGE, $700 PER PATIENT LESS THAN U.S. HOSPITALS.

Health care reform, to be successful, must address the causes of these tremendous disparities in the costs of providing health care in the United States and in other developed countries. The reforms we've seen so far at the state and national levels simply ignore this fundamental problem.

Certificate of Need Legislation Ineffective

In theory, the certificate of need (CON) legislation is supposed to provide for review of hospital expenditures for new equipment or facilities. In practice, the people serving on the boards who review applications for new equipment and hospital expansion do not have the information they need to scrutinize such plans (ND State Health Council, p. VII-17). In some cases, hospitals avoid the whole process entirely by planning several phases of remodeling, all of which cost less than the dollar limit which would require review by the state CON committee. In some cases, corporations simply buy CONs (see the Medlantic story, p. 45).

Furthermore, CON legislation does not cover outpatient clinics. What will not be approved for hospitals can simply be placed in clinics, which are unregulated. The result? The city of Fargo, North Dakota, sports three MRI machines, all located in clinics or associated non-hospital businesses. We know that one MRI machine can serve about 100,000 people. The Fargo-Moorhead area has a metropolitan population of about 140,000 people. With three MRIs in the area, there is bound to be a problem keeping them busy, unless physicians overuse them and clinics overcharge for them. The cost of an MRI in Bismarck, ND, is about $600, plus $150 to read it. In Fargo, with its three MRIs and lots of choices about where to go for the service, the cost at all three facilities is about $1,000, plus $200 to read it. Obviously, the "market" has little to do with keeping Fargo MRI costs down.

ter·mi·nol·o·gy

prospective payment: an advance ment of payment for health care charges that are likely to occur (p. 121).

diagnosis-related group (DRG): system that reimburses health care providers fixed amounts for all care given in connection with standard diagnositc categories (p. 114).

adapted from HIAA *Source Book 1990*

Insurance Bars Access to Basic Health Care

Insurance companies, and this includes HMOs or PPOs, when they see their costs increasing, must either increase the amount of money coming in by raising premiums, or they must cut expenses. The quickest way to cut expenses is to prevent consumers from using insurance. Insurance companies do this in several ways. One is to refuse to insure those who have health conditions which are likely to lead to high medical costs, or to prevent these persons from entering the insurance pool in the first place by making the premiums so high the consumer cannot pay the cost. Another method of cutting expenses is to make consumers pay a deductable or increase the existing one. And a third approach is to ask consumers to also pay part of the costs of any medical expense, called a copayment. From a business standpoint, these methods are very effective. We know that consumers go to the doctor more often if they do not have to pay even a small part of the costs, and we know consumers sometimes go to the doctor more often than they need to. There are even some consumers who demand prescriptions when they don't need them. But doctors don't have to give consumers prescriptions they don't need nor do they have to order tests that consumers don't need. Plainly and simply, many consumers do not abuse their access to health care. In most cases, consumers simply want to know if they should be concerned about a problem. If consumers could make these kinds of distinctions on their own, there would be no need for primary care physicians.

We do know, however, that consumers who have no insurance and cannot afford medical care die at a greater rate than those who have access to health care through insurance. The whole purpose of insurance is to spread the risk of something happening—and its costs—to a large pool of individuals. Access to basic health care, something everyone needs, should not be determined by whether or not the consumer has managed to become part of a risk-sharing pool which depends for its survival on not needing to pay off.

Insurance is neither an effective or economic way of providing basic health care to consumers. That is not to say that insurance companies are evil, that they exist solely to rip off the public, that they have little concern for the consumer. Rather, it is to say that we have a complex system for deliver-

ter·mi·nol·o·gy

copayment: the amount of the medical bill the consumer is responsible for once the consumer's deductible has been paid (typically insurance covers 80 percent of the bill and the consumer must pay the other 20 percent).

deductible: the amount of money (typically $100, $250, and $500) that a consumer must pay for medical care before the insurance begins to pick up some of the costs.

pre-existing condition: any health problem for which a consumer received medical treatment before the effective day of the health insurance policy (some policies exclude any condition from 6 to 18 months before the effective date of coverage; for higher premiums, coverage can begin with the first day of the policy).

adapted from Robert N. Veres, pp. 34-35

Minnesota's Insurance Plan . . .

The Healthright package, which supporters say will eventually offer affordable health care to all uninsured Minnesotans, was signed April 23 by Gov. Arne Carlson.

The plan will impact virtually every sector of the state's health care industry (HF2800)

Funding for HealthRight

The main funding mechanism for Health Right is the 2 percent tax on health care providers. The 2 percent tax will first apply to hospitals starting Jan. 1, 1993, and will be extended to other health care providers and wholesale drug distributors starting Jan. 1, 1994.

The tax is on gross revenues, defined as all money collected from in- and out-patient services for hospitals and all money collected by other health care providers for services. Proceeds will go to the health care access fund which will be established in the state treasury.

Exemptions from the tax are medicare payments, medical assistance payments, nursing home and supervised care services, home care services, general assistance medical care payments, HealthRight payments, and payments received from another provider that has already been subjected to the tax.

From July 1, 1992, through Jan. 1, 1994, proceeds from a 5 cent increase on the cigarette tax—from 43 to 48 cents per pack—will be deposited in the health care access fund. Starting Jan. 1, 1996, a 1 percent premium tax will be applied to non-profit health services corporations.

This will include Blue Cross/Blue Shield, Delta Dental, and HMOs. Commercial insurers are currently taxed at 2 percent.

HealthRight also provides for the self-employed to deduct the entire amount paid for health insurance under the state income tax beginning in 1993.

The entire HealthRight plan is expected to cost the state $294 million annually by 1997 when enrollment stabilizes. Subsidies are expected to reach 160,000 Minnesotans and cost $254 million of that total....

Health Right benefits

By 1994, benefits in the HealthRight plan will include 100 percent coverage of outpatient services, clinic services, physician services, emergency transportation services, x-ray and lab services, and other services.

Other coverage will include:

- inpatient hospital coverage with a $10,000 annual limit and 10 percent co-payment for adults. (annual out-of-pocket maxi mums will be $2,000 per individual and $3,000 per family);
- outpatient mental health coverage up $1,000 per year for adults and $2,500 per year for children;
- full coverage for preventive dental and 50 percent coverage for non-preventive dental;
- a $3 co-payment for prescription drugs for adults, and
- a $25 co-payment for eyeglasses for adults.

To be eligible for HealthRight, families and individuals must be without employer-based insurance for 18 months and any other insurance for four months. They must also fit a residency definition that includes living in the state for the last six months....

Cost containment and state regulation

A number of measures designed to control the annual rise in health care costs are contained in the bill. The stated goal is to decrease *the rise* in costs by at least 10 percent each year over the next five years.

Cost containment authority rests mainly with the commissioner of the Department of Health, who will receive recommendations from the newly-formed Minnesota Health Care Commission....

Health commissioner's duties

The commissioner is charged with collecting data on health care spending from providers and group purchasers and is authorized to issue fines and obtain court orders for those who do not comply.

Expenditures on medical equipment, capital projects, or new specialized services that exceed $500,000 must also be reported. All major spending of providers is to be reviewed

Lacks Substantive Reform

in conjunction with the Minnesota Health Care Commission. Providers that do not cooperate in cost reduction and insist on performing procedures that are not the most clinically effective for the cost, would be mandatory screened on any future major spending.

Statewide and regional limits on growth in spending are also to be developed, and the state divided into four or more regions to foster health care planning and delivery.

The commissioner is also to promote research, experimentation, and the development of practice standards, and to designate centers of excellence for high-cost and specialized procedures and to establish minimum standards for those procedures....

Health care access commission

The 25-member commission—composed of four insurers, six providers, four employers, five consumers, three labor union representatives, and the commissioners of Commerce, Employee Relations and Human Services—will serve in an advisory capacity to the commissioner of Health, and will submit a plan for controlling growth in health care costs. Ten of its members are appointed by the governor....

Mandatory medicare reimbursement

The existing practice by physicians of charging up to 20 percent more than Medicare reimbursements for their services will be phased out. Starting in 1996, Medicare reimbursement will be considered payment-in-full....

Insurance reform

HealthRight also aims to enhance the ability of small employers and individuals to afford health insurance by limiting the current "experience rating" system used by insurers and by providing pooling mechanisms for smaller groups to access cheaper rates.

Experience rating is how insurers currently vary their rates for small employers and individuals based on factors such as gender, age, occupation, and health history. These reforms move in the direction of "community rating," whereby everyone shares equally in the burden of their community by paying equally into their insurance pool.

The stated objective is to eliminate all rating practices based on risk by July 1, 1997....The success of insurance reform is vital to avoid wholesale shifts onto the state plan....

Reform of rural health delivery

Isolated hospitals with 20 or fewer beds that are determined to be sole community hospitals and have exhausted local sources of support would receive grants.

Hospitals of 100 or fewer beds that are not located in a city of the first class and would otherwise close as a result of the provider tax would also receive grants.

Minnesota House of Representatives
pp. 17-20

Income per Month ($)	Monthly Premium ($)* Household Size					
	1	2	3	4	5	6 (or more)
500	8	-	-	-	-	-
660	14	11	-	-	-	-
840	24	18	13	-	-	-
1,020	45	29	21	16	-	-
1,200	65	42	25	25	19	-
1,400	95	62	39	29	29	22
1,575	127	85	55	44	33	25
1,750	-	95	77	49	49	37
2,060	-	167	111	72	58	58
2,300	-	-	156	101	81	64
2,600	-	-	210	140	114	91
2,850	-	-		194	154	125
3,125	-	-	-	253	169	138
3,450	-	-	-	-	235	186
3,675	-	-	-	-	297	250
3,900	-	-	-	-	-	265
4,200	-	-	-	-	-	340

* estimates of 1994 costs to the insured

Providing Everyone Needed Care

One of Shevtsov's first observations concerned the United States' inadequate provision of medical care for those who can't afford health insurance. "We wonder how this can be the case when your country is so rich," he said.

Crouse concurred, questioning whether the United States uses its tremendous wealth and resources wisely. "We keep patients with little or no brain function alive for months or even years at enormous expense, while countless children are needlessly ill or dying of easily preventable illness simply for want of immunizations, adequate prenatal care, or basic medical care."

...Shevtsov suggested, "Just as we need a little more capitalism in our system, perhaps you need to incorporate some socialist ideas in your system. Both of our countries must build and shape our health care to serve the needs of the people, not the needs of the state or the current system."

Joseph Moriarity
"The Duluth-Petrozavodsk Connection,"
pp. 21-22

The most striking feature of British medicine is that the English do less of everything—spending money, performing surgery, prescribing drugs, and doing technological procedures. This economy is partly due to rationing imposed by the system, but it is also due to inherent conservatism that says one ought to do only what works.

"Face to Face"
Robert H. Anderson,
p. 565

Dr. James S. Todd, chief executive officer of the American Medical Association, says there is a lot of unnecessary and expensive care that could be eliminated. "We provide treatments that have virtually no possibility of success," he says, "but because there is a possibility [that it might help], the public expects it and the doctors do it. We have to eliminate what I call "'care at the margins.'"

Patrick G. Marshall
p. 668

ing health care to consumers in this country, a system that is comprised of parts which are not well suited to deliver what consumers need, a system that is wasteful and difficult to change. Moreover, with any complex system, the efforts to bring about change quite often generate unexpected results.

The Failure of Prospective Payment

Ever since its inception, Medicare and Medicaid have been strongly criticized for being too expense and wasteful. That may be so, but the federal government has made several attempts to adjust the program to eliminate the problems, only to be invariably met with criticism from whoever's ox is gored.

Our government, instead of monitoring what hospitals pass on to patients in the form of higher hospital costs, has devised a form of reimbursement for Medicare that encourages hospitals to shorten the length of time they keep patients. When Medicare was first instituted, the government reimbursed hospitals for whatever they billed for the care they provided. There was no control over what the hospital charged. In the early 1980s, the government developed the diagnostic related group (DRG) system, a form of prospective payment, for Medicare patients. With this system, a hospital is paid a set fee for providing care for a patient with a given condition. The sooner the hospital discharges a patient, the more money the hospital gets to keep.

Utilization review tries to reduce hospital costs by decreasing the number of patients, (by manipulating the denominator of this equation). The high costs of the hospital day, of course, are really buried in the numerator, the capital investments and operating expenses of hospitals.

$$\frac{\textit{capital investment} + \textit{operating expenses}}{\textit{number of patients}} = \textit{cost of the hospital day}$$

The profiteers soon learned how to turn a fast buck from the DRG system. In a very short time, some doctors and hospitals learned how to code patient problems so that they received the maximum payment. A doctor no longer saw a patient in the emergency room for acute gastric distress. Medicare wouldn't pay for this. But Medicare would pay for a suspected heart attack, a condition with very similar symptoms. Coded as a suspected heart attack, even if the patient turned out to have a bad stomach ache, Medicare still paid for the care.

Some health care providers resort to out and out fraud in coding. Sisk (p. 84) noted that Medicare pays more for heart attack patients who are discharged alive than it does for those discharged dead. A study in

What to Look for in Health Insurance

1. Buy coverage tailored to your needs (this may not be possible if your employer is paying for part of your coverage.. If you are past child-bearing years, shop for a policy that does not cover prenatal care and delivery. Such a policy should be considerably cheaper than one with maternity benefits.

2. You can reduce your insurance costs immediately by increasing the deductible. You can decrease your premium even more by increasing the cap on out-of-pocket expenses. Many companies have done both of these things to keep employee insurance costs as low as possible.

3. Do not cancel a health insurance policy until you have coverage—in writing— from another insurance company. If you change policies and let one policy lapse before becoming insured by the second company, there is much more likely to be problems with pre-existing conditions and waiting periods.

4. Look carefully at the cap on out-of-pocket expenses. This is much more important than the amount of the detectable. Some companies begin accruing a new deductible on January 1st of every new year, regardless of whether the condition being treated is the same for which you've already paid one deductible. For example, if you break your leg in November, you will pay the maximum out-of-pocket deductible for the year you broke your leg, and on January 1 of the next year, your insurance company will start accruing a second deductible for the same condition. So if your maximum out-of-pocket expenses per year are $1,000, you will wind up paying $2,000 for a leg broken in November which is still being treated in the following year.

Some companies will continue to treat the broken leg as a single condition, and not charge you for a new deductible. This is a very important distinction.

5. Sometimes it is cheaper to buy catastrophic health insurance to cover expenses of over, say $5,000, and combine this type of insurance with a lower cost plan that covers expenses only up to $5,000. You will need to shop carefully to determine if this will save you money.

6. The premiums for the same health insurance coverage may very radically from company to company. The same coverage, for example, may be cheaper through one spouse's employer than the other. For example, one of our group was purchasing insurance for $110 a month from one company, but when she changed employers, she paid $40 a month for the exact same coverage. The employer was not paying more of the employee's insurance costs—the company with the lower premium belonged to a much larger insurance pool than the company with the larger premium.

7. When your monthly health insurance premiums approach $500 per month, consider buying bare-bones catastrophic insurance and putting the difference between the insurance premium and the $500 in the bank, essentially becoming self-insuring.

California showed that 23 of the patients listed as being discharged alive were actually dead when they left the hospital.

The DRG system, as a means of controlling costs, has failed miserably. Because it attempts to use length of stay to control hospital charges, instead of actually investigating the process by which hospitals arrive at their charges. The DRG system could be useful in bringing studies of outcomes across various institutions, but even this usefulness is questionable because the system encourages coding for maxium return rather than for the patient's actual condition.

We maintain that a rational health care system would allow a doctor to call a spade a spade and still be paid for the care provided. It is a waste of a doctor's time, much less his medical expertise, to have to play the game of finding a code that is reimbursable by third-party payers, all 1400 of whom have different rules. This system is so profitable that hospitals hire crews of people to pour over bills and be sure that every box of tissues and every whiff of oxygen is charged to the maximum allowable amount. This is no more than a shell game. But worse, it is costing consumers an inordinate amount of money and greatly decreasing the quality of the care they receive—although expensive advertising campaigns would have consumers believe otherwise.

Most importantly, the prospective payment system has done virtually nothing to stem the increasing cost of health care for the simple reason that it does nothing to contain the costs of what the hospitals charge patients for the services they do provide. In fact, what it has done is simply provide a convenient mechanism for hospitals to charge patients the same they always charged, but for a shorter period of time.

Prospective payment is such a fundamentally wrong approach to controlling hospital costs that it is almost ludicrous. And it has created a system in which no one—absolutely no one—questions the amount of money charged for given procedures. Only whether the procedures are covered or not covered. The result? Nurses who attend laboring women are a reimbursable expense by insurance companies. But insurance companies do not question what a hospital actually charges for that nurse. As a result, Dr. Lindemann has delivered babies in which the hospital has charged $795 for the attending

How to Read a Hospital Bill

If your insurance company handles your hospital bill, you will likely not see what you actually paid for your care, only a printout from the hospital telling you how much the hospital charged, how much the insurance company covered, and showing the difference, which you must pay.

Always ask your hospital to send you a detailed copy of the bill. The accounting office will probably send you only a summary of the charges, for the pharmacy costs, room and board costs, laboratory costs, etc. This is still not what you want. Ask for an *itemized* bill.

Ask the Hospital Accounting Department to Explain Each Item on Your Bill

Call the hospital accounting department and make an appointment to go over your bill and explain what each charge is for. Insist upon an appointment. Let them know you are serious. If you just drop in on the accounting deparment, they may be too busy to answer all your questions.

Write down the name of the person you are scheduled to see. You needn't tell them, but allow yourself several hours for this task. There are a lot of charges on an itemized hospital bill. As the person in the accounting department tells you what the charges are for, make a notation on a copy of the itemized bill. If the accounting people cannot explain what the charge is for, ask them to find someone who can.

Why do this? Because patients don't. Insurance companies check itemized bills for the kinds of charges they cover, not whether you actually received the care itemized. There is every possibility that there are charges on that bill for services you never received, but unless you can tell what you were charged for, you will not be able to determine the accuracy of the charges.

Go Home and Study Your Hospital Bill

After you have gotten all your questions answered, take your notes and your bill and go home. Chances are you will come up with more questions. Call the accounting department and ask to talk to the same person you visited with, and continue to ask questions.

As you study your bill, prepare two lists of questions or comments: one for your insurance company administrator and one for your hospital administrator.

For Your Insurance Company

- list any services or items you were charged for but never received
- ask why the insurance company pays, for example, $2.00 for an aspirin or $30 for sheets.
- ask how much the company spends on advertising.
- ask how many vice presidents the company has.

For Your Hospital Administrator

- ask for bills that you can read and understand
- ask why your room and board charge doesn't include things like slippers and shampoo, but instead tacks charges for these items on as "central service."
- ask what the hospital markup on supplies is (for example, what does the hospital pay for the aspirin it charges you $2.00 for?)
- ask how much the hospital spends on advertising .
- ask how many vice presidents there are.

Let Your Elected Representatives Know What You Found Out

If hospitals will not provide you with the information you request, ask your insurance company and your state insurance commissioner for help.

Then present whatever data you have been able to gather (including listing the kinds of information you have been unable to get from the hospitals, insurance companies, and the state insurance commissioner) and ask the same questions of your state and national elected representatives.

Some health insurance companies will reward consumers for bringing incorrect charges to their attention. Check if your health insurance company is one of these. If it is not, ask them why.

How to Read a Hospital Bill

Date	Item	Charge	Dept.
11/30	room charge A215-1	259.00	
-	ER charge	58.50	ER
-	extended service	81.50	ER
-	splint-short leg 10+OVR	39.00	ER
12/01	ankle, 3 views	78.00	X-ray
-	room charge A215-1	259.00	
-	ankle, 2 views	62.00	X-ray
-	poloroid films	30.00	X-ray
12/02	room charge A215-1	259.00	
12/01	IV loop	8.00	pharm
-	2C7417 secondary set	7.57	pharm
-	2C0123 IV set continu-F	10.27	pharm
-	232074 D5 LR 100 ml	18.50	pharm
-	jelco 12-16-18-20 GA	8.14	pharm
-	dress, trnsprnt 10 & 14	3.75	cent. serv.
-	admission kits-adult	8.75	cent. serv.
-	admission kits-adult	8.75	cent. serv.
-	ace bandage 6-in.	7.75	cent. serv.
-	ice bag disp.	10.75	cent. serv.
-	sox-surg. knee med	12.00	cent. serv.
-	urinalysis, comp (81000)	13.50	lab
-	chem prof-13 (80016)	47.25	lab
-	CBC/diff (85022)	27.00	lab
12/02	231074 secondary set	7.57	pharm
-	231074 D5 .45 (2)	18.75	pharm
-	injection site	7.17	pharm
-	2C00005 IV set w/1 Y sit	8.77	pharm
12/03	room charge A215-1	259.00	
-	jelco 14-16-18-20 GA	8.14	pharm
-	jelco 14-16-18-20 GA	8.14	pharm
-	injection site	7.17	pharm
-	jelco 14-16-18-20 GA	8.14	pharm
-	280088 D5W 50 ml	111.66 (6)	pharm
-	cefazolin 1 gm vial (2)	85.98 (6)	pharm
-	IV admixture	-- (6)	pharm

Date	Item	Charge	Dept.
12/01	PAR care/15 min.	124.00 (4)	int. care
-	nisp/day	33.00	int. care
-	ECG-st A'S	62.00	resp. ther.
12/03	dress trnsprnt 10 & 14	3.75	cent. serv.
12/04	mon inj H20 1500 ml	7.75	cent. serv.
-	mon inj saline 500 ml	7.75	cent. serv.
-	ace bandage 4-in.	5.75	cent. serv.
-	shave prep kit	5.00	cent. serv.
-	shampoo	2.00	cent. serv.
-	teri-tred slippers	2.00	cent. serv.
-	cotton roll, sterile	17.75	cent. serv.
12/03	oxygen-hourly (3 hr min.)	21.00 (3)	resp. ther.
-	initial set-up RT	22.50	resp. ther.
12/04	OR MA-2 hrs	971.00	OR
-	major-on call	260.00	OR
-	cautery	34.50	OR
-	minidriver	46.00	OR
-	tourniquet	25.00	OR
-	PK ortho minor pack	61.00	OR
-	blades, scalpel	10.00 (5)	OR
-	prep tray, large	13.50	OR
-	blades, scalpel	4.00 (2)	OR
-	gloves-microptic	8.00 (2)	OR
-	drape towels	30.00 (4)	OR
-	suction tubing	2.50	OR
-	suction cannister	4.00	OR
-	cautery hand cont disp	11.50	OR
-	cautery plate	6.50	OR
-	sponge ratec	7.00 (2)	OR
-	sponge 4 x 8	3.50	OR
-	eschmarck, reusable	6.00	OR
-	owens cloth	3.50	OR
-	softroll, 4-in.	2.00	OR
-	bone screw, sm cort ca	181.50 (11)	OR
-	bone plate, sm frag	41.50	OR

Date	Item	Charge	Dept.
-	anes-1 hr, 30 min.	104.00	anes.
-	general set-up	121.50	anes.
-	ventilator, anes	39.50	anes.
-	non inv BP cuff & EKG	57.50	anes.
-	ETC02 conn-elbow	4.50	anes.
-	pulse oximeter	23.50	anes
-	breathing circuit, disp	16.50	anes
-	endotracheal tubes	11.50	anes
-	masks-adult	8.00	anes
-	ventilator tubing	2.00	anes
-	yankauer suction	2.00	anes
-	LR 500-1000	19.50	anes
-	anectine 2 mg, 20 ml	11.13	anes
-	brevital 100 mg	11.78	anes
-	metubine 2mg, 20 ml	35.63	anes
-	fentanyl per cc	14.24 (4)	anes
-	room charge A215-1	259.00	
-	gait training (1-15 min)	48.00 (2)	PT
-	trapeze full frame	64.00	PT
-	propofal 10 mg/ml, 1 ml	27.15	pharm
12/05	misc. PT supplies	69.75	PT
12/03	gait training (1-15 min)	48.00 (2)	PT
12/05	ascriptin 325 mg tab	22.60 (20)	pharm
-	meperidine inj all stre	109.10 (10)	pharm
-	heparin flush 10 U/cc	54.10 (5)	pharm
-	glycopyrrolate .4 mg (2)	10.36	pharm
-	acetaminophen/cod 30 mg	18.72 (16)	pharm
-	hydroxyzine 100 mg/2cc V	113.30 (11)	pharm
-	RX 115489 (take home drugs)	20.55	pharm
-	RX 115490 (take home drugs)	7.45	pharm
-	egg crate mattress	16.00	cent. serv.
-	4 x 4'S sterile	2.25	cent. serv.
-	ace bandage 4-in	5.75	cent. serv.
-	4 x 4'S sterile	2.25	cent. serv.

This is an itemized bill for a patient who broke her ankle at 9:00 p.m. on a Thursday night. She went to the emergency room, and from there was admitted to the hospital for surgery the following day, a Friday She was released from the hospital the following Tuesday.

Questions:

1. The room and board charge is $259 per day, yet the hospital has tacked on an additional $533.00 in "central service" charges, making the effective room and board charge considerably more than $259 per day.

2. Why was this patient charged for two admission kits? For an egg crate mattress that she never used? Why is there a charge for an injection site? Why was she charged for extra time in the emergency room when she was being admitted to the hospital, and there was no reason to delay moving her from one place to the other?

3. A patient should be able to read and understand what charges are for. What are the common names of the drugs given, and what were the drugs for? What's "major-on call" for which this patient was charged $260?

The Most Important Question of All:

How much do the hospitals pay for all this stuff?

What kind of tourniquet costs $25.00? What does the hospital pay for the 4 drape towels this patient was charged $30 for? Or the sterile roll of cotton for $17.75? Or the 4-inch by 8-inch piece of gauze (called a sponge) for $3.50? Or the egg crate mattress for $16, which was available in local stores for $9?

Summary of Charges

(the type of bill hospitals usually supply if asked by consumers for information about hospital charges)

room & care	1,295.00
ER	179.00
X-ray	170.00
pharmacy	779.60
central service	533.00
laboratory	87.75
intensive care	157.00
EKG	62.00
respiratory therapy	43.50
surgery	1,336.50
anesthesia	415.50
physical therapy	229.75

We believe hospitals should be required to make public what they pay for the supplies and services which appear on patient bills. We suspect that sometimes markup is well over 100 percent (one representative from a hospital management consulting firm heatedly told us that by merely stating this suspicion, we could be sued).

Don't misunderstand us. We're sure that with the proper accounting techniques, the hospitals can show that it does indeed cost them $2 to provide a patient with an aspirin. That's why we'd like to know what the hospital actually pays for the aspirin.

nurse—almost as much as he himself charges for a cesarean section. The insurance company pays the $795 without question, but then quibbles over how long Dr. Lindemann recommends the new mother stay in the hospital.

The Medicare and Medicaid reimbursement structure is presently being revised, and even though the American Medical Association (AMA) had direct input into the revision process, this organization is already screaming that the whole revision process is just a ruse to cut reimbursement schedules. We think the AMA should accept responsibility for its part in our health care crisis. Doctors should be working to put the medical decisions back in the hands of doctors and to bring about a more equitable reimbursement system—not uselessly squabbling over maintaining the status quo.

We know that primary care providers, a critical component in keeping health care costs down by providing needed preventive care, are paid inadequately under the present reimbursement system. The new reimbursement system makes an attempt to correct this disparity. The payment disparity illustrated in our narrative about the radiologist and the primary care physician (page 107 in this chapter), is a good example of the kinds of problems RBRVS tries to address. We believe there may well be good reason to decrease the amount paid for such a procedure. But the AMA would have the consumer believe otherwise.

Even though the hospitals and the AMA are complaining loudly that Medicare and Medicaid do not pay enough to cover their costs for treating patients, we know that the sudden rise of the for-profit hospital at the hands of corporate medicine took place largely for the simple reason that the first Medicare program paid hospitals so generously that astute businespersons could see that there was lots of money to be made taking care of these patients. With Medicare and Medicaid to back up a system in which many people were insured privately and generously by programs provided by their employers, the hospitals could hardly lose.

We find the AMA's irate indignity over a 16 percent decrease in certain physician fees for Medicare less than convincing when we as consumers have faced 25 to 40 percent increases in our health insurance premium rates year after year. We suggest the AMA stop pretending that a health care system as inequitable and irrational as ours is going to undergo effective reform while physician fees remain "income neutral," the euphemism for unchanged. We are all victims, and we will all need to accept changes in the status quo as we work on effective reform.

The Nature of Complex Systems

Lynne V. Cheney, in *Tyrannical Machines: A Report on Educational Practices Gone Wrong and Our Best Hopes for Setting Them Right*, discusses how large bureaucracies take on a life of their own. While her subject is education, her conclusions about unwieldy bureaucratic systems are equally appropriate to our failed health care system.

> Philosopher William James might have blamed what he called "institutionizing on a large scale." As James described it, ways of doing things that are well justified in the beginning tend, when established widely, to become "tyrannical machines...." Practices that began by filling needs become detached from their original purposes, even counterproductive to them. Having been adopted on a large scale, however, these practices take on a power of their own. (Cheney, p. 1)

The main reason our hospital costs are so much higher than any other developed country's is a systems problem. Tinkering with it tends to produce unexpected results because this is the nature of large, complex systems. Of course, those unexpected results are skewed somewhat by people who are intent on milking the system for all the dollars it can. These problems, however, are not the fault of the system, but the people who use, and abuse it. And these problems are no excuse for failing to address what is wrong with the system. Unfortunately, we are presently going through a period of political paralysis dominated by big money and special interest groups.

$$\frac{\textit{capital investment} + \textit{operating expenses}}{\textit{number of patients}} = \textit{cost of the hospital day}$$

We believe a major factor in the skyrocketing cost of our health care has been the takeover of the system by corporate America. A second reason is that no one—absolutely no one—is looking closely at the kinds of charges that are passed on to consumers as hospital operating expenses to be factored into insurance premium increases. And finally, the very size of our health care system along with the many billions of dollars behind it make change exceedingly difficult.

A New Role for Insurance Companies

We believe that insurance companies should be heading some of the efforts to abandon failed cost-cutting maneuvers like prospective payment and work toward effective monitoring of the actual charges they pay for the day. We believe insurance companies have at their disposal the information, expertise, and the ability to be able to monitor and spot hospital and physician charges which are simply too high.

- Why do insurance companies choose to fixate on controlling the length of stay, many times to the detriment of the patient, instead of the unnecessary costs of many hospital procedures?

- Why do insurance companies refuse to pay private physicans for performing given procedures in their clinics at half what the hospitals charge? Why, instead, aren't the insurance companies asking the hospitals why they are charging twice as much for these procedures?

We're not suggesting that insurance companies just stop paying for these procedures, throwing the costs back on the shoulders of the consumer. We're suggesting that insurance companies have at their disposal the kinds of data that could help the medical profession and policymakers take a long, hard look at

- the development of practice guidelines, such as do we need CAT scans followed by MRI scans, and what constitutes the delivery of quality health care,

- what medical procedures actually produce some measurable improvement in health compared to the cost of the treatment,

- the inconsistencies in reimbursement policies,

- the apparent inability of insurance companies to recognize and approve for reimbursement new, oftentimes cheaper and better ways of delivering health care, and

- THE COST OF THE HOSPITAL DAY.

We Are All Victims

We need to recognize that we are all victims of the tyrannical systems. It is no longer acceptable to simply pass unregulated costs on to consumers. The health insurance industry has the knowledge, the expertise, and the data to make valuable contributions to the development of meaningful health care policy in conjunction with state and federal legislative organizations.

The question is—and it is a critical one—can the health insurance industry revise its mission to meet the needs of consumers and participate in the development of a national health care system that denies basic health care to no one. Or will the health insurance industry fall victim to the inability of large systems to adapt and survive?

We presently have a health insurance industry which

- often does not pay for preventive care,
- pays inordinately high fees for procedures like MRI scans, which can often be unnecessary and unnecessarily expensive, even though there are an excess of machines competing for customers,
- pays those physicians providing basic health care little or nothing for the time they spend with patients, forcing them to gain compensation for their services by performing procedures like laboratory tests, x-rays, and surgeries, and
- produces mountains of incomprehensible claims forms consumers cannot understand.

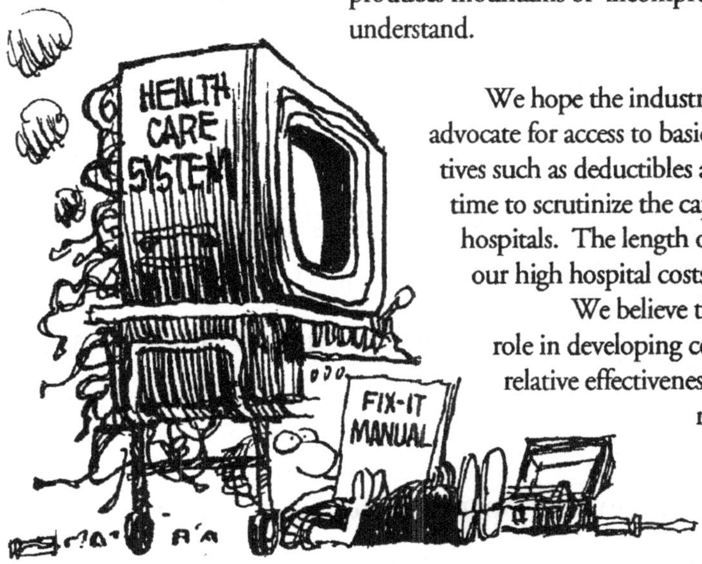

We hope the industry will find within itself the strength to advocate for access to basic health care for everyone, with no disincentives such as deductibles and copayments for basic health care. It is time to scrutinize the capital investments and operating expenses of hospitals. The length of patient stay is clearly not the problem with our high hospital costs in this country.

We believe the health insurance industry can play a vital role in developing consensus about what basic health care is, the relative effectiveness of treatments in relation to cost, in documenting how expensive it is to discourage consumers from seeking preventive care instead of treating the aftermath of disease, and in designing uniform claims forms consumers can read and understand.

Chapter 3 Summary

Problem #1:

Insurance companies and managed care organizations such as HMOs and PPOs ration health care.

Issue:

Access to basic health care is diminishing because we try to cut costs by depriving consumers of care.

Action:

A basic level of health care should be free and accessible to everybody.

Problem #2:

The insurance industry has the data available to participate in the medical community's assessment of the effectiveness of various medical procedures and treatments.

Issue:

The insurance industry should be working with the medical community to evaluate the outcomes of procedures and treatments, both in and out of hospitals.

Action:

Insurance companies should revise reimbursement practices, evaluating preventive procedures and scrutinizing the costs of health care relative to improved results.

Problem #3:

For certain procedures, insurance companies will reimburse only hospitals.

Issue:

Many insurance companies will reimburse only hospitals for some procedures which can be safely performed in physician offices for one-third the cost.

Action:

Insurance companies need to develop ways to quickly identify those procedures which can be more economically performed in doctor's offices than in hospitals.

Problem #4:

There are over 1400 different insurance companies offering health care coverage.

Issue:

Consumers cannot read or understand most hospital bills and insurance reimbursement forms.

Action:

Involve the insurance industry in designing uniform claims forms that consumers can read and understand.

Chapter 4

The Nursing Shortage

Chapter Contents

Narratives

Discussion:

The Nursing Shortage That Isn't

Chapter 4 Summary

Bulletin Boards

Action Guides

Nurse's Training: Paper vs. Experience

Over the past 20 to 30 years, the training of nurses has undergone some very significant shifts. In the past, nurse's training consisted of two or three years of training in a hospital along with the book work. The nursing school graduate of a two or three year training program was eligible to take the examination which allowed them to call themselves Registered Nurses (RNs).

Nursing programs run in conjunction with teaching hospitals associated with universities were in a position to combine their nurse's training with regular university studies leading to a four-year degree in nursing. As more and more four-year degree programs developed, two- and three-year nursing programs closed. Typically, with four-year programs, the nursing student attends classes at a regular university campus, taking regular university courses in the sciences, and then transfers to a hospital setting in the last two years, probably even including some rotations in psychiatric hospitals.

In other words, the program to train persons to take the examination to become a registered nurse has shifted from two to three years of largely practical experience in a hospital to two years of university study, plus two years of sojourns in several kinds of hospital settings. This in and of itself would be no problem, except the shift in nurse's training has created serious problems for nurses who have graduated from the older, more practice-centered programs. Professional organizations often assume that four years of training has to be better than three, and three better than two. Nurses with two- or three-year degrees who wanted to enter four-year programs and earn university degrees in nursing found themselves forced to repeat information they might have covered in their nurses training classes in a university setting, and found themselves required to even repeat the practical training as well. Registered nurses with three-year degrees would be forced to go to school three to four years to get a university degree in nursing.

In time, many employers began requiring four-year nursing degrees regardless of a person's experience. If registered nurses with three-year degrees took a few years off to raise a family, they might find it difficult to return to their profession. For example, in the state of North Dakota, the legislature passed a law that prevents anyone with less than a four-year degree from becoming a registered nurse. Currently registered nurses with two- or three-year degrees will continue to be licensed, but if they move to another state and continue to work, allowing their registration to lapse in North Dakota, they will not be allowed to renew their registration if they return to the state. Even if they have kept their registration current in other states.

These situations embody the classic conflict between practice and theory. The four-year programs have substituted book learning for practical experience, and the substitution is not always beneficial. In any art—and medicine, including nursing, is one—the practical experience is equally as valuable as the theory.

Consumers need to know that paper degrees are good, but in certain situations practical experience is better. A laboring mother is much better off in the hands of an experienced, competent obstetrical nurse than a person who has read a lot of books and really prefers to look at fetal monitors rather than examine the patient.

- **persons who can provide good quality health care generally have a background that includes both book learning and much practical experience**
- **those evaluating health care need to understand that the art of medicine arises largely from experience, not book learning (See Chapter 2)**

A Nurse! My Kingdom for a Nurse!

It wasn't too many years ago that when I was in the delivery room with a patient, I had three nurses there to help: one for the baby, one for the mother, and one for me. Now when I am in the delivery room, which today often also includes the father, in some hospitals I have one nurse to help me, and if I am extremely lucky, two.

If I have two nurses helping, one is usually looking after the baby (applying blue dye to the baby's belly button, putting the silver nitrate into the baby's eyes, putting the identification bands on the baby) and the other nurse writes everything down in the medical charts (time of birth, when the placenta is delivered). If I have only one nurse helping me, she has to do everything.

Not long ago, I had just finished a delivery. The nurse who assisted me was finishing up with the first mother when I began helping the second patient. I hadn't worked with the nurse assigned to assist me with this second delivery. I was concerned because I knew some hospitals had a policy of hiring inexperienced nurses because they can pay them less. In theory, these newly hired nurses are trained on the floor. In practice, some nurses worked without adequate training, and often the nurses themselves realized this and were unhappy about it. In some situations, I have no way of controlling, or even knowing in advance, whether I will be assisted by adequately trained nurses. However, I was soon to find out.

The two-minute-old baby had been taken over to the warmer and the patient's husband was sitting in a chair near his wife. Blood was spurting from my patient's vagina in a stream the size of a garden hose. I was standing to the patient's right side with my right hand in her vagina and my left hand on the top of her uterus, messaging and squeezing for her life and mine. The nurse noticed nothung and was at the warmer, single-mindedly putting the baby's identification bands

ter·mi·nol·o·gy

hemorrhage: excessive bleeding.

pitocin: brand name for oxytocin, a hormone which stimulates the uterus to contract, and hence decrease the flow of blood.

uterus: the womb, a mostly muscular organ to hold and nourish the growing baby.

vagina: the muscle-and-membrane passage between the uterus and a woman's outer body through which the baby is delivered.

adapted from *Taber's*

on its wrist and ankle, for all the world unaware that the mother was hemorrhaging a mere eight feet away from her.

I tried to gently arouse the nurse from her reverie by telling her "I think we're going to need some oxytocin now."

"Where is it?" she asked.

"I don't know, but they usually keep it somewhere in that red cart over there on the other side of that curtain."

My patient had a large episiotomy, but more importantly, her uterus was soft and not contracting to stop the flow of blood. I began messaging her uterus from the outside while I put pressure on her cervix internally to try to stem the bleeding until I could give her oxytocin, a hormone to cause the uterus to contract.

The nurse disappeared behind the curtain where I could see her feet and ankles. I noticed that she had stopped and was standing still. I assumed she is busy drawing the oxytocin and getting it into the syringe. After a minute or two she asked me again "Where is it?"

"I don't know. The nurses usually get it there."

Her question shattered any illusions I might have had about my patient getting the medication she needed in a timely manner. She wasn't drawing the dose of needed oxytocin—she couldn't even find it. Furthermore, she was still standing immobile behind the screen as if there were no real need to hurry in finding the oxytocin.

"If you can't find it there, go out on the floor and ask the other nurse," I prompted.

She disappeared for another minute or two and came back with the oxytocin vial, shook it down, broke off the top of the ampule, attached the needle to the syringe, placed the needle in the vial, drew the oxytocin carefully into the syringe and meticulously removed all the bubbles from the syringe. In the meantime, my patient continued to hemorrhage a stream of blood the diameter of a garden hose.

The nurse walked over and carefully placed the oxytocin intramuscularly into my patient's left leg and I sighed with relief. In an attempt to keep her from getting any more nervous and disoriented than she already was, I suggested "I think we're going to need an IV now."

The nurse walked out of the room and came back in a couple of minutes with the IV starting kit and a bag of saline (salt) solution. By now it is

ter·mi·nol·o·gy

ampule: small glass container for hypodermic solutions which can be sealed and its contents sterilized.

antecubital: in front of the elbow, at bend in arm

cervix: the lower part, or neck, of the uterus, which extends into the vagina.

episiotomy: during labor, surgical cutting of skin between vagina and rectum to prevent tearing of this tissue.

intramuscularly: into the muscle.

IV: abbreviation for intravenous, meaning within or into veins.

oxytocin: a hormone that stimulates the uterus to contract.

adapted from *Taber's*

obvious that this nurse is inexperienced in obstetrics, clearly inadequately prepared, and inappropriately scheduled for this particular type of nursing. In defense of nurses, they are sometimes forced by hospitals to work nursing services they are unfamiliar with, and most nurses are very uncomfortable about this.

Since I am quite sure by now that this nurse is inexperienced and lacks the training to work obstetrical care, I am now in a very precarious situation. If I speak sharply to her or embarrass her in any way, the quality of her work may degenerate even further. I also have the father to think about, who is sitting in the chair watching this slow-motion drama. I apprehensively observe the nurse applying the tourniquet to the patent's left arm so she can locate the veins. I know this nurse is relatively new to the obstetrical floor, but I had no idea what her nursing background is or where she came from. And, I might add, it is not unusual for doctors to know relatively little about the new nurses they work with. The administrative nurses hire them, but I have never seen either an administrative nurse or a hospital administrator in the delivery room with me observing whether or not the nurses they hire are adequately trained.

The nurse attempted to start the IV. She was unable to get the IV into the vein she chose, and in the process, destroyed it so she couldn't use it. She did the same thing to a second vein.

Before she could destroy another vein, I suggested "maybe you'd better go get another nurse to help you."

She left and came back with the nurse who had helped me with the previous delivery. The second nurse tried to start the IV in my patient's other arm, and failed both times.

Despite the oxytocin shot, and my vigorously messaging her uterus, my patient is still spurting blood in a stream the size of a garden hose. My patient is well on her way to bleeding to death and we can't get an IV started! Moreover, the nurses seem unable to recognize the seriousness of this situation and therefore don't realize they cannot continue indefinitely to poke a needle unsuccessfully into my patient's arm. The problem has to be solved.

I finally tell them "I think you'd better get the nursing supervisor in here." The first nurse went to try to find the nursing supervisor while the second nurse continued to try to find a vein for the IV. By now, of course, even somebody who is an expert at starting IVs is going to have a hard time

ter·mi·nol·o·gy

syringe: instrument, in this case a hypodermic needle, for injecting medication into vein.

vein: blood vessel carrying blood deficient in oxygen back to the heart, and then to the pulmonary artery to the lungs of oxygenation.

vial: a small glass bottle for medicines (synonym for ampule).

tourniquet: length of rubber tubing tied around arm to put pressure on veins. By restricting the flow of blood with the tourniquet, the veins expand and the nurse can more easily insert an IV into the vein

unit of blood: 450 grams, or about a pint.

adapted from *Taber's*

Safety Considerations

Staffing Policies

Hospitals try to keep their costs down by keeping staffing at a minimum. Some hospitals try to keep costs down by hiring inexperienced personnel.

Wasteful—And Risky— Blood Bank Policies

Years ago, it was thought that if a person only needed one unit of blood, they didn't need a transfusion at all. The hospitals in which Dr. Lindemann practice still operate under this old assumption and send letters to doctors who order only one unit of blood, informing them that they are not practicing medicine properly. As a result, doctors generally order—and use— two units of blood, doubling the risk for hepatitis and AIDS.

Packaging and Locating Medicines to Avoid Confusion

Because medicines are often packaged in similar looking containers, many hospitals stock the delivery room only with the medicines needed for the baby. For example, the vitamin K (aqua mephyten) which is given to every newborn baby comes in a brown ampule shaped just like the brown ampule of Ergotrate, a brand of methergene used in some hospitals.

It is not unusual for oxytocin to be someplace else than in the delivery room. But nurses need to know where it is.

The obvious solution is to have the pharmaceutical companies package the medicines in different looking containers. But instead of correcting the problem, many hospitals now keep the mother's emergency medical supplies outside the delivery room.

It is better to keep the mother's emergency supplies in the delivery room and put the baby's supplies, none of which are used in emergencies, in the nursery. When the baby goes to the nursery to be bathed, these non-emergency medications can be given.

- **if you do not understand hospital policy, ask for an explanation**
- **if the policy appears to be merely for the convenience of hospital staff, do not hesitate to request an exception to standard operating procedures**
- **every patient needs someone to advocate for them (see p. 84)**

because many of the best veins have been damaged by attempts to insert a needle into them. My patient has now lost so much blood that her blood pressure is falling and her veins are beginning to collapse, further complicating the problem.

I don't know how long it took the nursing supervisor to appear, but it certainly seemed like five or ten minutes. After a couple of more attempts, we got the IV started in the antecubital vein. This is a big vein, but since it is located on the inside bend in the elbow, it is not an ideal spot for an IV. But now we could get some fluid going into the patient and some more oxytocin.

My patient was still bleeding faster than we were able to replace her fluids with an IV tube, a tube only about the diameter of a ten-penny nail. But we finally got some contractions and the bleeding began to slow down. We were trying to get another IV started to begin replacing the blood loss, but before we could accomplish this, my patient had become ashen gray and very sleepy. She was on the verge of passing out and going into shock.

During all this time, her husband had been extremely patient, but he now asked "Is she going to be all right?"

"Yes, she's going to be all right," I assured him, although I felt much more like ranting and raving about the conditions that had put us in this predicament in the first place. I feared that five more minutes of these kinds of delays and my patient would be dead. The nurse who could efficiently put wrist and ankle identification bands on the new baby, but couldn't find the oxytocin or get an IV started, spent a good bit of her time carefully recording the events that were taking place in my patient's medical chart—a chart which will report "the IV was started at 1400 hours by the nursing supervisor." There will be no indication that there was a problem.

The Most Dangerous Time in a Hospital

Persons going to hospitals should know that there are two times in these institutions when services may be poorly coordinated:

- shift changes, and
- mealtimes.

More precipitous deliveries (when the doctor isn't called in time to get to the hospital) occur at these times than any other.

Why? Because those monitoring a patient are passing information along to another person. For example, a nurse may report to the nurse on the next shift that the patient really ins't in labor—something the nurse going off duty checked perhaps an hour or so ago. By shift-change time, the patient may well be in active labor.

It is not always easy to tell when a patient is in labor or when labor starts. So staff must check these patients often. Because there are a lot of details to take care of at shift-change time, patients sometimes go longer than they should without being checked on.

Patients should always speak up if they think they have a problem. But patients may need to be more persistent in their questioning at shift-change time because there are more opportunities for miscommunication and errors then.

- **Do not hesitate to ask for help when you need it.**

- **Do not hesitate to ask to talk to a supervisor if you cannot get your problems solved.**

Life in the Page Lane

Nurses can play a very important role in preventing obstetricians from missing the deliveries of their patients. This is the place that experience working a regular nursing service becomes very important. No amount of textbook learning can substitute for the kind of knowledge an obstetrical nurse gains by working the floor. The kind of knowledge that helps obstetricians avoid what is called precipitous deliveries., those births where the physician doesn't get called in time to get to the hospital.

My beeper goes off and I notice that the number I'm supposed to call is a few digits off from the number for the obstetrical floor. I think that's a bit odd, but I get to a phone and give the number a try.

"This is Dr. Lindemann. Do you have a message for me?"

"A message? No-o-o-o."

"Sorry. I was wondering why someone would be paging for me on this number."

Before primary care nursing, the ward clerk always paged the doctors. There was only one person doing the paging and the person who answered the phone when you responded to a page was the same ward clerk who had initiated the page for the nurse in the first place. You knew immediately who needed you and why. True, you needed the ward clerk to be sure you got the correct nurse on the phone, but the person answering the phone knew who you were supposed to talk to and got them.

As often as not when I return a page now the person who answers the phone doesn't know who paged me or why. I can spend a lot of time on hold while the person who paged me is tracked down. And when a mistake like this one is made, it takes longer to find out what is needed. In this situation, there is no mechanism for preventing the problem from occurring again because nurses, forced by bottom-line motivated decisions to be the jack of all trades, are more and more being forced into the position of being master of none.

Five minutes later I get beeped again at this same number. If a page is an emergency, the caller adds a number one behind the phone number. There is no number one, so I can only assume that a nurse somewhere needs to check on something with me. I didn't have any patients ready to deliver, so it didn't seem likely that someone on the OB floor was trying to get in touch with me. I go ahead and call the same number a second time.

"Hello again. I'm still getting paged at this number."

"I have no idea what's going on, Dr. Lindemann. I'll see what I can find out."

A few minutes later I get another page at the same number.

"Have you got any idea who's paging me at this switchboard number yet?"

"I'll bet it's Mary on the OB floor."

"What? She's been on the OB floor for years. Why's she paging me at this number for, for pete's sake?"

Needless to say, I wasn't off the phone long before my beeper was at it again, this time with the OB floor number. Even after all this, the number I was given to call was still incorrect—the prefix was wrong. I dialed the correct OB floor number and asked for Mary.

"What's the problem, Mary?"

"Oh, Dr. Lindemann, I've got one of Dr. Shank's patients here and he doesn't answer his page. Can you come over here and give us a hand?"

I found myself wondering if possibly this nurse was dialing the wrong number for Dr. Shank, who even as we spoke might well have been sitting at home waiting for a call he was never going to get.

"O.K. How's the patient doing."

"She's seven centimeters dilated and having contractions every ten minutes."

"I'll come on in, but I want to return some videos on the way. I should be there in about ten minutes. Do you think I have time?

"Yes."

As I'm standing in line at the video store, my beeper goes off. I leave the store as fast as possible, and from the store to the hospital, the beeper goes off six more times, although there is still no number one in front of the digits indicating an emergency. By the time I got to the hospital ten minutes later, the patient had delivered her baby without a doctor present.

At first glance, I am the person at fault here, because after all I was asking this nurse to proffer a medical opinion about whether this patient was going to deliver within the next ten minutes. When the nurse told me the patient's contractions were ten minutes apart and she was seven centimeters dilated, I had no reason to doubt the accuracy of the information I was given, or to doubt the nurse's opinion that I could safely delay my arrival at the hospital for ten minutes.

When I did arrive at the hospital, the head nurse was wringing her hands and complaining that what more could she have done, they had called me 8 times. The implication was that the nursing staff should not be held responsible for their part in this precipitous delivery. Of course, six of those calls came to me in my car on the way to the hospital, one minute apart.

When I checked the fetal monitor, I discovered that at the time I talked with the nurse who called me, and had been told that the contractions were ten minutes apart, they were actually three minutes apart. Had I been given accurate information about this patient, I would never have gone to the video store. This baby was this patient's third child, and you cannot watch a woman who has given birth to several children from the nurse's station. When my patient screamed "I have to push!," she was alone and the nurse assigned to her was at the nurse's station, possibly writing the lengthly reports they must spend so much of their time doing these days. In defense of nurses, when ward clerks handled a lot of the paperwork tasks, the nurses could spend more time on the floor checking their patients and less time creating a paper trail.

Let me emphasize that I am not questioning this nurse's medical opinion of the situation. Had I known the correct data about this patient's condition—that her contractions were not ten minutes apart, but three—I would have gone to the hospital immediately.

In many hospitals, whenever a patient delivers a baby without the doctor being there, a review board investigates the situation. As part of this investigation, I had written a letter to the review board indicating that the

Fetal Monitoring: Overkill

The [fetal] monitors come in two forms. External monitoring relies on two sensors strapped to the woman's abdomen. One contains an ultrasonic device that detects the fetus's heartbeat while the other senses contractions. Internal monitoring, which can be used only after the water breaks, passes sensors through the vagina—an electrode that is attached to the fetus's scalp to pick up heart rate and a pressure sensor at the end of a tube in the uterus.

The events are displayed as squiggly lines on a video screen and recorded on a long scroll of paper. As the mother's uterus contracts, the fetus responds by increasing its heart rate. Physicians once believed that subtle changes in the heart rate could signal fetal distress. But they are no longer so sure what small changes mean. Nor are they sure that, in the case of extreme distress, they can do anything about it.

By itself, use of the electronic fetal monitor adds only a few hundred dollars to the cost of having a baby. Using the monitors can even appear to save a hospital money, because a single nurse can track the progress of several women in labor. Moreover, in crowded hospitals, the use of electronic monitors may be better than relying solely on nurses with stethoscopes, who may be too busy to check the fetal heart rate often enough....

At the first sign of "distress" or "something unusual" on the fetal monitor, many doctors will wheel a woman into the operating room for a quick C-section, which adds $3,000 or more to the cost of having a baby.

If after birth a baby is slow to develop, or is imperfect in any way, many obstetricians fear that they will be staring at the tracing from the monitor in court, blown up into poster size, as a jury listens to two experts argue over what the tracing means and as attorneys ask, "Why, doctor, didn't you perform a Caesarean section at this point, when you can clearly see by the tracing that the fetus was in distress?"

Obstetricians say that some patients, knowing of the close association between electronic fetal monitoring and increased chances of a Caesarean delivery, ask not to be put on the monitors.

"I say, 'Fine, if you don't want to be monitored, then sign this release,'" said an obstetrician who asked not bo be identified. "They look at the release and say they're not going to sign it. And then I tell them, 'Well, then you're going to be monitored.' Because I just can't take the risk...."

"One cannot be criticized for doing a C-section. But one can always be criticized for not doing a C-section," said James Powers, an obstetrician who practices in the Washington area....

It was once supposed that subtle changes in the heart rate of the fetus could tell physicians much about what was happening to the baby....Now...obstetricians say they do not know what the subtle changes in fetal heart rate mean, if anything.

"It's like reading tea leaves," said...an obstetrician...." We've discovered that fetal heart rate doesn't tell us very much."

William Booth

A-1, A-14

fetal monitor results, at the time I talked to the nurse who called me, showed that labor was much farther along than was reported to me. The patient's chart indicated that over an hour had elapsed between the time the nurse actually checked my patient and the first of the eight phone calls the head nurse was so upset about. Somehow the hospital review board had lost this letter.

In subsequent meetings, the head nurse made it very plain that she regarded this as my problem. The nurse had, you see, tried to call me eight times. The review board members asked me what I thought should have happened to prevent this situation. To the head nurse's disgruntlement, I answered "Examine the patient!"

Does this kind of thing happen often? In some form or other, yes. Sometimes I am called several times by a nurse to report that a fetal monitor is registering distress, that is, the baby's heart rate is going down. This can be normal and not really fetal distress. A nurse experienced in obstetrical practice knows this. Nonetheless, if the nurse is upset about fetal distress at this stage of a delivery, I must go to the hospital to verify that the lower heart rate is not ominous.

At other times I have not been called when a patient's water has broken and there has been mecomium in the fluid—a definite sign of problems. The fetal monitor, however, under these circumstances, might register no fetal distress. The technology simply reports the increase in heart rate and whether or not there are contractions. The person monitoring the patient must make the determination about the meaning of that piece of data.

My point? The nursing profession and our medical system have gradually increased the amount of book learning required for nurses, sometimes at the expense of practical experience. Hospital administrators, in a effort to save money, sometimes hire inexperienced nurses or temporary nurses. These nurses are not incompetent. But the successful practice of nursing requires a kind of experience and commitment that comes neither with book learning nor the modern business practice of casting employees in the role of interchangeable cogs in a wheel.

Ending the Three-Day Labor

When I relocated my practice in 1981, I asked the hospital staff about their infant and maternal mortality and cesarean section rates. I wanted to know how their outcomes compared to the national averages.

I was told the section rate was 15 to 16 percent, which concerned me because I considered it higher than it should have been. There had also been 2 maternal deaths and 3 infant deaths the previous year for this metropolitan area which had a population of about 30,000, and a hospital which had 350 births per year. The national average at this time was about 8 maternal deaths per 100,000 live births and 2 infant deaths per 1,000 live births, so these rates appeared to be higher than they should be, and I considered them a possible sign of problems.

Once I knew these statistics, I reveiwed the hospital records, in part to find out the way the doctors and the hospital handled their patients, but also to see if by their comments, the nurses indicated whether they were amenable to changes in procedures. I discovered I was very fortunate to be in a community where the staff of nurses were willing to try different procedures to help their patients, and they were very good at monitoring labor.

At this time, there were three main reasons for cesarean sections. About one-third of the cesarean sections were repeat sections, that is, performed on those women who for some reason had had cesarean sections for their previous deliveries , and then automatically had cesarean sections for their subsequent deliveries. About one-third of the cesarean sections were performed because labor was termed "non-progressing." And about one-third of the cesarean sections were performed because the baby was in a breech position or in distress.

I had come from a medical community in which doctors did not automatically assume that once a woman delivered a baby by cesarean section she had to deliver her others the same way. This procedure is called vaginal birth after cesarean (VBAC). At this time VBACs had been practiced widely throughout the world, but relatively little in the United States. In fact, a conference on VBACs had been held at the National Institutes of Health in 1979 (see Cesarean Childbirth), and the procedure had been found to be safer than subjecting a woman to a second cesarean section (although today the risk of a second cesarean section is less than it was in 1979). In this community and for a number of miles around this community, no one was doing VBACs.

Since one third of the cesarean sections in this community were performed because of previous cesarean sections, this appeared to me to be a place where I could noticeably reduce what I considered a high percentage of cesarean sections. Because the VBAC procedure was new to this community, I was very careful to explain the advantages of the procedure to my patients. And since the mortality rate for cesarean sections at this time was higher than for vaginal deliveries or for VBACs, some of my patients chose to have VBACs.

I was also able to reduce the number of patients who were having cesarean sections because of "nonprogressing" labor. When I first went to this hospital, I discovered I was to have no internal uterine pressure catheter (IUPC), a device for internally monitoring the mother's uterine pressure. Having trained in a large hospital where we had this kind of equipment at our disposal, I was a little concerned. I learned, however, that these devices were unnecessary when I had a staff of nurses assisting me who could tell false labor from real labor, something a fetal monitor cannot do.

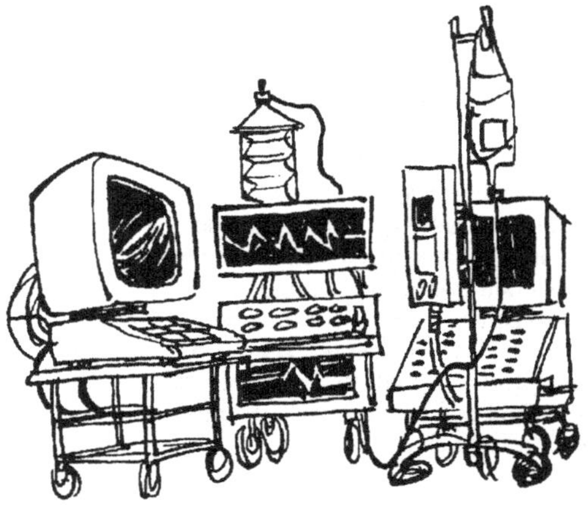

In normal labor, the contractions should dilate the cervix one centimeter per hour for women having their first baby, and about 1.5 centimeters per hour for women who have already had a baby. If the contractions dilate the cervix for five to eight centimenters, but no more, we call the labor non-progressing. The fetal monitor measures the heart beat of the baby and the contractions of the mother. But a woman can have contractions which do not dilate the cervix. The monitor can't tell the difference between these two kinds of contractions.

With latent labor, the woman is having contractions, but there is practically no dilation of the cervix at all. The woman can't sleep because the contractions keep her awake. She is often hungry because we haven't allowed her to eat anything for fear we may have to do emergency surgery, where she could accidently vomit under anesthesia and get stomack contents into her lungs. She hasn't slept much at all, possibly for two or three days, so she is

Too Many Cesarean Sections

...the broad assumption that labor which does not conform to a statistical norm is abnormal and requires therapy has led to the common term "failure to progress in labor." Failure to progress is frequently classfied as dysfunctional labor and placed in the category of dystocia, when it may, in fact, be false labor or prodromal labor or otherwise not abnormal. The benefits of cesarean birth for that component of dystocia called "failure to progress" are poorly suported in the literature. Furthermore, the efficacy of interventions such as ambulation, rest, sedation, oxytocin stimulation, or emotional support in treating "failure to progress" and dysfunctional labor, rather than early resort to cesarean delivery, has not been adequately assessed.

U.S. Dept. Health and Human Services,
Cesarean Childbirth
p. 343

Many obstetricians, particularly those in Brazil's major cities, have such a strong preference for delivering babies by Caesarean section that their patients have a vaginal birth only by a fluke....In hospitals affiliated with the public health insurance system, the rate is double the national average—or 66 percent. The priciest private maternity hospitals report that 80 percent or more of their births are by Caesarean....

"The Caesarean is the best delivery procedure for Brazil's socio-cultural environment," says Carlos Antonio Barbosa Montenegro, director of one of the chief maternity teaching hospitals in Rio. Brazilian hospitals ordinarily do not have regular round-the-clock staffs of residents and nurses ready to watch over a labor until the doctor arrives for the final stages. Instead, the routine is for private doctors to bring their own teams, including a nurse and anesthesiologist, with them to the hospital to perform the delivery.

"It's often impossible to get my team together when a woman goes suddenly into labor," says Montenegro, who also has a private practice. "The anesthesiologist has a second job, the nurse is visiting her mother out of town...." Moreover, Montenegro says, many hospitals don't have fetal monitors and other technology to handle emergencies that develop in the course of labor.

In Rio especially, Montenegro notes, "it is simply impossible for me to agree to a single unscheduled delivery." Well-to-do doctors "live in terror," he says, because of Rio's perennial crime wave, which recently has included a spate of kidnappings for ransom of upper-middle-class Brazilians. "I can't go out at night safely. I can't park my car on the street at night in front of the hospital without having it stolen," he explains.

Julia Preston
p. 6

Too Many Cesarean Sections

A study completed in 1988 by Dr. Sidney Wolfe of the Public Citizen Health Research Group in Washington, D.C., of the cesarean birth rate in 10 states indicates that almost 500,000 cesarean section births are unnecessary. Dr. Wolfe indicates that this wastes well over one billion dollars a year.

Health Letter
"Waste Not, Want Not,"
p. 7

Following a cesarean delivery, more than 98 percent of women in the United States undergo a repeat cesarean for any subsequent preganancy. This practice began in the early 1900s to avoid the risk of uterine rupture at the scar site during labor.

U.S. Dept. Health & Human Services
Cesarean Birth,
p. 10

Wealthy women are 73 percent more likely to give birth by Caesarean section than are poor women, a study in the July 27 *New England Journal of Medicine* reported. Jeffrey B. Gould, M.D., of the University of Berkeley School of Public Health, and colleagues studied 245,854 Los Angeles County birth certificates from 1982 and 1983, and 1980 census statistics on income.

They found that the incidence of Caesarean births—which was independent of the mother's age, whether she had had children before, or the baby's birth weight, race, or ethnic group—steadily increased with a women's family income level. The rate of Caesarean births in women with a family income over $30,000 was 22.9 percent, the rate of women whose family income was below $11,000 was 13.2 percent, and the overall rate was 17.8 percent.

News Clips
"And the Rich Get C-Sections,"
p. 533

Increases in cesarean rates are influenced by availability of physicain and hospital services and these, in turn, are subject to influence by government policy and incentives. When the impetus for medical development is strong, as it has been in developing regions of Canada and France, the cesarean rate increase appears to rise in association with investments in specialist services and hospital technology. With conservative government policy, of which the Netherlands is the best example, access to surgically equipped facililities and obstetricians is controlled by insurance reimbursement and programmatic early identification of high risk mothers....

In the United States, obstetricians rather than midwives and general practitioners usually deliver babies. The rates of cesarean births in this country and those in Western Europe correlate roughly with the use of obstetricians' services.

U.S. Dept. Health & Human Services
Cesarean Birth,
p. 99-100

Check Your Hospital's Cesarean Rate

Ask your doctor what percentage of his or her deliveries are cesarean sections. If the percentage given is high or low, ask what might account for this.

Ask the hospital where you plan to deliver your baby what percentage of their births are cesarean. Then call your state health department and ask for the division that keeps track of state vital statistics. Compare the percentage of cesarean births the state has on record for your prospective hospital to the figures the hospital gave you. If the discrepancy is large, ask both the hospital and the state record-keeping office to explain the difference.

The rate of cesarean sections can vary significantly from hospital to hospital. The following table compares the cesarean section rate for six of the large hospitals in North Dakota.

In the United States, a Caesarean section—withdrawing a baby from a mother's uterus through an incision in the abdomen—is usually performed only when a pregnancy has problems: when the fetus is in a breech position with its feet down, for example, or when a difficult labor drags on to the point of posing a risk for the baby and mother. The rate in the U.S. is 23.8 per 100 deliveries and has been fairly level since 1986, according to a report issued in July by the National Center for Health Statistics.

Julia Preston
p. 6

City	Pop.	Hospital	Total Births	C-Sections	
				No.	%
Fargo & West Fargo	71,947	Dakota	211	50	24
		St. Lukes	597	135	23
		St. Johns	190	39	21
Minot	32,843	Trinity	282	141	50
		St. Josephs	181	48	27
Grand Forks	43,765	United	608	116	19

Data taken from the North Dakota State Department of Health and Consolidated Laboratories *A Guide to Hospital Charges by Diagnosis Related Group 1990*, pp. 30-31. You may have to ask for the data by DRG rather than by description.

exhausted. By the time productive contractions do begin, she is physically unable to endure the process and her body is dysfunctional. Many caesarean sections are performed because latent labor is treated as if it were productive labor. By the time real labor begins, the patient is worn out and possibly frantic. Or her husband is frantic and demands that I do a cesarean section.

I have found that with non-progressing labor, it is often better to plan to allow my patients to rest and to allow them to eat while we wait for their bodies to get into gear.

I ask my patients if they would like something to eat. Women who are in active labor are usually not hungry, although those in protracted, non-productive labor often are. My experience with women in labor is that they can vomit just as well on an empty stomach as on a full one. As simple as it may sound, I have found that developing a plan for labor prevents a lot of last-minute caesarean sections and helps produce an uneventful delivery.

With the help of an experienced, knowledgeable nursing staff, I was able to bring the cesarean section rate for this hospital, which served an area with a population of about 30,000, down to 10.5 percent and maintain it there for three years. During this period of time we had no maternal deaths and no delivery-related illnesses in babies.

We didn't need the latest high-tech equipment. We didn't need $9,500 beds. We didn't need a skeletal staff composed exclusively of RNs. We succeeded because we had experienced nurses and staff who were able to spot signs of trouble and alert doctors appropriately, we had a regular staff of caregivers who worked efficiently together and whose primary concern was the patient's welfare. The American consumer needs to know that quality health care cannot be bought—for any price. Quality health care will only surface when caregivers are allowed to make the medical decisions only they are qualified to make, and caregivers are allowed to concentrate on what they do best rather than on making a profit and outglitzing their competition.

Hospitals Create a Nursing Shortage . . .

Hospitals employed 133,376 fewer full time employers to provide patient care but increased registered nurse staffing by only 37,500 full-time positions.

C. F. Mullinix
p. 14

Contrary to popular impression, the supply of nurses is not decreasing, nurses are not leaving the profession in droves and hospitals are not losing their grip on the labor market for nurses ...And the recent decline in nursing-school enrollments, troubling as it may be for the future, is not responsible for the current shortage.

In fact, the current shortage is the result not of a shrinking supply of nurses but of a rapid increase in demand for them...

One way hospitals reduced costs was by cutting staff—and hiring more registered nurses (RNs). To hospitals, RNs represent a great bargain. They are extremely versatile employees and need relatively little supervision. They can perform the duties of licensed practical nurses (LPNs) and nursing aides as well as their own. They can also substitute for other hospital personnel, such as physical therapists and even, in some circumstances, physicians. For these reasons, hospitals have found that it is more cost-effective to use RNs instead of other workers, even though the salary of an individual RN is usually higher than that of an LPN or other less skilled hospital worker

Robert K. Landers
p. 158-159

And Fill Gaps With Temporary Nurses

Joan Moss of the American Hospital Association reports that the hiring of temporary nurses from outside agencies has been "growing by leaps and bounds." Those institutions reporting severe shortages hired temporary nurses 59 percent of the time just to cover their vacant RN positions. And these nurses are paid more but often can do less because they are unfamiliar with the institution.

Robert K. Landers
p.p. 163-164

An AHA official was quoted as having cited "declining enrollment in schools of nursing, the negative image of nursing in the popular media and easier access to a wider range of professions for women as some of the factors behind the growing shortage of RNs in U.S. hospitals." In reality, none of these factors contributed to the shortage.

The increased demand for registered nurses instead had its origins in efforts to hold down rising health-care costs, especially the federal government's revision of the Medicare reimbursement system in 1983.

Robert K. Landers
pp. 161-162

The Nursing Shortage That Isn't

There is a loud cry that this country is experiencing a severe shortage of nurses. It may appear that this is the case, but the evidence clearly indicates that to a large extent, hospitals have created this shortage artificially by replacing many of the traditional hospital caregivers such as licensed practical nurses, aides, orderlies, and ward clerks with registered nurses.

Hospitals and the Bottom Line

Hospitals are now run as businesses, with business administrators, not doctors, making the decisions about what is purchased and who is hired. Hence, these decisions are based on maximum profitability, not improved health care. In fact, over the past 25 years, our medical care system has been taken over by large for-profit corporations, and this is one of the major factors in the increase of our health care costs (See Chapter 1).

What has this to do with the appearance of a nursing shortage? For one thing, hospital administrators have found that it is "cheaper" to replace LPNs, aides, orderlies, and ward clerks, with registered nurses. True, they have to pay the nurses more than the other employees, but nurses can do everything on a floor. This means that hospital administrators can ask the RNs to do the jobs of several persons and as a result, reduce their total number of employees.

Hospitals maintain that health care is labor intensive, and hence expensive. Moriarity (p. 454) claims that labor accounts for nearly 60 percent of a hospital's costs. Hospital management nearly always chooses to lay off employees to cut costs rather than search for other ways to economize, such as cutting down on remodeling or the purchase of unneeded equipment. In the United States, the average hospital utilization rate, that is, the percentage of available beds that are actually in use, runs between 50 and 60 percent (HIAA *Source Book 1990,* p. 86). The occupancy rate at for-profit hospitals runs about 10 percent less than this (Burns, p. 541).

Strangely enough, about the same time that hospital administrators began replacing hospital staff with nurses, the nursing profession developed the concept of "primary care nursing" as preferable to "team nursing." Primary care nursing, in theory, is supposed to encourage the nurse to take a personal interest in each

Primary Care Nursing . . .

A primary nurse's relationship with a client is based on the nurse's role as a professional. When the nurse explains her role as a primary nurse, with particular emphasis on the meaning of her title, she establishes herself as a professional and creates the bond that is necessary for a "contractual" professional-client relationship.

Marie Manthey
"An Expert Answers...,"
p. 23

Called Primary Nursing, this delivery system is notable for allocating responsbility, authority and accountability for the care of a small caseload of patients to a particular nurse.

Marie Manthey
"Primary Practice Partners,"
p. 58

And the Abuse of Nurses

Appelbaum and Granrose found that most hospital administrators they interviewed felt employing LPNs and aides was inefficient because they were limited in the tasks they could perform. They report talking to only one hospital administrator who believed that registered nurses should be used to provide professional nursing services, with aides and practical nurses providing auxiliary services.

Robert K. Landers
p. 162

"Nurses are being used for things they shouldn't be," says Lucille Joel, a professor at the Rutgers College of Nursing and a first vice president of the American Nurses' Association (ANA). "One of the important things to nurses...is the presence of support staff in the institution, so that they can nurse,' Joel adds. "They don't want to be abused. They don't want to be considered a multipurpose worker. They want to nurse, they want to lay hands on and care for people.."

Robert K. Landers
pp. 159-160

patient—something compentent nurses have been doing for years, even without this highly touted new practice model. In reality, this model has become a method for hospital administrators to cut their total number of employees.

Team Nursing

With team nursing, each hospital floor had a head nurse, and the nurses, LPNs, aides, orderlies, and ward clerks were responsible to her (or sometimes aides and orderlies reported to LPNs, who reported to the RN). LPNs and aides could feed people, give baths, empty bedpans, and make the beds. Orderlies were there to help with moving patients and the kinds of tasks that required brawn. Ward clerks took care of a lot of the paper work and directed traffic. The nurses were then free to pass out medications, and monitor and chart the patients' progress, calling the doctor when needed.

Nurses usually *teamed*, that is, all information was collected at a central location. The head nurses would make the rounds dispensing medicines. One nurse, usually the head nurse, was responsible for procuring the required medications in the proper dosages. With primary care nursing, each nurse often takes care of procuring and giving medications for assigned patients, creating additional opportunities for medication error. Head nurses, at the end of their shifts, commented on each patient in writing (called charting). Proponents of primary care nursing complain that

> team and functional activity based systems ignore individual professional responsibility and support bureaucratic controls and task-based work assignments. (Manthey, "Primary Practice Partners, " p. 58)

It appears to us that for Manthey, the real issue here is control. And the doctor: Mysteriously unmentioned.

Primary Care Nursing

With primary care nursing, a single nurse is assigned to a patient, and that nurse does everything for that patient, including emptying bedpans. The theory is that with a single nurse responsible for the patient's care, a special bonding will occur that will make the nurse patient-relationship more effective.

> The *essential ingredient* of the delivery system is the establishment of a responsibility relationship between a nurse and a patient....This relationship is established by an RN, who *explains her role* to the patient. (Manthey, "Myths," p. 55)

The puzzling aspect of this primary care philosophy is its emphasis on the responsibility of the nurse for the patient, as if nurses working in the team approach somehow don't exercise any real care in the performance of their duty to their patients. Just because a nurse performs some of the tasks for a whole floor of patients instead of all of the tasks for a few of the patients in no way dooms the

ter·mi·nol·o·gy

registered nurse (RN): state-licensed professional who directs care of patient, manages nursing services, and educates all levels of nursing staff.

licensed practical nurse (LPN) usually high school graduates or equivalents who have had a year of nurses training in an approved program and have passed the nationally standardized LPN exam given by the state.

orderly: male hospital attendent who assists nurses by lifting or transporting patients.

aide: women who do direct, non-medical patient care; sometimes called nursing assistants

ward clerk: person who performs secretarial duties, stamps charts, answers phones

adapted from *Tabor's*

team nurse to providing substandard, impersonal care to her patients. Primary care nursing is not going to make caring, devoted nurses out of uncaring, irresponsible persons, nor will it make nurses in any sense more professional. To our minds, the telling element of the definitionof primary care nursing is the emphasis on control rather than patient care. What primary care nursing obviously does is make a personal relationship into a "system," the antithesis of personal care. Primary care nursing also clearly puts the nurse in a position to "control" the patient's entire care. We see no mention of the doctor in Manthey's articles. Her silence on this issue is thunderous.

With nurses doing the work of the LPNs, aides, orderlies, and ward clerks, hospitals must hire a lot more nurses. There is no shortage of persons to care for patients, including RNs, if RNs were employed to do what they are trained to do. There has been an artificially created "shortage" of RNs because those in charge of hiring practices choose to hire nurses—and misuse them—instead of hiring, as needed, several levels of caregivers.

We believe there are two types of nursing services for which primary care nursing may well be more appropriate than team nursing: obstetrics and intensive care. To date, we have seen little attempt to fit the nursing service to the actual needs of the type of patient. Rather, what we have found is an attempt to force entire hospitals into a single model of nursing service, a service that just happnes to coincide with the current management policies of cutting down the number of hospital employees to save money.

The Hospital Role in this Shortage

Aiken and Mullinix (1987) have studied hospital practices in hiring nurses relative to the perceived shortage. They observe that hospitals have increasingly utilized registered nurses while decreasing total hospital full-time equivalents (p. 14). Indeed, the data shows that hospitals are not only substituting nurses for less skilled workers such as aides and licensed practical nurses, but also for workers with similar skills, such as respiratory therapy, physical therapy, and pharmacy. To hospital administrators, nurses, even at significantly higher salaries, are a bargain becuase they can do the jobs of several employees. While this data certainly indicates that the demand for nurses has increased because of the way hospitals now would like to operate, there has been no study of the appropriateness of substituting nurses for other hospital personnel.

Hospitals often use the excuse that with the more sophisticated technologies, they need to hire registered nurses to provide care. For a while, the government paid additional monies to hospitals for Medicare patients because the hospitals argued that these patients were sicker than the others and required more intensive

ter·mi·nol·o·gy

community hospital: all non-federal, short-term hospitals which are open to the public (except those which are part of an institution such as a university).
adapted from HIAA *Source Book 1990*

full-time equivalent: number of full-time staff plus half the part-time personnel.
Aiken and Mullinix p. 14

nursing care (Landers, pp. 161-162). When research indicated that there was no statistical basis for such a conclusion, the government stopped paying hospitals this additional money.

More Registered Nurses, But Fewer Caregivers

We now know that Medicare patients do not require any more intensive nursing care than any other patient at the hospital, although it is likely that *all* hospitalized patients are sicker now than they used to be simply because they are being discharged from hospitals after shorter stays. So while in 1968, only 33 percent of all hospital personnel were registered nurses, by 1986 that number had increased to 58 percent of all hospital personnel. And while the total number of registered nurses employed was increasing, the total number of full-time employees providing care to patients was decreasing radically. Hospitals employed 133,376 fewer full time employers to provide patient care but increased registered nurse staffing by only 37,500 full-time positions (Mullinix, p. 14).

The nursing shortage, then, is an artificially created one. Hospitals could hire LPNs, aides, orderlies, and ward clerks to assist nurses, but often choose not to. Instead, hospitals report that they have vacant registered nursing slots, and therefore there must be a nursing shortage. In the meantime, they often hire temporary nurses at inflated salaries. Oftentimes temporary hires are paid for out of different budgets than permanent employees, so the real cost of making a policy of hiring temporary RNs is difficult to track. And not necessarily cheaper.

Despite the need for hospitals to hire temporary registered nurses, a need brought about by what many hospital administrators consider an acute shortage, hospitals have been unwilling to make any changes in the way they operate. In 1983, a panel from the National Academy of Sciences Institute of Medicine reported that hospitals needed to improve career opportunities and the working environment for registered nurses. This included increasing salaries, involving nurses more in decisions about patient care, and in the management and governance of the institution. But observers note that hospitals haven't changed much, and they see little hope for change. Landers (p. 166) observes that "there is a big difference between perceived need for registered nurses and economic demand for them." That hospitals remain so intransigent in their employment practices indicates just how artificial this so-called nursing "shortage of the century" really is—otherwise hospitals would have reason to change their standard operating procedures.

Chapter 4 Summary

PROBLEM #1:

There is an increasing emphasis in nurse's training on book learning as opposed to practical experience.

Issue:

Nursing, like medicine, is largely an art which requires extensive practical experience as well as academic study.

Action:

Remove unreasonable barriers which prevent two- and three-year nurses from practicing their profession and upgrading their degrees.

PROBLEM #2:

Primary care nursing has replaced team nursing in many hospitals.

Issue:

Primary care nursing allows hospital administrators to replace aides, orderlies, and ward clerks with nurses, who can do all these jobs..

Action:

Hospitals should hire persons with training appropriate to the task and let nurses devote their time to doing what they are trained—and paid—to do.

Problem #3:

Some hospital administrators keep permanent, full-time staff to a minimum, filling in with termporary nursing staff.

Issue:

Chronic short staffing requires regular use of temporary nurses who are skilled, but nonetheless often unfamiliar with their assigned areas, seriously affecting the quality of care provided.

Action:

Require hospitals to use nurses appropriately and hire aides, orderlies, and ward clerks to do non-nursing tasks.

Chapter 5

Doctors, Lawyers, and Liability

Chapter Contents

Bulletin Boards

Action Guides

Narratives

Discussion:

Neither Fast Nor Fair

Chapter 5 Summary

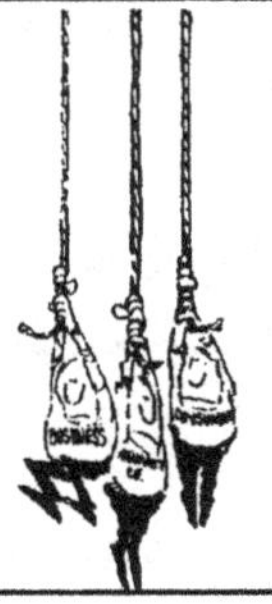

Catch As Catch Can

The trouble with litigation as a method of social justice is its randomness. It only compensates for certain kinds of misfortune, compensates erratically (sometimes inadequate, sometimes overgenerous) even for those and eats up most of the proceeds while redistributing them.

Michael Kinsley
p. A23

(Advertisement in *Minnesota Medicine*)

What's happening to doctors today is enough to make you sick. Medicine has become big business. Being a skilled physician is simply not enough any more....

And we can show you how "clinics without walls" give physicians the bargaining power of a network while retaining their autonomy, their patients, and their integrity.

Broeker, Geer, Fletcher & LaFond
p. 382

There has never been a malpractice insurance crisis in this country. What we have are crises of unaffordable health insurance, runaway health care costs and special interest legislation trampling the rights of injured victims of malpractice.

The only crises in this country with respect to health care are (1) the obscene cost of our annual bill ($675 billion projected for 1991); (2) the fact that 33 million Americans are forced to go without health insurance due to the unaffordable costs; and (3) the disadvantaged and innocent victims of medical malpractice who can neither afford to lobby Congress for special interest legislation nor afford to obtain health care for injuries caused by negligent health care providers.

Consider the actual case of a woman paralyzed by negligent surgery, with medical bills and future health care needs costing $1.6 million. In a state such as Virginia, where I am a practicing attorney representing victims of medical malpractice, recovery is limited to a maximum of $1 million. This woman can't even get her medical care paid. Moreover, she recovers nothing for permanent injury, mental anguish or pain and suffering. Who speaks for her?

William E. Artz
p. 4

EXHIBIT A: EXAMPLE OF MAULPRACTICE
(MALPRACTICE)

If It Works, Don't Fix It

Did you ever wonder how problems with patients were resolved before the lawyers and insurance companies ensconced themselves as arbiters of right and wrong in medicine? In most cases, if there were problems with a procedure, they were taken care of at no cost to the patient. Very simple.

Years ago anesthesia used to be flammable. And at times something would cause the anesthesia to explode. If the anesthesia exploded in a patient's face, doctors and the hospital personnel took care the problem, and sometimes that included plastic surgery and several months of care. Doctors and hospital personnel were able to express remorse for things that they wished had not happened, things that often were largely beyond their control. And the problem was taken care of. This system worked for years and years. The only difficulty was that lawyers weren't making any money suing doctors and insurance companies weren't making much on liability insurance.

Now lawyers have interceded on behalf of the patient and said that if a doctor is willing to correct a problem without charging the patient, the doctor is admitting guilt, and as a result, liability insurers will classify the doctors as uninsurable.

So what happens now? My patient was in the operating room, prepped and draped. The lights were off. We were ready to start surgery. The patient is paying by the minute for the anesthesia, and the cautery isn't working properly.

"Could you check the cautery and see why it isn't working," I asked the nurse.

"We have a lot of different machines, a lot of different pads, and they aren't interchangeable. I'll see what I can do." She changed the pad to the machine in the dark under the draping.

The cautery started to work, but not well. We kept having to turn up the current throughout the procedure. Suddenly I heard the sickening crackle of arcing electricity. We immediately stopped what we were doing and checked for the source of the problem. We couldn't find any burns on the patient, but just the same we didn't continue with the cautery procedure. When surgery

ter·mi·nol·o·gy

cautery: electrically heating tissue to prevent bleeding.
adapted from Tabers, C-28

Litigation Corrects Few Problems

The doctors said Murrey, 68, had died of an undiagnosed stomach ulcer that burst during surgery. The ulcer was akin to a "ticking time bomb" that could have gone off at any time, they said....

It was not a burst ulcer that killed Murrey, who won the Purple Heart and Bronze Star during World War II. Rather, Murrey died after massive bleeding when doctors accidentally cut an artery near his small intestine during surgery and mismanaged the resulting complications, the inspector general's report indicates. VA officials now describe Murrey's death as a "therapeutic misadventure...."

Among the records pulled were those of Thomas Murrey, who had been admitted for what had been expected to be routine prostate surgery. During his two days in the operating room and intensive care unit, the VA doctors made at least 15 mistakes or errors in judgment, including an excessive use of narcotics and sedatives, improper provision of fluids, inadequate temperature monitoring and poor supervision of residents and nurses, according to consultants who reviewed the case....

While Barbour [Galen L. Barbour, the VA's associate medical director] described the North Chicago situation as an "aberration," he acknowledged the fact that VA officials were aware of warning signs at the facility for at least three years, yet were unable to make improvements.

Michael Abramowitz
p. A4

Donald Billig, a heart surgeon once at the center of a controversy over medical care at military hospitals, has had medical licenses reinstated in several states and is practicing medicine at a clinic in Southwest Washington.

In a brief interview yesterday, Billig said he is voluntarily refraining from performing surgery but is licensed to practice medicine in New York, Massachusetts, Pennsylvania, Texas and the District of Columbia....

The 60-year-old Billig...was convicted by a military court in 1986 for the negligent death and involuntary manslaughter of three patients at Bethesda Naval Medical Center. The proceeding yielded evidence that he had severe vision problems in one eye.

After serving 25 months of a four-year sentence at the federal penitentiary in Fort Leavenworth, Kan., the Navy-Marine Corps Court of Military Review overturned the conviction on the grounds that the evidence did not prove guilt beyond a reasonable doubt....

His two-year search for work ended eight months ago when he was hired at the Prompt Care Walk-in Medical Center, in the 400 block of M Street SW. One of three doctors there, Billig practices general medicine.

Gabriel Escobar
p. A12

was completed and we removed the cautery pad, we found a small, third degree burn.

Now that leaves me with a bit of a mess. In the first place, this is an attractive woman who now has a third-degree burn where it will easily be visible. While I am still trying to figure out what I'm going to tell this woman's husband, the nurses have already called in the liability management team for directions on what to do.. Note that before we begin taking care of the patient, the liability problem has to be addressed. The liability team is even called in before we contact the plastic surgeon to assess the problem.

Before lawyers, liability carriers, and tort laws encouraged patients to allow an adversarial relationship to be established between themselves and doctors, patients usually got the care they needed until the problem was resolved. The family was happy, everybody was happy, and there were few lawsuits. Now, instead of taking care of the patient, we have tediously lengthy processes that really don't solve the problems, and doctors are often held responsible for many happenings which are in many instances beyond their control.

The National Data Bank

Although the law provides that the information contained in the Data Bank is confidential and intended for authorized entities only, it would not be unduly cynical to assume that it is only a matter of time before the Data Bank reports are made available to anyone who wants access to the information. For example, the Public Citizen Health Research Group, founded in 1972 by consumer advocate Ralph Nader and directed by Sidney Wolfe, M.D., has already called for changes to the law that would provide direct consumer access to this information. Moreover, although the American Medical Association was successful in having language inserted that provides limited direct access by a plaintiff's attorney, access remains an issue, since a physician can (and probably will) request his or her own data file, making the document potentially subject to discovery by other parties....

Furthermore, if malpractice data are made available to consumers, the public may be alarmed by the number of malpractice claims filed against physicians in the United States and may make erroneous assumption about the state of the health care delivery system. As practicing physicians know so well, a malpractice claim does not necessarily equate with incompetence or negligence. Moreover, certain specialities or areas may have a higher incidence of claims as a result of treating higher-risk cases or other factors.

Kristin Larson
p. 36

Olender [attorney for the woman bringing the charges against a doctor and hospital] threw a spotlight on the little-known National Practitioner Databank, a computer bank started last year by the federal government to collect information on doctors who are disciplined and those who settle or lose malpractice cases. And he showed how a doctor could avoid being reported, especially if he had smart lawyers who knew how to navigate the system....

As the case headed toward trial, the parties negotiated a possible settlement. Then, the defense lawyers offered this deal: the hospital would pay damages, if Dennison [the woman charging the doctor with malpractice] dropped the doctor from the lawsuit first. Dennison agreed....the hospital agreed to pay Dennison $485,000....

While the client had agreed to drop Dr. Blank from the lawsuit, this provision of the settlement rankled Olender [the woman's attorney]. It meant that Blank would not be reported to the new national databank, which was designed to protect consumers. Under the rules, if the doctor is dismissed from a case, there is nothing to report.

Databank officials said that insurers, rather than plaintiffs in lawsuits, are the ones with the official responsibility to report the names of doctors. Their obligation to report is triggered only when they pay money on behalf of a doctor to satisfy a malpractice settlement or judgment.

Saundra Torry
p. 5

All's Fair in Love and War

I believe that doctors can prevent a lot of problems with their patients if they will take the time to talk to them, despite what the liability insurance companies say. There are more than enough opportunities for miscommunication in the treatment of any patient. If doctors will take the time to talk to unhappy patients, they can often find out what's really bothering them.

Exhibit 1

Dear Dr. Lindemann:

I am writing to let you know that AA contacted me last week about the matter that came up...regarding the piece of gauze she passed after her delivery....Her phone call was very pleasant, but she did request that the Clinic pay her $600 in addition to writing off her bill. I have referred this to the insurance company for handling, and I have recommended that we pay the $600....

I think this matter can be quickly resolved, now that AA has decided to get it taken care of. I have recommended that we act expeditiously and the Clinic agrees. If a payment is made to AA, even though it is extremely small, the company will probably have to file a report with the National Practitioner Data Bank, so one of the claims people there will probably be in touch with you about this.

I simply wanted to advise you of recent events and to let you know we are hoping to get this resolved within the next two weeks or so.

Sincerely,

Exhibit 2

Dear Dr. Lindemann:

I have just returned from two weeks out of the office, so I apologize for the delay in responding to your letter. You are correct about the mix-up regarding these two patients. Indeed, I had assumed that your letter to me regarding AA was about BB. I had therefore assumed you were at least somewhat familiar with the background.

BB was a patient of Dr. X's, but it is my understanding that you delivered her baby. I am sending you copies of portions of her Clinic chart and the delivery records from the hospital. You will see on her Clinic visit that she reported having passed a piece of gauze six days after her delivery. No further foreign body was seen and her exam was normal. However, she reported continuing abdominal pain and bleeding and these symptoms continued throughout the summer. Ultimately she required a D&C. She has done very well since. Dr. X was very reassuring to her in telling her that he did not expect her to have any long-term problems.

Dr. X. told me that he was not even convinced that her bleeding and pain were related to the gauze, but said he couldn't be sure of this. It seems clear that whatever problems she had as a result of this were quite limited. However, it is also my experience that when a retained foreign object is involved, a patient is almost sure to get something for it, if a claim is made. I think the $600 BB was willing to accept is quite reasonable and well worth getting this resolved.

I should also point out to you that BB did not make any formal claim at all, and simply telephoned me to discuss her request for payment. Thus, there has been no claim made against you, and we are considering it to be an informal claim against the Clinic. As a result, even the very small $600 payment will not have to be reported to the National Practitioner Data Bank as a settlement.

After you have looked at the attached records, please feel free to call me with any additional questions.

Sincerely,

So a letter from a lawyer about a patient who wants to file a complaint against me is very upsetting (Exhibit 1). Especially when the lawyer is threatening to report me to the National Data Bank over a $600 claim. For a patient I don't even know.

What's the beef, you say? That's certainly trivial enough that any good office manager could get it straightened out in no time. Actually, that's just the problem. They can't. Any more than my office manager can get an insurance claim paid to a doctor from one of my referrals to him (see "Simon Legree is Alive and Well," p. 104).

The real story here? I had just left the clinic referred to in this letter to open my own, independent practice. These letters came from the clinic lawyers and quickly followed my severing my relationship with that organization.

The first letter was about someone the clinic lawyer thought was my patient, but never had been, even when I was at the clinic. But notice how casually we as doctors can be reported to the National Data Bank. The patient in the second letter (Exhibit 2) is also not mine, but a patient of a doctor still there—a doctor who had called me personally and requested that I assist with one of his deliveries. No, I didn't deliver the baby, but was there to offer any guidenace or advice as needed. In fact, I left as soon as the baby was delivered, leaving the patient in the clinic doctor's care.

EXHIBIT A: EXAMPLE OF MAULPRACTICE (MALPRACTICE)

Now, I always check a patient after delivery to be sure there aren't any stray pieces of gauze left around. This wasn't my patient, so I may not have checked—I frankly don't remember. But there's no reason to believe that the patient's own doctor, the clinic doctor, couldn't have left the gauze there as well since these final checks are performed at the end of a procedure.

The problem here? There's no point in trying to blame someone. The whole situation is trivial beyond comprehension, but lawyers can threaten to report doctors to the National Data Bank and, like the managed care folk, not be responsible for the consequences of their mistakes. The lawyer, as soon as she discovered her own mistake, quickly revised her perception of the case from compelling to weak.

In case you missed the legal subtleties here—not at all hard to do—let me explain. The first patient was actually filing a claim against the doctor, alleging malpractice. So any payment made by the insurance company, even a sum as small as $600, would be reported by the insurance company to the National Data Bank as a paid claim against the doctor. On the other hand, the second patient simply wanted her clinic bill reduced by

$600, so according to the letter of the law, this was not an incident that needed to be reported to the National Data Bank.

Used as a political weapon, the National Data Bank will not provide the kind of information it was intended to gather. In this situation, I have no opportunity to find out what really happened with this clinic doctor's patient Even if I had still been a member of the clinic staff, I would have had little opportunity to correct the problem because this was not my patient. Had this second patient indeed been in my care, I would have talked with her and tried to find out what the real problem was, and why she continues to have problems. As the clinic doctor admits, the gauze was very unlikely to have anything to do with her complaints. Actually, the clinic doctor knows full well—and knows that I know—the gauze had absolutely nothing to do with her complaints.

The real point of this lawlerly exchange is purely political—patient welfare plays no part in this scenario. The message was now that I no longer belonged to the clinic, I was competition. And very vulnerable.

Litigation—or the threat of it—has solved no medical problem here. It has merely provided a convenient vehicle for demonstrating my vulnerability as an independent practioner. And allowed a patient to haggle over and reduce a clinic bill after the fact, in essence paying the patient to shut up.

How Much for a Life?

Unfortunately, after 15 years of state-based initiatives, the tort reform movement has been effectively stalled in most states....In Florida, the cost of liability insurance adds $1119 to the cost of delivering every infant. In New York and Arizona, the cost is $607 and $447, respectively.

Martin J. Hatlie
p. 584

..only about 10% of the children with cerebral palsy receive anything from malpractice suits, even though such cases account for some 60% of the damages paid in successful malpractice claims against obstetricians....

Some 9,500 U.S. babies are diagnosed annually with cerebral palsy. Dr. Freeman notes that only around 10% of such cases result from oxygen deprivation...

It [the state of Virginia's no-fault compensation program] identifies only a small group of babies who are permanently and totally impaired both mentally and physically as the result of asphyxia at birth. Virginia has taken those babies out of the legal system and will offer them compensation from a special fund set up by taxing obstetricians, hospitals, and other physicians. But all the other babies with CP, who are mildly or moderately impaired but able to ambulate, don't quality. Only the worst of the worst are eligible...

We know asphyxia causes only 4% to 8% of CP, so 92% of these children are not currently eligible for compensation. The money obstetricians now pay for malpractice could be used instead to give every child with CP the right to draw up to $250,000 for excess expenses. Under our proposed plan, all families who have a child with CP could apply to a no-fault compensation system similar to workmen's compensation for such expenses as braces and wheel-chairs....Sweden has a no-fault policy, and New Zealand has a complete no-fault policy for all medical claims....

Edward M. Wallach
pp. 15-16

A hospital and two other defendants have agreed to pay $750,000 in the death of a 7-year-old girl who was admitted to the hospital to have her tonsils removed and died from an overdose of anesthesia.

Lawyers for both sides on Monday described the out-of-court settlement as the largest monetary settlement in Minnesota history for the wrongful death of a child....

Eisberg said most wrongful death cases for children in Minnesota probably are settled in the range of $150,000 to $200,00, with some as low as $75,000 and some as high as $300,000.

AP, Minneapolis
"Cities Hospital Agrees ...,"
p. B1

In the past, attorneys' associations have fought any efforts that would limit a patient's ability to bring a case to trial or place a cap on awards, saying it violates patients' rights.

Proponents of the bill, however, contend that the current system, with its long delays and high legal fees, denies many injured patients the chance for fair compensation.

They cite a 1987 General Accounting Office report showing that, in cases closed in 1984, it took an average of 25 months, and as long as 11 years, from the date a claim was filed until final resolution. In more than half the cases, plaintiff legal fees took more than 30% of payments to the injured party. Plaintiffs also were responsible for paying other expenses, such as court costs and costs of obtaining evidence.....

Suggested alternatives include a fault-based administrative system. Under this proposal, a state would establish an agency with exclusive jurisdiction to review medical liability claims. Patients injured by negligence could receive full payment for out-of-pocket damages, but pain and suffering and other non-economic damages would be limited. The agency would be required to coordinate with state licensing and disciplinary official to identify and discipline negligent physicians.

Laurie Jones
p. 24

"Dead Babies Aren't Worth Much"

I cannot emphasize enough the difficulty I have with the constraints put on me by liability insurers and the threat of malpractice to express my pain to my patients when a baby dies. Especially when I consider it a preventable death.

You always worry with a high risk pregnancy. When you have a patient with high blood pressure who continues to smoke anyway, even when pregnant, added to obesity and infertility problems, you're in there rooting for your patient and the baby. Once they get to the hospital, you hope nothing untoward happens. The patient is on a fetal monitor. You should be called if there are problems. In one such case, the nurse reading the monitor strip recognized it as bad. She reported it to the doctor on duty, who pronounced the reading good. The nurse knew otherwise, but for some reason, did not ask another doctor or call me anyway. The baby died. Who's liable here? I would be the one blamed, even though two other people made poor decisions. But that's not the worst part of situations like this. The people who made the poor decisions don't have to face my patients. I do.

In another instance the nurses watched the fetal heart rate, which should be 140 or 130 beats a minute, drop and drop. Even when the heart rate dipped to 60 and then 20 over a period of hours, they just watched the strip disappear. The baby died. After this incident, a few of the nurses took some training in fetal monitor strip reading, but I still have to face the family and report that their baby died.

One of my patients came to me after losing two other babies. She had a blood incompatibility problem similar to the RH factor. Her first baby was born early and ill, but survived. Her second baby was born dead. When she came to me, she was pregnant a third time. By carefully following the condition of her amniotic fluid, we were able to have her carry her baby as long as possible and then induce her to deliver a healthy baby that lived.

The Legal System Misses the Point

During the fifth month of the patient's third pregnancy, she began experiencing bleeding and painful cramping. Ultrasound testing and examination by her physician failed to reveal the cause of the problem. She was instructed to go home and stay off her feet. Later that day, the patient began to bleed heavily and was taken by ambulance to the hospital.

An examination by a second physician also failed to reveal the reason for the bleeding. The patient was discharged the following day with instructions to get plenty of rest. Still, her bleeding and cramping worsened.

Her husband drove the patient to the emergency room the next day where she was examined by a third physician. He advised her to go home. The husband rejected this advice and insisted that she be admitted to the hospital. The patient was transferred to the labor and delivery ward.

Upon her arrival on the ward, a nurse said, "What are you doing here? The doctor told you to stay home and rest." Another nurse told the patient that if she miscarried at this point in her pregnancy it would not be a baby, but a "big blob of blood."

The next morning the admitting physician stood outside the patient's room and yelled that he did not want her for a patient, because he could not continue taking on the workload of the patient's original physician. Prompted by the patient's husband and a nurse, he apologized for the outburst and told the patient he would take care of her until he left for a vacation at noon.

In great pain, the patient believed she was having labor contractions. The physician performed a sonogram and abdominal examination, but not a pelvic exam. Although the patient was hysterical and insisting she was close to delivery, the physician left for his vacation, 20 minutes before the end of his shift. Before he left, he advised the patient's husband to calm his wife down.

The patient began delivering. Seeing the baby, her husband kicked open a glass door to get the attention of the hospital staff. Two nurses wheeled the patient to a delivery room and delivered a one-pound baby girl.

Observing neither a hearbeat nor any respiratory activity, one of the nurses announced that the baby was stillborn and placed the infant on an instrument tray. Ten minutes later, the patient's physician arrived and checked the baby for gender. He made no further examination of the infant.

About a half hour later, the husband touched the infant's finger. His grasp was returned. He summoned a nurse, who determined the infant was alive and rushed her to a neonatal intensive care unit where the infant died 12 hours later.

The patient and her husband sued the physicians and hospital, alleging violation of the standard of prenatal care, failure to recognize signs of an imminent premature birth, and delay in treating the infant after birth. They claimed severe emotional distress due to the negligent treatment of both mother and infant.

The trial court granted summary judgement for the hospital and physicians, based on the plaintiff's failure to furnish an expert witness within the 180-day limit.

The parents appealed the decision, contending the case came under the "common knowledge" exception to the rule requiring expert testimony in malpractice actions. The Iowa Supreme Court upheld the trial court's determination that certain conduct by the physicians and hospital could only be properly addressed with expert testimony. This included the question of whether faster or more heroic action would have saved the infant's life. Also, there was no evidence that the patient's treatment caused or could have prevented the premature birth....

The Digest,
p. 4

This case is particularly compelling as an example of how tort law has repeatedly failed to deal fairly and humanely with the victims of malpractice, much less stop the damaging actions from continuing.

Not long after her delivery, I received a call from a lawyer on her behalf. He wanted to know if I would testify for her in a lawsuit against the doctor who cared for her when she lost her second baby. But, according to him, he was really under the gun on this one. According to the law, you only have two years to file a claim against a doctor if the baby is delivered dead. As he put it, "dead babies aren't worth much." He really preferred babies born with defects. When the babie lives, but has a birth defect, the law allows a family up to 22 years to file a claim.

Lawsuits don't solve the problem. They don't adequately compensate the families or provide the kinds of supportive care families need in these kinds of situations. It is often very difficult to really place the blame on any one person, although the law tries. Doctors are prevented from expressing remorse over poor outcomes, much less mistakes. And the results of lawsuits are often illogical and notoriously inconsistent.

Lawsuits for liability, placing the blame on some scapegoat, have no place in a health care system that puts quality of patient care above all else.

Too Many Specialists

The fact remains that for the overwhelming number of diseases and illnesses, few specialists are needed, particularly when compared to the need for direct, primary, personal, and family services. The impetus to find new sources of money, new markets, and new customers has far more to do with expanding health technology and increasing specialization than does patient-service priorities.

Richard Kunnes
p. 50

An interesting study of how the trend toward specialization has intensified the problem of the shortage of doctors and the high cost of treatment was provided some years ago. In 1952 at Cape Canaveral, 16 doctors, only three of whom were specialists, served a population of 40,000. By 1964, there were 117 doctors representing most of the specialties, and they were having tremendous difficulty in serving a population of 170,000. Although the ratio of physicians to the population had increased by more than 40 percent, the income of the doctors had skyrocketed for providing fewer services.

La Roche, quoted in Ruth Mulvey Harmer
p. 40

The cost of medical services is also increased substantially by defensive medicine—those practices adopted by providers primarily to avoid liability risk. Studies done by the American Medical Associations's Center for Health Policy Research have shown that the current liability system creates strong incentives for physicians to order additional laboratory tests, roentgenograms, and consultations to confirm their medical judgments, as a protection against future liability claims that may result if optimal treatment outcomes are not experienced.

Martin J. Hatlie
p. 584

The economic evolution of health care removes the physician further and further away from the patient's life. What had formerly been a private relationship between two individuals has been reshaped into a major industry, involving some fifty medical specialties and subspecialties and more than seventy ancillary technical occupations.

Richard Kunnes
pp. 86-87

...69 percent of respondents in a recent survey agreed that "people are beginning to lose faith in their doctors." The percentage is up from 62 percent in 1982. The good news is that only 10 percent of respondents with a personal physician said they were losing faith in their own doctor, down from 15 percent in 1983.

News Clips
"Image Boosting,"
p. 49

Patients' loss of faith in the medical profession has led to litigious actions and malpractice fears. In part, this may be due to patients' unrealistic expectations of a perfect outcome. A loss of faith on the patient's part, as well as a lack of adequate discussion on the physician's part, are to blame.

To improve our image, we just resume our role as patient advocates—a role that, for some reason, has been lost in the sweep. As a first step, we should spend more time conversing with and listening to the patient. Medicine seems to have lost its humanitarian focus and taken on characteristics of big business. Profit, for example, has become more important in some circumstances than quality care. We must push for more humanitarian medicine.

Edmund C. Burke
p. 5

Neither Fast Nor Just

In almost every discussion about the high cost of medical care, the subject of liability comes up. Before medicine became a big business, consumers often had a personal relationship with a doctor, sometimes a very longstanding one. In fact, a doctor may well have seen not only the patients' parents, but also the patients' grandparents. You've got it. The old general practitioner.

This person's training? Medical school, internship and possibly residency, then out into the real world to practice medicine. Many of these doctors, after practicing general medicine for a few years, went back to school to specialize. They became the pediatricians, the internists, the orthopedic surgeons.

Everyone a Specialist

What ever happened to the old general practitioners? During the 1940s, medical school curriculums were revised. Doctors no longer had to go out in the real world and practice medicine before specializing. They simply finished up their internship and began their specialized training. Medical schools, by changing the structure of curriculums, were no longer producing general practitioners. For many years, people started going to internists simply because there were fewer and fewer general practitioners around to take care of colds and the flu. Of course, there was subtle pressure on the consumer to believe that they needed a more highly trained physician to take care of their flu and colds than general practitioners. Finally, the medical schools developed a specialty to fill the gap left by the old general practitioners, and called it the family practice physician.

The point of this trip down memory lane? Well, for one thing, that doctor that now treats your cold and flu has sunk a lot more money into medical school than your general practitioner or yore, so you are charged more. Now, you might also argue that with the additional training, consumers are getting more for their money when the internist treats their colds and flu. On the other hand, you could just as easily argue that the general practitioner, with ten or twenty years of practical experience, may be equally qualified to treat your cold or flu, and in some cases, the experience might be a greater advantage than the schooling. We have developed a system of training doctors that at great expense makes specialists out of everyone. The important question is do we get better care for all this extra expense? We think the answer is obviously no.

The Family Practice Physician

Officially created in 1969, family practice is a relatively new medical specialty. But its roots extend back to the general practitioners of days past and draw on the spirit of the "horse and buggy" doctor who made house calls, tended to the sick and was a trusted family confidant.

Before World War II, most physicians in the United States were general practitioners [GPs]. These physicians typically took one year of training in a hospital after finishing medical school before hanging up their shingle to practice. The end of the war saw the rise of specialization in medical practice, with a decline in the number of GPs.

Eventually, these changes led to a shortage of general practitioners—doctors who could manage common health problems and coordinate a patient's health care within an increasingly complex medical world....

Unlike general practitioners, family physicians complete a full three-year residency in family practice, making them eligible to take a board-certifying examination. This length of residency training follows four years of medical school and is the same length required to become an internist or pediatrician....

Nationally, family physicians provide more health care to more people of all ages than any other specialty. For example, family physicians take care of more children under age 17 than do pediatricians and treat more patients over age 65 than do internists....

Like general internists and pediatricians, family physicians do general physical exams and diagnose and treat acute medical problems like ear infection, pneumonia, sprains and vaginal infection. They also care for people with chronic medical problems like hypertension, diabetes, cancer and heart disease.

Most simply put, family physicians differ from pediatricians and internists in that they take care of both adults and children. But they're also more likely to handle problems in the fields of dermatology, minor surgery, office orthopedics and office gynecology.

Jay Siwek
p. 15

There is a second important point to notice about this subtle shift in how medicine is practiced. The old general practitioner who had treated the members of your community for years and years knew all about you—far more than any specialist could find out about you in taking a medical history. Don't get us wrong. Medical histories are important. But no medical history can substitute for knowing a patient as part of a family or community. The medical system we have allowed to develop has irrevocably and we suspect irretrievably severed the relationship between a family doctor and the community.

The result. The specialists treating you, because they don't know your family or you as part of the community, have no background information to provide the kind of perspective that may well be critical to effective diagnosis and treatment.

Tests Substitute for Community

In this day and age, then, when doctors see you for the first time, chances are they're looking at a blank slate. So they run the basic tests. And what they see may be ambiguous. But since they don't really know you, they can't rely on their knowledge of your lifestyle to help them clear up some of the ambiguities. So they run some more tests. And because they don't really know you, they have to be absolutely sure that your condition isn't some exotic disorder that a knowledge of your lifestyle and place in the community might shed some light on. So they run some more tests because they have to cover all their bases. And then, because they don't know you well enough to know that you won't sue them if you're unhappy about something, they run some more tests.

To make the problem worse, the medical system we have allowed to develop does not consider taking care of people's colds and flu very significant work. We know this because insurance and Medicare reimburse doctors relatively little for providing these services. In fact, the reimbursement rate is so poor that the doctor is hard pressed to spend much time talking to you at all—something that in many cases is what is really needed instead of prescriptions or tests.

Did some of these community-based general practitioners sometimes miss important clues that led to some bad outcomes for patients? Sure they did. On the other hand, do specialists, because they more than likely have little real knowledge of your and your lifestyle, sometimes miss important clues that lead to bad outcomes for patients? Sure they do.

Medicine is not a perfect science, as we've discussed in Chapter 2. Whether patients have bad outcomes because their doctor lacked specialized training, or

How to Choose a Doctor

It was when the hemorrhage had cost me about two-thirds of my blood, and I ended up in the emergency room, that I remembered the fax. I asked the attendants to call my specialist. Because he was out of town, I requested that my pertinent records be faxed to the hospital. Scared, I didn't know how much longer I could remember hematocrits, specific dates, and dosage of the new medication I'd obtained for anemia and to aid in digestion....

...the office personnel refused to send my records. They said they didn't have the time or the manpower.

What I learned that terrifying weekend was not to judge a physician by his medical competence or background alone. You've got to look further....

The Staff

The first line of defense in your emergency will be the people who answer the office phones. To prevent I-can't-be-bothered lines at your life-and-death moments, check out the office staff. Listen for clues and use your instincts. Assess their phone rapport. When you call, are you put on hold for long periods of time? Are your messages taken accurately? Are your questions for the doctor relayed in an effective manner or are you told to just come in?

Telephone Counseling

....Days before my hemorrhage, I phoned in my symptoms—nausea, vomiting, cramps, aches. The nurse who fields calls told me "that sounds like the flu." Despite my insistence that somehow this felt different, she called me back after consulting with the doctor, told me I had the flu and to drink clear liquids.

Vacation Coverage

....I had been told years ago that when my physician leaves town his office partner covers for him....

But when the emergency room physician phoned my doctor's office, he was told that my doctor was out of town. The partner, reporting he knew nothing about my case, refused to inform the emergency room doctors attending me in any way....

Bedside Manner

The specialist who cared for me in the hospital was well-informed and thorough. He was also dogmatic, dour and distant. He suggested an uncomfortable and potentially deadly diagnostic procedure....Doctor X became angry, even more distant and curt....

Dr. Y...let six phone calls interrupt our interview—two to chat about golf games, and one each to agree to read a colleague's paper, to make a luncheon appointment, to talk about his ability to still do surgery despite having his arm in a cast, and to talk to a hospital resident....

Although Doctor Z had a caring attitude, great listening skills, an interesting perspective and an excellent reputation, he was mired in the bureaucracy of a local hospital. To get an appointment to see him, I had to send my records ahead and beg....After several "He'll get back to you" phone calls, I simply gave up....

I found a physician I like....Someone I can talk to, who allows me to take an active part in my care, who has an efficient and effective support staff, who doesn't wither if I don't march to his orders, who admits what he occasionally doesn't know, and who can find the time to research answers.

Candyce H. Stapen, p. D5

hematocrit: quantity of red blood cells in given volume of blood.

adapted from *Tabor s, p. H-21*

- **If you think you have more than the flu, insist on seeing the doctor.**
- **Insist your doctor explain your care fully.**
- **If you can't get answers to your questions, go to a different doctor, and if necessary, a third or fourth doctor.**

because their specialist doctor is a virtual stranger and is unable to spend enough time with them to catch important clues is irrelevant. The results are the same.

Sometimes medical outcomes are poorer than doctors had hoped for no matter how good the care they provided. But we have allowed a system to develop in which patients expect the optimum outcomes and doctors dare not admit that the results of a given procedure are less than 100 percent perfect. Such a system denies doctors the chance to express remorse to the patients when outcomes, for any number of reasons besides physician error, are less than perfect.

In some very important ways, our health care system is set up to prevent consumers from knowing about problems with doctors. State Medical Boards, for example, usually do not tell consumers about actions against doctors, even if consumers call and specifically ask for this information (Glazer, "Policing the Professions," p. 291).

Furthermore, our health care system has degenerated into a pattern which requires doctors to employ lawyers to manipulate the problematic situations in the doctor-patient relationship. Consumers should know that the lawyers for companies which provide liability insurance specifically instruct doctors not to engage in discussions with patients who are unhappy about their care. Doctors, if patients show anger, are supposed to cut off all communication and refer the patient to the insurance company. Doctors are told by insurance companies that if they reduce fees because a patient complains about a treatment or procedure, the doctors are admitting guilt. In fact, such a practice seriously jeopardizes a doctor's ability to procure liability insurance.

A health care system which handles its problems with doctors in a manner such as this is inefficient and outrageously expensive, not only in dollars, but also in terms of man's inhumanity to man. In effect, this approach prevents the real problem between the doctor and the patient from ever being

solved. It simply puts a price tag on the disagreement, and makes many third party manipulators rich in the process.

We know that when doctors keep patients informed, when doctors take the time to explain the patients's choices, and the patient takes the responsibility for the decision—including the risk—consumers are less likely to hold the doctor responsible for outcomes that are beyond the doctor's control. That is not to say that doctors who are indeed supplying substandard care should not be identified and prevented from continuing to practice harmful care. Rather, that is to say that patients, if they are informed about their treatment and if they have taken the responsibility for the decisions about their care, would less likely fall into the trap of allowing third parties to set up an adversarial relationship between doctors and patients. Lawsuits do not solve problems with substandard care. They simply make all health care much more expensive than it need be.

Separating Poor Outcomes from Malpractice

We've briefly discussed the kinds of problems that are created by the disappearance of the family doctor and the proliferation of specialists, and how this situation can contribute to making the practice of medicine, not a perfect science to begin with, even less perfect. To make any sense out of the whole issue of medical liability, we must maintain a clear distinction between malpractice and poor patient outcomes. The outcomes may be poor—that is, less than had been hoped for— but that does not automatically indicate that the care provided was substandard or the provider incompetent.

With malpractice, the issue is physician or hospital care that actually harms the patient. There must be a direct causal relationship between care which was clearly substandard by commonly accepted practice guidelines and the bad outcome. Politics and angry patients should have no bearing on determining what malpractice is or is not. Unfortu-

THE MEASURING OF HEALTH CARE

nately, our health care system has no mechanism for quickly and effectively spotting incompetent physicians or deadly hospitals and correcting the problems.

Lawyers ignore this problem, but argue that no consumer should be denied the right to sue. Large court awards for medical problems supposedly caused by doctors or hospitals have gained a lot of publicity in recent years as the cost of liability insurance has skyrocketed. But these well-publicized awards come about only after ten or twelve years of wrangling in the courts, and the actual amount of money which makes it into the family coffers is often greatly reduced after the lawyers take their cut. The only persons who never lose in liability cases are the defense lawyers. The consumer making the claim may lose, the lawyer representing the consumer may lose the case and thereby the contingency fee, but the lawyer defending the doctor (or whoever is being sued) never loses. The defense lawyers, regardless of the outcome, always get paid.

Does tort law actually improve patient care? We think not. We believe that the lawyerly concern for the inviolate right of consumers to sue for damages and this groups's vigorous attempts to fight putting caps on jury awards to consumers is a misguided effort. The important issue is not whether consumers can or cannot sue, but how can we develop a system to quickly spot dangerous doctors, nurses, and hospitals and either correct the problem or put them out of business. Lawyers, a group of professionals who could contribute much to reforming our system to do what needs to be done, have been strangely quiet about this fundamental and critical issue.

We feel that lawyers, like insurance companies, have a valuable role to play in health care reform. As with insurance companies, however, the critical question is whether lawyers can overcome the tyrannical machine of our legal system, a legal system which quibbles over points of law while many consumers go without the medical care they need . A legal system which fails to quickly and effectively deal with harmful health care providers. A legal system which fixates on assigning blame rather than getting consumers the health care they need. A legal system that we feel must develop efficient, effective, and quick ways to humanely

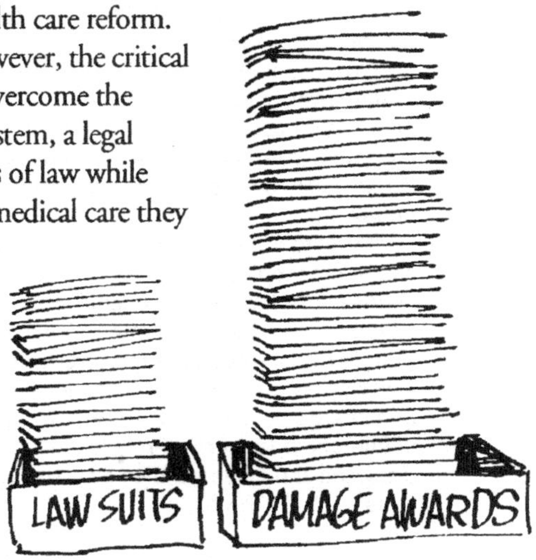

Peer Review: The Good-Old-Boy System

In the 1950s, many local medical societies decided to establish grievance committees in response to increasing threats of legal action. Theoretically, it was a good idea, but practically, these committees had little power over offending doctors. The severest action any could take was censure, suspension, or expulsion from the society. And most kept these actions secret.

Furthermore, some of the doctors who were approached began suing the grievance committees. In Cleveland, an opthalmologist sued the Academy of Medicine of Cleveland for $700,000 because the committe had "merely suggested to the doctor that he lower his fee in one case." The doctor was awarded the full fee in court.

Ruth Mulvey Harmer
p. 99-100

A commission of the American Bar Association yesterday recommended that systems for disciplining lawyers—most of which operate in great secrecy—open their proceedings to public view....

In the District, Maryland and Virginia, the vast majority of complaints against lawyers never become public. Closed-door proceedings are held, and the complaint general remains secret until a panel has found the lawyer guilty of some violation. Even then, secrecy may prevail if the lawyer is given a "private" reprimand.

"You cannot ask the public to trust a system which they cannot see and which operates in secret," Raymond R. Trombadore, a Sommerville, N.J., lawyer who chaired the commission, said at a news conference yesterday....

"The irony that lawyers are protected by secret proceedings while earning their livelihoods in an open system of justice is not lost on the public," the ABA commission found.... "The fox is still guarding the chicken coop," said Kay Ostberg, the group's acting director. She charged that there is an inherent conflict of interest in lawyer self-regulation and said discipline should be handled by state legislatures.

Saundra Torry
p. A1, A17

We have long insisted that only peers are qualified to judge other physicians' practices. Now, Rep. Greenfield and others have made clear their willingness to champion review of physicians by physicians, instead of by bureaucracies, nurses, or for-profit ventures. Surely it is unwise to pass up this opportunity to demonstrate our concerns about quality care and our willingness to use our expertise to better our profession.

Richard B. Tompkins
"MMA Could Ensure...,"
p. 41

As long as policing is a job for insiders, there is little likelihood that the peer review committees will be effective in weeding out the doctors whose performance constitutes a danger to public health and to financial secirity. And many outside watchdogs have done little better. The insurance carriers have been in an excellent position to identify dishonest and incompetent doctors, but they have done little—even Blue Cross and Blue Shield.

Ruth Mulvey Harmer
p. 107

Frances Conley was one of the first fully tenured female professors of neurosurgery in the United States. She was on the faculty of Stanford University Medical School, she reported to the man who had first hired her there 25 years ago, a man who she says "had tremendous respect for me." In the world of medicine, which is dominated by men, she had broken through the glass ceiling.

Two years ago, her mentor retired, and Conley's supportive work environment changed when he was temporarily replaced by someone Conley describes as "very arrogant. He cannot accept the fact that women were created for anything other than to feed him, clean up after him and provide him with sexual gratification."

On May 22, Dean David Korn of the medical school informed her that he intended to appoint this person to the position permanently, because the school did not have the funds to continue the nationwide search for an outside replacement. Conley, 50, resigned....

Judy Mann
p. B3

monitor the quality of our health care system and assure consumers that they receive the care they need—or go the way of the dinosaurs.

Talk to Your Doctor

If patients believe the treatment they receive is below standard, consumers have few choices. First, we recommend patients talk to the doctor about the problem. We suspect that in many cases, patients really don't want to face their doctor about complaints, either because they do not like confrontation, they do not know how to discuss a problematical situation, or they feel they shouldn't question a doctor.

One of our primary goals is to encourage patients—to give them permission, if you will—to ask questions of their doctors and to become active participants in choosing which treatment options to pursue. We suggest that if a doctor discourages patients from asking questions, whether by making fun of the questions, ignoring the questions, or by gruffness in manner, the patients should seek a second opinion from another doctor. Or a third. Or a fourth.

We think the liability insurance lawyers recommending to doctors that they cut off communication with angry patients leads to all kinds of serious problems, not the least of which is the threat of a lawsuit. We believe that many of the problems doctors have with liability suits could be avoided if doctors spent whatever time it takes to fully explain procedures—and risks—to their patients and work with patients to accept the responsibility for their treatment choices.

If consumers cannot resolve the problem by talking over the situation with their doctors, what choices do they have?

- They can file a complaint with their insurance company,
- They can file a complaint with their state medical board.
- They can report the problem to their state Professional Review Organization (PRO). See page 69 to locate your group.
- They can report problems to their state consumer protection agency, and
- They can find a lawyer and sue the health care provider.

Medical Review Board Actions

Because states vary in their enforcement of disciplinary procedures, a high rate in one state does not mean doctors there are worse than those in other states; it may mean such states are more diligent in investigating complaints.

Disciplinary Acts Against Physician,
Washington Post Health,
p. 5

State	Serious Actions	Rate/1000 Physicians	State	Serious Actions	Rate/1000 Physicians
Missouri	98	9.3	Washington	25	2.30
Iowa	41	8.91	Texas	69	2.23
Oklahoma	39	7.70	Delaware	3	2.16
Alaska	5	6.62	Montana	3	1.13
Georgia	65	5.67	Wisconsin	20	1.04
Kentucky	36	5.49	Maine	5	1.01
Colorado	37	4.98	North Carolina	26	1.01
West Virginia	16	4.71	New Mexico	6	1.01
South Carolina	28	4.71	Arizona	15	1.88
Indiana	43	4.63	Rhode Island	5	1.86
Ohio	91	4.01	New York	108	1.80
Utah	13	3.95	California	133	1.74
Mississippi	13	3.59	Kansas	8	1.69
Oregon	22	3.49	North Dakota	2	1.68
Minnesota	34	3.34	Nevada	3	1.65
Illinois	79	3.00	Maryland	24	1.48
Idaho	4	2.89	Alabama	10	1.47
Louisiana	24	2.76	Tennessee	13	1.30
South Dakota	3	2.75	Dist. of Col.	5	1.29
Wyoming	2	2.71	Pennsylvania	29	.96
New Jersey	53	2.64	New Hamp.	2	.84
Arkansas	10	2.61	Hawaii	2	.74
Vermont	4	2.52	Massachusets	15	.72
Michigan	44	2.41	Nebraska	1	.32
Virginia	31	2.33	Connecticut	0	.00
Florida	70	2.30			

* includes: medical license revocation, suspension, and probation
† source: Washington Post Health, 18 June 1991, p. 5.

Only the state consumer protection agency has the interest of the consumer as a primary goal. And these organizations are subject to the same political pressures as our elected representatives.

The problem is that all of these alternatives are usually quite ineffective in identifying dangerous doctors, nurses, or hospitals and correcting the problems quickly before other patients are hurt.

Peer Review Doesn't Work

The professions have always vigorously defended "peer review," that is, the effectiveness of doctors (or engineers, or lawyers) judging doctors (or engineers, or lawyers). The argument is that non-professionals would not understand the issues, and therefore are incapable of making an informed decision in problematical cases. Studies have shown, however, that the peer-review process is ineffective. It's true that a hospital's peer-review committee can revoke a doctor's privileges, but in a town with several hospitals, the doctor can simply move on to a different one. On the other hand, in a town with only one hospital, the doctor can be driven out of business by jealous doctors on the committee (Glazer, "Policing the Professions," p. 294).

There are several reasons state boards are so ineffective in tracking down incompetent doctors and putting them out of business. First, these boards are funded by the licensing fees for the state, and most are expected to operate on only a portion of these fees. They are chronically underfunded to perform any regulatory actions. Second, investigations require lengthy, costly research. And finally, these boards are composed of doctors who are very hesitant to censure fellow doctors. Sometimes the board members themselves are not the best doctors. One report indicates that "more than 97 percent of the complaints that are valid on their face never see the light of day (Glanzer, p. 292)."

> Doctors are regulated by state medical boards. The boards derive their power from state laws giving them the right to grant and revoke licenses. Individual state laws lay out the boards' powers, the types of violations for which they may punish incompetent or miscreant doctors, and the types of penalties they may impose. The American Medical Association and its affiliated state medical societies also issue ethical codes to be followed by their members but which have no legal force. (Glanzer, p. 291).

Access vs. Right to Sue

Adrienne Schultz doesn't deliver babies anymore. She can't afford to.

Malpractice coverage for the prenatal clinic at the House of Ruth, the 6th Street NE shelter for homeless and battered women where Schultz works, would run $46,000 per year....So the physician takes care of the women up to their eighth month and then turns them over to one of the local hospitals.

The Amendment to the Physicians Free Clinic Assistance Act of 1986 would....protect obstetricians who volunteer their services from malpractice suits except in cases of obvious negligence....

The D.C. Trial Lawyers Association is not unsympathetic to the inadequate state of local health care. But president Patrick M. Regan says his group opposes the measure "because we know the intentions of the Medical Society lobby. We're convinced that they are going to attempt to use legislation of this type to do away with the physicians' responsibility under the law for their negligent acts."

...Washington attorney Sandra Robinson testified on behalf of the Trial Lawyers. "Basically," she said, "it is our position that [the bill] cuts off the rights of poor and indigent persons who can't afford private medical care to sue if negligence has occurred and it appears to discriminate in that sense."

Such opposition is echoed by other sources. Says Sid Wolfe, head of the Public Citizens Health Group: "Poor people are already second-class citizens. I would say you're patching up a failed system on the backs of the poor. This is a desperate, impossible kind of alternative to more fundamental reform. Either you don't get adequate care, which is unacceptable, or you give up your rights, also unacceptable."

Sandy Rovner and David Streitfeld
p. C5

In the past, attorneys' associations have fought any efforts that would limit a patient's ability to bring a case to trial or place a cap on awards, saying it violates patients' rights.

Proponents of the bill, however, contend that the current system, with its long delays and high legal fees, denies many injured patients the chance for fair compensation.

They cite a 1987 General Accounting Office report showing that, in cases closed in 1984, it took an average of 25 months, and as long as 11 years, from the date a claim was filed until final resolution. In more than half the cases, plaintiff legal fees took more than 30% of payments to the injured party. Plaintiffs also were responsible for paying other expenses, such as court costs and costs of obtaining evidence.....

Suggested alternatives include a fault-based administrative system. Under this proposal, a state would establish an agency with exclusive jurisdiction to review medical liability claims. Patients injured by negligence could receive full payment for out-of-pocket damages, but pain and suffering and other non-economic damages would be limited. The agency would be required to coordinate with state licensing and disciplinary official to identify and discipline negligent physicians.

Laurie Jones
p. 24

Unfortunately, after 15 years of state-based initiatives, the tort reform movement has been effectively stalled in most states....In Florida, the cost of liability insurance adds $1119 to the cost of delivering every infant. In New York and Arizona, the cost is $607 and $447, respectively.

Martin J. Hatlie
p. 584

Glanzer (p. 292) continues that studies show that state medical boards are ineffective in dealing with the problem of incompetent doctors:

> Recent examinations of the California and Maryland state disciplinary systems support the impression that incompetent physicians are seldom plucked from the medical profession as soon as they are detected. In both states, only a tiny minority of consumer complaints are acted upon, and only a fraction of those lead to disciplinary action against the doctor. Those complaints that do lead to penalties take years to reach a conclusion. During that time, the accused doctor continues to practice, and any complaints against him remain secret. What's more, very few of the disciplinary actions that are taken against doctors are for incompetence or negligence, presumably the primary concern of any patient....Over-prescribing drugs to patients, drug abuse and alcohol abuse accounted for about three-fourths of the disciplinary actions taken by state boards.

Lawsuits Fail to Police the Profession

Tort law allows individuals to sue someone for wrongful acts and be compensated for the damages. This law allows consumers to sue manufacturers as well as persons providing services such as doctors and hospitals for damages. And there is some evidence that more and more people are suing for damages and that the awards given by juries are much greater than they used to be. In 1977, there were 437 medical malpractice suits filed in federal courts. By 1987, that number had increased to 1,783. According to a study by the Rand Corporation, the increase in tort filings has been seen primarily on the federal level, where there have been a number of mass-injury cases filed against the producers of asbestos, for example, or the Dalkon Shield (Cooper, p. 329).

So while the increase in claims filed may not be as great as it appears if one looks only at the federal filings, there is evidence to support the claim that jury awards have jumped significantly. A study by the Institute for Civil Justice found that the average size of awards, adjusted for inflation, in Cook County, Illinois, rose from $52,000 in 1960 to $1,179,000 in 1980-1984, and in San Francisco, from $125,000 to $1,162,000 in the same period. Furthermore, successful claims in both areas for medical malpractice and product liability increased from 25 percent to 50 percent. (Cooper, p. 329).

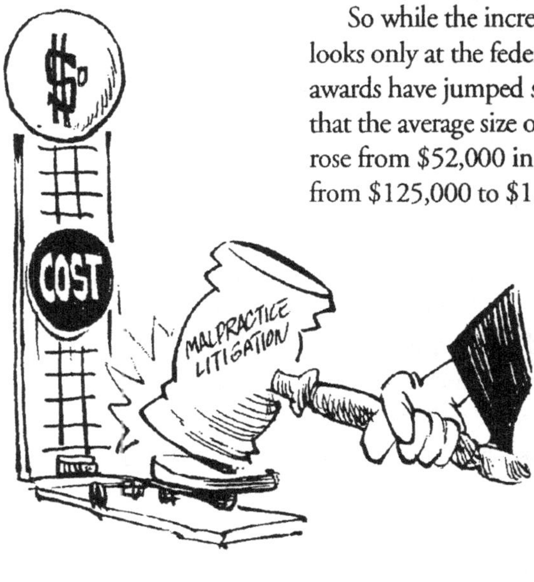

Has the increase in awards and the increase in successful claims improved our health care system? We think the answer is obviously, no. A study in California of hospital adverse events during the middle 1970s indicates that for each malpractice claim filed, there were believed to be 10 other injuries caused by negligent care. (Localio, et al., p. 245). In this study, 280 patients among 31,429 were identified as having adverse events caused by medical

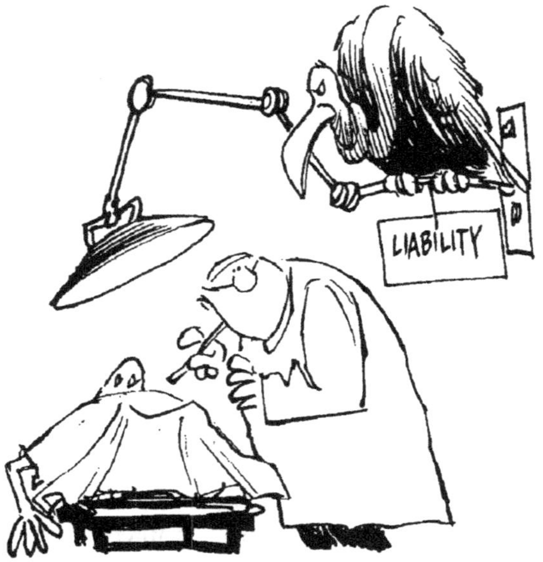

negligence as defined by the study, but only 8 of the 280 filed malpractice claims. The study concludes that "Medical-malpractice litigation infrequently compensates patients injured by medical negligence and rarely identifies, and holds providers accountable for, substandard care" (Localio, et al., p. 245).

There are those that maintain the fear of liability suits has made doctors more careful and has forced doctors to change the way they practice medicine. The assumption here is that any change is a change for the better. Again, we believe this to be an erroneous assumption. Much is made over the seemingly unnecessary laboratory tests doctors order in their practice of "defensive medicine." But consumers hear less about the enormous increase in cesarean sections performed by doctors, which can in large part be attributed to fear of liability. Yes, cesarean sections are sometimes performed when there is a good chance the baby could be delivered vaginally. Why? Because the records show that patients don't often sue doctors over cesarean sections. Most suits evolve out of babies delivered vaginally. The result? Consumers pay more for the delivery. Consumers are subjected to the increased risk of surgery. And consumers pay higher insurance premiums to cover the costs of the increase in cesarean sections.

Have consumer malpractice suits effectively removed dangerous doctors and hospitals from the health care arena? We believe the answer is no. While a few consumers have won large rewards, most do not. In fact, the majority of consumers who have been actually harmed by medical malpractice never even file claims. But consumers have ended up paying for all this malpractice litigation with higher insurance premiums and higher doctor and hospital fees (Cooper, p. 338).

Consumers Kept in the Dark

Despite all the claims that medical liability suits keep doctors on their toes, consumers are deliberately prevented from having access to the results of many of the procedures for identifying doctors or hospitals which perform poorly. The investigations made by state medical boards are private. Only if a doctor is found guilty of some morally offensive behavior such as drug addiction or having intercourse with patients—seldom is the issue malpractice itself—does the record become public. Knowing the reluctance of state medical boards to actually censure a doctor, that means that much of the information about the competence of doctors is unavailable to the public.

If a consumer calls the state or county medical association to ask for a recommendation for a doctor, the consumer cannot assume that that doctor is competent.

> Joyce Palso...was among those who were enticed by advertisements for cosmetic surgery....even though before the operation, Palso had done everything she could think of to check her doctor's medical credentials. It seems that none of the government or medical authorities she contacted warned her that Dr. James Dean had 11 malpractice suits filed against him at the time of her operation. (Glazer, p. 293).

The state of California, where Joyce Palso had her surgery, handles consumer complaints through a Board of Medical Quality Assurance. With an estimated 50,000 to 80,000 complaints annually, in 1988, only 42 physicians had their licenses suspended or revoked. Of these 42 cases, only 12 involved incompetence or negligence. The rest were for things like criminal convictions or drug abuse (Glanzer, p. 294).

To help address some of these issues, the federal government established a national Practitioner Data Bank to provide a national collection center for information on professional conduct and competence and malpractice claims. This Data Bank opened September 1, 1990. By April of 1991, liability lawyers were arranging settlements conditional on taking doctors names off settlement papers so that their names wouldn't appear in the National Data Bank (Torry, p. 5). See our narrative on page 171 about the politicization of the process.

Not that the information in the National Data Bank is directly available to consumers anyway. Public Citizen and Dr. Sidney Wolfe has published some of the data so it is available to consumers.

Capping Malpractice Awards

There have been a number of efforts to reform the tort system, most notably by putting a cap on the amount of money juries can award. Many states have set up alternative forms of settling disagreements by arbitration. Some doctors feel that arbitration does not protect the doctor from automatically being considered guilty—it just puts a monetary value on the disagreement.

None of these suggestions address the real problem here. We need to efficiently identify incompetent doctors and dangerous hospitals and prevent further harm.

Dr. Sidney Wolfe believes that doctors sitting on a state disciplinary board are not going to be willing to censure their colleagues. Instead, Wolfe thinks states need to give licensing boards disciplinary clout, increase the funding for the boards so that they may do their job, give state boards the necessary powers to obtain records against accused doctors, grant them emergency powers to suspend licenses, and require periodic recertification of doctors (Glazer, p. 296).

We believe that reform of medical malpractice requires that the issues of negligence and outcomes be separated. The issue is not whether a patient has been harmed, but whether the problem, whatever the cause, is addressed and corrected. A SYSTEM OF ARBITRATION SHOULD BE THE FIRST LEVEL OF PROBLEM RESOLUTION, WITH THE EMPHASIS ON THE OUTCOME. A physician should not be prevented from showing compassion for the patient. Arbitration could address the problems earlier than litigation, when the problem may be more easily correctible, and certainly for less money.

Consumers would still have the option of litigating the claims in court, but the decision to accept arbitration or file a claim in court must be made first. The results of arbitration would be binding, Consumers could not go to court just because they were unhappy with the results of arbitration. Nor could they arbitrate if they were unhappy with court results.

Instead of liability insurance, doctors and hospitals could contribute to an arbitration pool, and costs of correcting problems paid for from that pool.

Correcting Harmful Practices

Arbitration, with lawsuits as an option, must be combined with an effective and quick means of identifying harmful practices, whether they are dangerous hospitals or harmful practitioners, and putting a stop to the continuation of problematical situations.

We know that peer review does not work. Whether it could work if it were more heavily funded is questionable. We are virtually certain it cannot work in secret, as it purports to do now. We believe that the process of reviewing harmful practices requires public scrutiny, and requires the input from many many consumers. Token consumerism usually fails because the consumers are so outnumbered by the professionals, and the appointments to these committees are usually political. We believe those serving on these boards should be limited to two or three year terms. And they should be elected rather than appointed by the political party in power. Election is a political process, but at least it would be open to the public

State medical boards should make public the kinds of data that help consumers decide for themselves whether they want to go to a particular health care provider. These kinds of information could include

- infection rates,
- deaths associated with simple procedures,
- units of blood used (adjusted for specialty, with adjustment explained in terms consumers can understand), and
- gauze and sponges left in body cavities following procedures.

And finally, no one—absolutely no one—is discussing how to take care of patients who, through no one's fault, have poor outcomes which require additional and sometimes long-term care. We consider this one of the most important issues to be solved in health care reform.

Only consumers can bring about the kinds of changes vested interests have clearly shown little desire to bring about—the kinds of reform that would actually address the problems, fairly compensate the consumers, and stop wasting the time of health care professionals in tilting at the shadows of malpractice. The court system has not been able to supply such a service. With poor medical outcomes, finding a victim to blame is irrelevant. Our health care system needs to be able to identify harmful practices quickly and effectively, and the system needs to be able to correct the problems quickly and effectively. Consumers need to have access to a fair, humane, and cost-effective way to correct problems which arise from their health care.

Consumers should be satisfied with nothing less.

Chapter 5 Summary

Problem #1:

Liability lawsuits set up an adversarial relationship between doctors and patients.

Issue:

Sometimes outcomes are simply poor outcomes. When planning their health care, consumers need to know what range of outcomes is possible—and that poor response to treatment does not equal malpractice

Action:

The health problems of consumers need to be taken care of, and blame—and hence malpractice suits—are irrelevant to providing that care.

Problem #2:

Liability lawsuits fail to stop the continuation of harmful medical pratices.

Issue:

Harmful practitioners may never be identified, and even if sued, are free to continue treating patients.

Action:

Health care reform needs to address how to efficiently identify harmful health care providers and correct the problems.

Problem #3:

Liability lawsuits fail to compensate consumers adequately, fairly, humanely, or in a timely manner.

Issue:

Harmful practice issues should be investigated, with concentration on correcting the problems; poor outcomes should be arbitrated.

Action:

Health care reform needs to remove the issue of blame from the issue of compensation, providing consumers with whatever care they need to solve the health problem.

Problem #4:

Make review of harmful practices an open and public process with meaningful consumer involvement.

Issue:

Consumers are capable of determining the quality of their care if they have the information they need to make informed decisions.

Action:

Data on outcomes for hospitals, clinics, and doctors should be readily available to consumers.

Chapter 6

We Don't Need Miracles—Just Basic Health Care

Chapter Contents

Bulletin Boards

Action Guides

Narratives

Discussion:

We Don't Need Miracles, Just Basic Health Care

Chapter 6 Summary

Rural vs. Urban Care

I believe DRGs have a role in limiting hospital stays and giving the hospital and physicians a tool for moving patients out of the hospital and into the nursing home, or out of the hospital and into the home care setting when the patient doesn't belong in an acute care setting. But there's a great difference between DRGs as they are applied to rural hospitals versus metropolitan hospitals. Metro hospitals typically have much better access to social service programs that can arrange home care, nursing home care, and outpatient programs. We don't have the same resources, and sometimes the hospital is the only safe place for a patient, even though hospitalization may not be necessary in terms of acute care. I'm concerned that officials who review rural hospital charts aren't keeping that in mind, I'm also concerned that some of the reviewers don't provide primary care and may not understand the role a rural hospital plays in caring for such patients.

Douglas D. Pflaum
p. 9

Gail Wilensky, administrator of the federal agency that supervises the federal-state Medicaid program, said of the hospital study that under the law, States are not obligated to pay a hospital's full cost—only the cost for efficiently and economically operated facilities."

Wilensky said that in many hospitals only 60 percent of the beds are occupied and when a hospital has a large number of unoccupied beds, its cost per patient rises sharply because overhead and related fixed costs are spread over fewer patients. Even though state Medicaid payments might be adequate if the hospital had more patients and therefore more revenue, they cannot cover costs per patient if the hospital has too many empty beds.

Spencer Rich
"State Medicaid Payments...,"
p. A5.

For eight badly burned firefighters, it made the difference between riding an ambulance 31 miles or 78 miles to the nearest hospital.

The difference was the Renville-Bottineau Memorial Hospital in Mohall, N.D.

But the 24-bed hospital is itself in danger of becoming a victim, fighting for its life against a financial squeeze that is tightening its grip on rural hospitals throughout North Dakota and Minnesota....As a Sept. 15 oil-tank fire near Sherwood, N.D., dramatically illustrates, proximity to emergency health care in rural areas is more than an issue of mere convenience.

Patrick Springer
"Many Rural N.D., Minnesota Hospitals...,"
p. A1

Hospitals and clinics across rural Minnesota are struggling to survive.

Wellness, for many, means driving to the nearest town large enough to support a doctor.

Lists of young physicians wanting to become country doctors do not exist....

Nationwide, Medicare and Medicaid payments for the elderly and poor must be equalized.

Minnesota doctors...are paid only one-third to one-fourth of what doctors in Miami and Los Angeles receive for Medicare cases.

Craig McEwen
p. C2

Denying Needed Care Wastes Money

Several years ago, one of my patients was seriously overweight—so overweight she couldn't get around easily, including in or out of a bathtub. Because of her weight, what would often be simple, pimple like eruptions on her skin, especially where her skin bears the entire weight of her body, developed into almost boil-like conditions.

Antibiotics certainly helped alleviate the infections, but sometimes these areas needed to be squirted periodically with warm water or soaked in warm water to clean them out and help the healing process. If she could only have gotten in and out of a bathtub, she could have taken care of this herself. Since she could not, she was unable to provide the care she needed for herself.

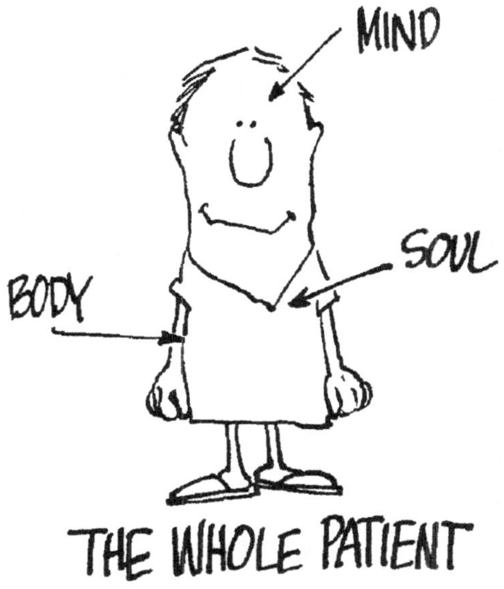

She appeared in the emergency room with a fever of 101° F and, according to her, unable to move. She was sent home with the advice to soak in a tub, even though she told them that she could not get in and out of a tub.

The kind of care this woman needed most people could have provided for themselves. But our health care system is unwilling or unable to deal with someone who cannot take the advice provided. Her only choice would have been to hire a home health care worker to irrigate her infected areas. In this instance, insurance would not pay for this care, nor would the welfare system. The county could have provided the service, but would have charged her as much as $82 per visit to provide the simple care that she needs.

As the health care system now operates, it is unable to accommodate the simple kind of care this patient needs. It can only refuse to help this patient until her condition becomes so serious—and so expensive to treat—that she must be hospitalized. Her only other alternative is to pay an exhorbitant amount of money to obtain this very basic, preventive care she could not provide herself.

Those who cannot provide the kind of care they need—no matter how simple—should not have to go without health care until they are so sick that they need acute care.

$600,000 Sewer Gas

No matter how you cut it, we doctors are often the ones to take the rap. When people read about liability suits in the newspapers and magazines, the culprit always seems to be the doctor. Even though the doctor sometimes has very little control over the hospital conditions under which they operate—they have 100 percent of the liability for the results.

One of the hospitals I deliver babies in recently remodeled their obstetrical floor to the tune of $600,000. This organization created eleven obstetrical rooms. These are the rooms that needed the $7,500 beds purchased six years ago replaced by $9,500 beds. When I asked why the old beds needed replacing, I was told that the new beds raised up higher and lower than the old beds, so nurses didn't have to bend over as much and patients could get in and out of the beds more easily. Both the $7,500 and the $9,500 beds were what we call labor, delivery, recovery, and post-partem (LDRP) beds, that is, all-purpose beds. It used to be that women delivering babies were moved around from room to room, depending upon whether they were in labor, were about to deliver, in the recovery room, or back to their own room after delivery. This required a different bed for each stage of delivery. Both the $7,500 and the $9,500 beds were LDRP. The increased cost of the new beds really had nothing to do with the older beds being less all-purpose than the new ones.

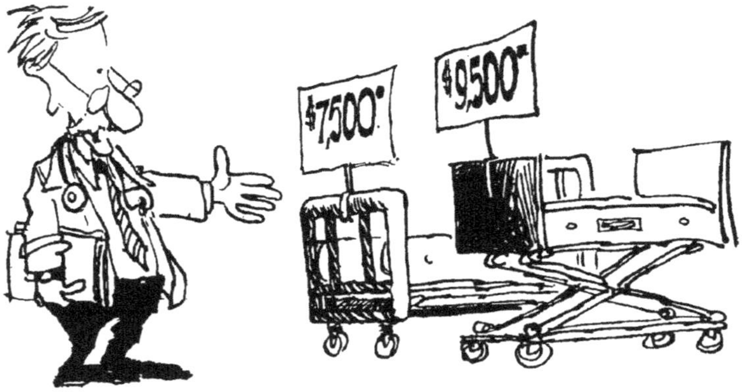

The hospital decided to hold a reception to show off its newly remodeled unit. As I walked through the obstetrical unit during the reception, I noticed the door to one of the rooms was being kept conspicuously closed. As I walked past it, I caught the unmistakable odor of sewer gas. Now, I have delivered babies at this hospital for nine years, and for some reason from time to time there has been a problem with sewer gas. Evidently the $600,000 remodeling job did not include solving the sewer gas problem. I frankly don't know how the new mother and her family in that room could stand it, but of course no one was admitting that solving the sewer gas problem might

have been more important the installing a jacuzzi or replacing perfectly good beds with more expensive ones.

Unfortunately, one of my patients had the gall to deliver during the reception, and the head nurse didn't want her party disturbed by something as messy as a real live birth. After some consternation, they found an available room several floors away which was not set up for obstetrical use. I'm not sure what the regular purpose of this room was, but I can assure you it was no bigger than a closet because there was barely space for me and a nurse to stand beside the delivery table.

My patient was delivering three weeks early, and I was not happy to be so far removed from the obstetrical floor with a risky birth. And so far away from trained obstetrical nurses if we ran into trouble.

As I delivered the baby, I realized the baby had difficulty breathing. Three nurses were looking in the observation window while I was struggling to get the new mother's bleeding stopped and trying to resuscitate the baby. We couldn't get the tube inserted into the baby's throat to get the breathing started. The nurse then tried to insert a tube from a Delee suction trap into the baby's throat, but was shoving the tube clear into the baby's stomach, which was counterproductive. The tube can paralyze the diaphragm, preventing breathing. By now the mother realizes the baby is in distress and becomes frantic. Luckily, a medical student happened by and I was able to have her round up the neonatal intensive care doctor.

The charge nurse stopped by after the reception was over and generously asked if there was anything she could do to help. She held the sutures while I repaired the episiotomy.

Did this $600,000 remodeling increase consumer insurance rates? You can bet your bottom dollar it did. Did this $600,000 remodeling improve the quality of care being offered? Doubtful.

A System Prone to Fraud

Housed in shabby, nondescript storefronts along the most desolate blocks in the city, the clinics are called mills because, for the official New York State Medicaid reimbursement rate of about $11 per patient visit, doctors there grind routinely through dozens of patients in a single hour. Often, exams consist of nothing more than taking a person's name, temperature and Medicaid information....

...she stood in line at the mill with two of her four children for two hours, waiting to see a doctor for a severe respiratory infection. Three minutes after she finally entered, she came out with prescriptions for three popular and expensive drugs.

The drugs, given to many patients at this clinic, were Naprosyn, Tagamet and Proventil. Naprosyn is an anti-inflammatory drug that can cause internal bleeding. Tagamet is used for ulcers or the type of bleeding that can be caused by improper or extensive use of Naprosyn. Proventil has been highly successful in treating asthma.

"[The doctor] took my temperature and gave me blood tests," she said. "She really checked me out...."

In New York, whose Medicaid reimbursement rates are the nation's second-lowest behind West Virginia, doctors receive $15 for a routine electrocardiogram. But a doctor treating a patient on Medicare, the federal health program for the elderly, would receive $45 for precisely the same service. If the patient had private insurance or paid himself, the bill would be more than $100. For an initial office visit, a doctor can receive $63 under Medicare in New York, more than five times what Medicaid pays....

"My entire goal in life was to become a doctor and return to the Bronx to treat my people," said Luis A. Diaz Jr., 38. Born and raised in the South Bronx, he spent his youth watching classmates slowly disappear, lost to drugs and guns and, more recently, to AIDS....

More than once, he says, he was offered jobs by owners of the Medicaid mills, through advertisements and acquaintances at the hospital where he trained.

"Two-, three-thousand dollars a week for three days' work," he said, sadly shaking his head. "They just wanted me to front by signing prescriptions and making an occasional visit. That's a lot of money. But what they were doing in the mills was everything I was against. Sixty patients an hour. Even whores spend more time with their clients."

Finally, he decided to open his own office, with a colleague in pediatrics. He said he craved the time to treat patients properly, advise them on preventive medicine and above all to follow them over the course of their illnesses.

"I wanted to make a difference," he said. "I know it sounds stupid, but I thought I could."

But not with Medicaid patients. Despite his professed desire to treat the people with nowhere else to turn, Diaz quickly realized that, if he hoped even to pay the rent on his modest office, medicaid patients were luxuries that he simply could not afford.

Michael Specter
p. A1, A8

Putting the Squeeze on Doctors

The state of North Dakota pays me a total of $463.70 to insert a Norplant implant in women eligible for Medicaid assistance.

Wow, you say, I'm making a bundle on that 30 minute procedure. In fact, I'm making such a bundle on this procedure that the state of North Dakota has put considerable pressure on me, and I presume other doctors who perform the same procedure, to reduce my charges for this service.

The problem with this approach? I have to pay $350 for the Norplant implant. But I have been unsuccessful in convincing the state Medicaid office that they should not be pressuring me to reduce my fee for the implant, but rather, pressuring the pharmaceutical company to reduce their fees for their product.

What does the state of North Dakota get for the $113.70 left over after I pay for the Norplant implant? For the next FIVE YEARS *I will be responsible for Norplant's product. I will take care of the patient, her phone calls, and any of her problems with irregular bleeding. In short, the state of North Dakota is getting a much better deal from me than from Norplant.*

Doctors, because they deal directly with patients, are an easy target for those who think medical care is too expensive.

Health Care a Social Issue

"Social pathologies such as the breakdown of the family structure, chronic unemployment, poverty, homelessness, substance abuse, violence and despair wind up in the emergency rooms, intensive care units, and morgues of our hospitals...." "The United States, more than any other developed country, is paying dearly for its social problems once they become medical problems."

Spencer Rich
"Tracing Medical Costs," p. A21.

People without health insurance have lower life expectancies, and their babies are much more likely to die before the mother leaves the hospital....the infant mortality rate for uninsured patients was 31.4 deaths per 1,000 births, compared with rates of 6.3 per 1,000 for the commercially insured, 5.5 per 1,000 for HMO members, and 10.6 per 1,000 for medical assistance patients.

News Clips
"Infant Mortality and the Uninsured,"
p. 49

Last year, 38,100 babies in the U.S. died in their first year of life—two-thirds of them within their first month. With an infant mortality rate of 9.1 deaths per 1000 live births, the U.S. ranks a dismal 20th among industrialized nations....

About 25 percent of all infant deaths, plus half of the deaths due to low birthweight, are preventable *just* with prenatal care....

"Prenatal care does not mean costly, high-tech 'frills....'" "It's the basics, and they work. A key cause of low birthweight, for example, is lack of prenatal care. About 80 percent of women at risk for delivering a low birthweight baby can be identified at their first prenatal visit...."

Parade Magazine

Infant mortality is not a health problem—it is a social problem with health consequences....Look at Japan: It reveres its pregnant women—even giving them the right to sit on a bus for free—and guarantees prenatal care to all. The result? Japan has the lowest infant-mortality rate in the world.

Parade Magazine,

Maternal Mortality Rates
(per 100,000 live births)

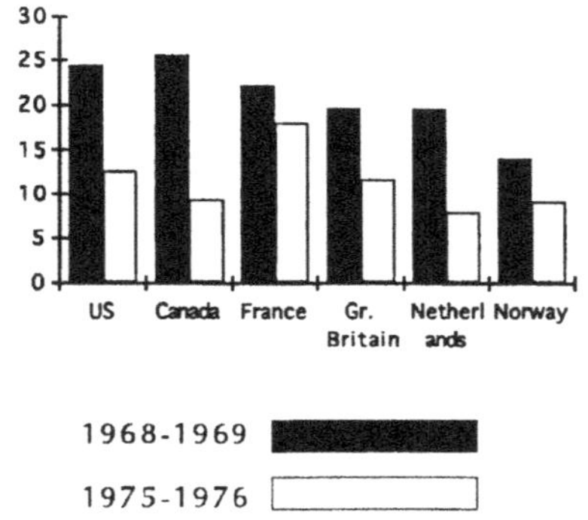

Infant Mortality Rates
(per 1,000 live births)

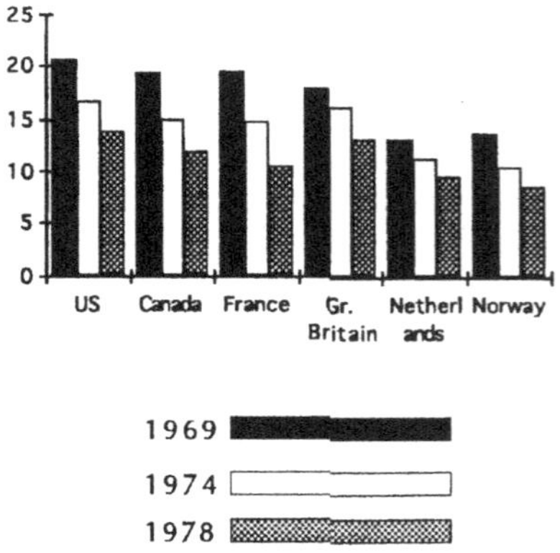

Treat the Patient, Not Just the Symptom

In this age of medical miracles, consumers might think that the spectacular story of a mother carrying her own daughter's child and hence delivering her own grandchild might constitute the great moments in our practice (Wheeler, p. A 1). And these are great moments. But for me, the greatest challenges often don't take the form of the spectacular. Often, the greatest challenges are meeting the needs of ordinary patients. Despite the media attention to miracles, most of us are struggling very hard to meet the needs of ordinary patients in a health care system that does not value ordinary care.

When I have a patient from a family which is dysfunctional, I have more than a single patient. I have a whole family to treat, regardless of my specialty. But our health care system chooses not to reward the time I spend with my patients to overcome the inadequacies of our miracle-lined health care system. Yet it is a kind of medicine I find personally very rewarding. And a kind of medicine which I know ultimately saves society millions of dollars.

A social worker called me and asked if I would see a former patient of mine who was again pregnant and not gaining any weight. The doctor she was seeing was unable to make any progress with her. This was a family who already had four children, and social services had placed one of the children in a foster home. They were trying to take the other three children away from the family.

The mother was a heavy smoker, she had not gained weight during her pregnancies, her babies were born early and had been too little, and she had failed to bond with some of them after birth. The mother now lived 75 miles from mu office, but her husband did bring her in for me to see before she delivered this fifth child.

The first time I saw my patient and her husband, both were very unhappy with the situation. The husband had been extremely suspicious of me at the initial interview. And why should't he be. Doctors are the persons who usually trigger the system which takes children away from parents. However, I was able to observe him in the waiting room with his children and he was at ease with them and treated them appropriately. I spent a good deal of time talking with the mother about cutting her smoking down so she would have a healthier baby. I observed the father each time she came, and he continued to interact normally with his children.

Do You Know Someone Who . . .

In medical school there are some really troubling situations that you don't get much advice about how to handle. Doctors are just sort of shoved out the door and expected to somehow cope with what I realized, after many years in practice, were some fairly stereotypical patients that our health care system has no effective method of dealing with. The abused person and the drug abuser.

I suspect physical abuse whenever a woman comes into my office with very vague complaints of abdominal pain or irregular periods, and the husband won't let his wife out of his sight, even in her obstetrician's office. He does most of the talking during the initial interview, and he never leaves her side, even during the internal exam. He tends to everything, asks lots of questions, and takes over the entire visit.

I suspect physical abuse whenever a woman comes into my office with obvious bruises on her body and will admit nothing. If I question her about her relationship with her husband, she will insist there are no problems, even though she may appear to be agitated when she tells me this. There are probably many reasons these patients won't talk, but I suspect they fear reprisal or do not fully understand or admit what's happening to them.

I suspect physical abuse whenever a patient comes into my office with a list of 500 complaints and a 40-pound medical history. The complaints are generally of the type that the little toenail on her left foot throbs once or twice a week. Sometimes on the 500th visit she will drop a hint about what is going on in her life, but she will often get angry that she has allowed some of her secrets to escape.

I suspect mental abuse when a patient comes into my office time after time for vague abdominal pain. Only after lots of procedures is she really able to talk about what's happening in her life. Often, these patients come from large, close-knit families where relatives give the patient no privacy. She's afraid to move.

I suspect physical abuse when a mother brings in her little girl for a vaginal discharge or vaginal bleeding. Almost invariably, I am told the child has fallen on an innertube stem or a pencil at the babysitters. I don't know about you, but I've never seen anyone land on an inner tub stem.

I suspect drug abuse when a patient comes to my office with some vague complaint and tells me what prescription drug with addicting qualities that she needs to fix the problem. This patient is upset all of the time and expects the doctor to make them un-upset and gets angry when she does not get the drug she wants.

I suspect drug abuse when a patient calls and insists on being seen immediately. She has lots of abdominal pain and tells me that 125 mg Demerol and 125 mg of Vistaril makes her headache and abdominal pain go away. Tylox also works well. All three of these drugs have a large addictive component. These patients are generally not dangerous, but will create a ruckus if they do not get what they want. If they get the drugs they want, they will be around forever. If I send them away without the drugs they want, they never come back.

I suspect drug abuse when the very skilled user telephones between 5 and 6 p.m., when the regular receptionist is gone and I'm trying to finish up at the office and get home to dinner. Some doctors, because they are tired, harassed, and know they are in for a time-consuming process to determine that the patient really does not need the requested drugs, will go ahead and prescribe what is asked for.

As a physician, I find these situations very frustrating. If I suspect physical, mental, or drug abuse but my patients deny it, I have few options. If the patients admit the problem, I can offer them treatment. Our health care system does not provide an effective procedure for dealing with these social problems. Yet I know that if I refuse to give the drug abusers the prescriptions they ask for, they will just go on to another physician and probably finally get what they want.

The delivery was unremarkable. The mother was still smoking, but she had cut down and her baby was full term, normal weight, and healthy. However, after her delivery, the mother became severely depressed, which is what I had suspected had been occurring after her previous deliveries. With the severity of her depression, she was totally uninterested in her children, which contributed to her inability to bond with some of them.

I contacted the social worker who had referred her to me and we discussed the situation at length. It was my feeling that we could rely on the father to be the primary parent. He had overcome his initial suspicions of me and by now I had been able to observe his interactions with his children on several occasions. The social worker agreed with me, and she brought the family in for counseling. The mother went to work, and by doing shift work, each parent could be home to take care of the children, each accepting total responsibility for the children part of the day. The next time I saw my patient, she had overcome her depression problems and they had worked through a lot of the difficulties that had made the family dysfunctional. Once she overcame her depression and had some time away from home at work, she was able to successfully bond with her children.

Not long ago I got a frantic call from this woman on a Sunday evening. She was pregnant again and she had noticed a decrease in fetal movement. Again, she had not gained weight and she was smoking more. Her husband brought her to my office the next day, and we talked for several hours. Even though she had a considerable drive to come to my office, she kept her appointments, gained weight, and delivered a healthy baby.

Was this a miracle? Not by today's standards. Does our health care system recognize the value of this kind of intervention? No. I am unable to charge for the time I spend talking with her—only for performing specific procedures. But I found my care of this patient very rewarding because I believe I have saved a family and improved the home environment for eight people. The long term effect of this kind of intervention could well span 50 to 80 years. At a savings to society of hundreds of thousands of dollars in social services, from prevention of child abuse to prison sentences.

A rational health care system—one based on everyday need instead of expensive miracles—would reward doctors for providing this kind of relatively inexpensive but very effective intervention.

Appropriate Care vs. High Tech Care

The United States has achieved a modest improvement in its infant mortality rate by relying on high-cost medical technology rather than low-cost expansion of prenatal care for pregnant women, according to a report issued yesterday by the National Commission to Prevent Infant Mortality.

The report called for a "one-stop shopping" system of delivering prenatal care to the estimated 3.1 million women—roughly one-third of those who become pregnant annually—who don't receive adequate care while they are pregnant because they cannot or do not navigate the bureaucratic obstacles.

"We can't expect a pregnant woman, often very young, sometimes shockingly uninformed about her own body, to take six bus trips from one office to another to apply for Medicaid, to apply for WIC...then to one office for a pregnancy test, another for parental care, and later a third clinic for immunizations," Sen. Bill Bradley (D-NJ) a commission member, said in testimony before the House Select Committee on Children, Youth and Families....

Researchers at the commission, which was created by Congress in 1987, speculated that the drop in the infant mortality rate in 1990 was due largely to the introduction of a new drug, Exosurf, which speeds up the maturing process of the lungs of low-birthweight babies. Those babies still must spend weeks in the hospital—at a cost estimated at $14,000 to $30,000 per infant.

"It's not that we're not spending money," Bradley said. "It's that we're spending money at the wrong time." He said the cost of prenatal care for all unborn children could be as little as $500 million, as opposed to $2.5 billion for the treatment of low-birthweight infants.

Paul Taylor
p. A19.

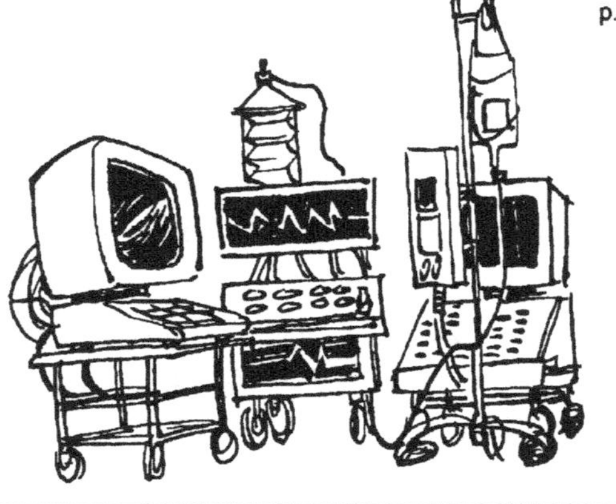

Four years ago, the people of Alabama learned that their state had the highest rate of infant mortality in the nation. For every 1,000 babies born, more than 13 died within the first year. In some rural counties, the number of deaths was twice the state rate—comparable to conditions in Third World nations....

Figures just released from 1990 showed that the state's infant mortality rate dropped precipitously, to 10.9, down from 12.1 the year before and within reach of the national average of 10....

Alabama officials credit the decline to a dramatic expansion in Medicaid programs that has brought thousands of expectant mothers into the public health system in the past two years. Coupled with the flood of recipients has been an increase in fees paid to obstetricians and hospitals for prenatal care and deliveries.

In addition, a special program in a third of the counties "locks in" pregnant Medicaid recipients to a particular physician, waiving their right to choose any doctor they please. In this type of managed care program, the physician is required to follow patients carefully throughout pregnancy or forfeit a Medicaid reimbursement from the state. As a result, more pregnant women are receiving comprehensive prenatal care, the key factor in reducing infant deaths, disabilities and babies born prematurely, officials say....

In 1986, Alabama Medicaid had been paying $425 for a delivery. In 1986, 26 of 67 Alabama counties offered no obstetrical care for anyone....

Herrmann [Alabama's Medicaid commissioner] immediately raised the reimbursement for prenatal care and delivery to $1,000, a figure that in October will rise to $1,700 for rural deliveries. That will make it one of the highest Medicaid rates in the nation and close to the regional rate for private patients.

Robin Herman
p. 8

See No Evil, Hear No Evil . . .

Our highly touted health care system that is so great at producing miracles often fails miserably in treating common problems. Over and over again I see patients who have recurring pelvic pain, but seem unable to get any relief. They go from doctor to doctor, are subjected to test after test, only to be told that the tests show everything is all right. Therefore there can't possibly be anything wrong with them. Many are simply patted on the shoulder and sent away with the same trouble they came to the doctor for. If they persist in seeking treatment for their pain, they risk being labeled hypochodriacs when they may well not be, or worse, they risk being labelled neurotic when they may well not be, and sent to a psychiatrist.

Recently I had a 30-year old woman come into my office who had been trying to get relief from her pelvic pain for six months. By now she had a fairly lengthy medical history, and what she told me didn't match exactly what the history said, but her story was interesting. The first thing you think of in this situation is pelvic inflammatory disease. In other words, she is sexually active and she had caught something. The treatment is fairly straightforward. You put the patient and her sexual partner on a course of antibiotics.

Why hadn't somebody during my patient's six-month attempt to get her pelvic pain treated diagnosed her problem? Good question. At the first clinic she went to, the first thing they did was an ultrasound to be sure she had no ovarian tumors. The ultrasound didn't show anything wrong. The clinic, nonetheless, made a good deal of cash in the process. Her problem, alas, remained undiagnosed. The ultrasound had not made her feel any better.

The second clinic she went to ran a urinalysis and a urine culture. These tests turned up nothing. She was told that because the tests came out fine, there was nothing wrong with her. When she went back a second time still complaining of pelvic pain, she was told she had a bladder and vaginal

Personal Care: The Missing Element

Critics cite waiting lines in Canada, which they say are caused by the Canadian single-payer system. In fact, Canada has few waiting lines; the Canadians never have to wait for emergency care. Waiting lines exist primarily for specialized high-tech procedures, such as heart bypass surgery. It's true that the United States provides more of these procedures than Canada, but it's unclear that our citizens are any healthier as a result. The Rand Corp. found that 40 percent of heart bypass operations performed in the United States were unnecessary. This means many Americans paid for an expensive procedure and were exposed to serious risks, yet received no health benefit.

Those who focus on rationing in Canada tend to ignore the rationing Americans face daily from their insurance companies. Unable to control runaway medical inflation, insurance companies protect their profit margins through rationing. Their tactics include denying care, even when prescribed by a physician, increasing cost sharing and refusing to cover preexisting conditions. The high co-payments and deductibles force hard-working families to wait months before they can afford to go to the doctor, while skyrocketing insurance company premiums are pricing more and more Americans out of the health care system.

Marty Russo
p. A19

The intricate machinery of our health care system can no longer grasp the threads of experience....Too often, payers, physicians, and health care executives do not share common insights into the life of the patient. We acknowledge that our common interest is the patient, but we represent that interest from such divergent, even conflicting, viewpoints that everyone loses perspective. As a result, the health care system has become an organism guided by misguided choices; it is unstable, confused, and desperately in need of a central nervous system that can help it cope with the complexities of modern medicine.

Paul M. Ellwood
p. 1550

Jerome Paulson, a George Washington University physician, wrote the *New England Journal of Medicine* in February to say, "It is impossible to calculate what is lost at the personal level every time a patient is forced to change physicians. Patients may not tell a new physician, whom they do not know well or trust, about family stress [or other problems]...the physician will not have in-depth knowledge about the patient's family, psyche and other factors that are crucial..."

Victor Cohn
p. 22

infection, and treated for it. Of course, the medication didn't make her feel any better.

Upon examination, she exhibited the classic signs of subacute pelvic infection. Her uterus and ovaries were sore. She remembered that some time ago she and her hsuband had been both treated for some kind of infection. I prescribed an antibiotic for both her and her husband and told her to return in 10 to 14 days, or sooner if she didn't feel a lot better.

She had spend $1,300 dollars on the two clinics who ran tests and didn't diagnose her problem. In fact, they actually told her that since the tests were fine, there was nothing wrong with her. The clinics expect to get paid even though they claimed there was nothing wrong with her, and even though she told them repeatedly that she still had the pelvic pain.

This woman didn't need a miracle. Nor did she need gold-plated technology. What she needed was a doctor who recognized subacute pelvic inflammatory disease.

Miracles are nice. But most consumers need effective, affordable, basic health care more than miracles. There is ample evidence that fewer and fewer of us can afford what the great majority of us need—good quality, basic health care.

The Three Basic Reform Plans

Hey and Carlson (p. 13) report that there are basically three types of health care reform bills before Congress. One, which essentially depends upon the "market," relies on the private sector and insurance companies to adjust the problems with our present system. The bills of Representative Nancy Johnson (H.R. 1565) and Senator John Chafee (S. 1936) represent this approach. They note that this system appears to be less favored than the other two approaches.

The second approach is characterized by a single payer, government-sponsored system similar to the Canadian one. Bills introduced by Representative Pete Stark (H.R. 650/651), Representative Marty Russo (H.R. 1300) and Sen. Bob Kerrey (S. 1446) represent this approach.

The third approach is employer-based and has been dubbed "pay or play." Bills introduced by Senator George Mitchell (S.1227), Representative Dan Rostenkowski (H.R. 3205), and a bill yet to be introduced in Congress by the National Leadership Coalition for Health Care Reform (NLCHCR) represent this type of reform. Under this system, employers must offer insurance to their employees or pay into a fund to cover them.

As we've said many times before in this book, the market will never solve our health care system problems. If anything, the market has demonstrated very well that expensive, profitable services will be provided at the expense of less profitable, needed services. Proponents of the market approach complain that all we need to do is "incent" efficiency, and the market will respond. We disagree. The government has tried adjusting the Medicare system repeatedly, and a slight change here simply unleashes all kinds of problems someplace else. Complex systems—and our present health care system is one—are not amenable to subtle adjustments.

The problems of the market approach to reform are evident in the bills of Rep. Johnson and Senator Chafee (Hey and Carlson, p. 12). Like our existing health care system, these bills provide for no mandated basic benefits. Furthermore, many of the details such as how much copayments and deductibles would be are left suspiciously unaddressed. In addition, the kinds of preventive care we have talked about, including prenatal care and well-baby care, are not provided. Nor is coverage provided for all consumers.

The employer-based proposals of Senator Mitchell, Rep. Rostenkowski, and the NLCHCR (Hey and Carlson, p. 12) caps personal out-of-pocket expenses for acute care at $3,000, a figure we consider to be much too high. Rep. Rostenkowski's bill does not address tort reform. Neither the market-based reform bills nor these pay-or-play reform bills address the problem of long term care for those who need it. As our population ages, this is becoming an increasingly important problem.

The government-sponsored, single-payer reform bills provide universal coverage, pregnanacy-related care, well-child care, and long-term care. They also provide for outpatient prescription drugs, whereas only one of the market-based and pay-or-play bills addressed this problem. The cap on out-of-pocket expenses is as low as $2,000 for a family of three, which is certainly lower than the pay-or-play reform measures, but again, something we consider a problem. We believe a certain level of care should be absolutely without cost—the types of care we know saves thousands of dollars in the long run. The level of care to be provided without cost to consumers needs to be clearly defined. What preventive care is provided? At what cost? What kinds of care will require co-payments? We encourage consumers to press their elected representativers for very specific answers to what types of care will be provided. This is a critical issue in health care reform.

Health care reform is a political issue. Consumers need to let their elected representatives know what consumers want and need in health care.

We Don't Need Miracles, Just Basic Health Care

The headline of the first issue of North Dakota's Blue Cross/Blue Shield newsletter screams "Miracles Don't Come Cheap" (Danovic, p. 1). There is no doubt—absolutely none—that the United States has the very best health care system in the world for producing miracles—IF YOU NEED A MIRACLE. Unfortunately, the great majority of us really just need some good, low-tech basic health care. Most of us want our earaches and sore throats treated, not liver transplants or triple coronary artery bypasses. But the health care system we have allowed to develop only wants to deal with miracles. Miracles are the big money makers.

The Standard Reform Approaches

Most articles discussing health care reform suggest cutting administrative duplication, cutting out waste, and cutting out fraud. We find these suggestions woefully inadequate. These are the types of things any business should do to cut down costs and operate more efficiently. These goals are commendable, but they can hardly be termed reform. The fundamental problem with these suggestions, no matter how effective they might be, is that they do not address the basic causes of the high cost of health care. They merely cut the fat from a system that is far too expensive, too wasteful, and ineffective in delivering basic, quality health care to everyone and always will be—even with the fat cut to the bone.

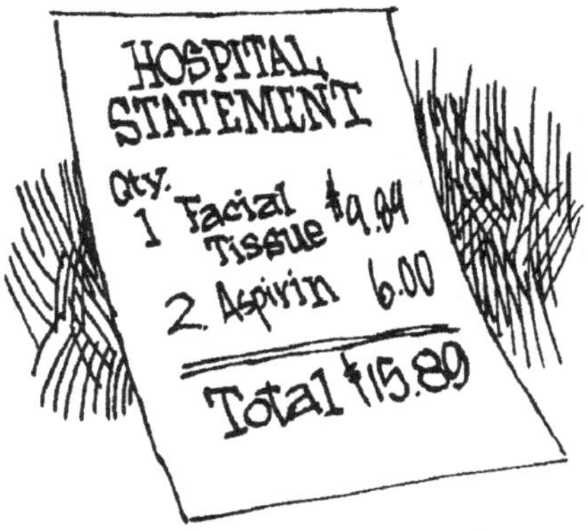

Let's face facts here—if the health care system we have were capable of providing basic, quality health care to every U.S. citizen—which we believe it should do—the system would already be doing it, as are the health care systems in other developed countries.

The present U.S. health care system CANNOT and WILL NOT EVER provide basic, affordable health care to every U.S. citizen because its goal is not the provision of quality health care to all, but its goal is to turn a profit. Oh, there are a lot of ads telling consumers that their friendly neighborhood clinic is just like home and miracles happen there every day—and this may well be true. But never for a moment believe that the provision of basic, quality health care for everyone is the primary concern of these enterprises. The primary goal is turning a profit. We believe, like many other critics of the existing health care system, that turning a profit and the provision of quality health care for all at a reasonable cost is a contradiction in terms. Before meaningful reform can be brought about, we must, as a nation, decide what our priorities are—the fulfillment of a social need or allowing corporations to profit from consumer health problems.

Undervaluing Primary Care

Dr. Bates earned her medical degree at the University of Louisville School of Medicine. She returned to Blackey [KY]...because she wanted to work with mountain people....

...A few months after opening Dr. Bates was seeing 20 to 25 people per day, spending 20, 30, 45 minutes—whatever was necessary—with each patient. "I wanted to feel confident that they understood the problem and what they needed to do," she says. She often made house calls after office hours.

What wasn't coming as readily as patients was money. As a rural physician, she was reimbursed $12 by Medicare and $9 by Medicaid for routine office visits for which she charged $25. Forty percent of her practice was made up of Medicaid and Medicare patients. "I didn't use the system in a way you almost have to," she says. "I was supposed to do tests on patients they might not need just to bring in cash. But I can't prick a baby's finger to do a white blood count to determine that it has a sore throat if I can tell without doing it...."

In the first six months of 1989, Dr. Bates billed for $84,000 in services, but only collected $39,000...

...she received an attractive job offer from the director of Mountain Comprehensive Health Corp. If she would sign a three-year contract to work at the nearby clinic, all her student loans would be forgiven and the clinic would buy her medical equipment. "We'd talked about a job before, but she never offered to buy the equipment," Dr. Bates says of Lois Baker, executive director of the federally subsidized clinic. "That meant about $40,000 worth of debt wiped out. I had to take it. And I saw that the clinic's goal was to provide health care for mountain people, and that's my goal, too."

Jeannie Ralston,
p. 19, 20

The companies are finding that offering general medical services at in-house medical clinics, staffed by their own doctors or provided by contract medical firms, is a cheaper alternative to insurance rates that are rising 20 percent a year....

Jacques Sokolov, director of Southern California Edison's huge 10-clinic in-house system, said it employs 15 full-time physicians, 100 others part-time and averages 100,000 visits a year. It is linked to a health insurance system directly managed by the company, which negotiates low prices with outside doctors and hospitals. The two systems combined, he said, are expected to save the company $120 million from 1988 to 1992....

One [success story] is C&P cable splicer William Prevo, whose physical at the company's medical center showed he had colorectal cancer.

"In a matter of days I was in surgery, said Prevo, 56. "The doctor told me another six months and it would have been too late." The surgery, performed by an outside specialist, was paid for by the C&P health insurance plan.

Prevo had never regularly visited his family doctor for routine checkups because, under the company's health insurance plan, he would have been required to pay at least part of the costs. But when C&P began offering checkups free, he started going....

In addition to general physical exams, the clinicians [at Gillette] provide immunizations, sigmoidoscopic exams, electrocardiograms, minor surgery and checkups every two years for workers under age 35, annually for those over 35. "About 85 percent take them; they could go to their own doctor and use the company insurance to pay for it, but it would cost $200 to $300" and most of this is not covered by the insurance, said Greer.

Spencer Rich
"Employees Becoming Pharmacist, Physician,
p. A1, A4

We have been at public discussions of health care costs where hospital representatives admit that their hospitals and clinics are wasteful and expensive. Their proposed solution? "Incent" efficiency. That is, devise a system which "pays" the hospitals and clinics to be efficient and they will be. We find this attitude repugnant. The hospital administrators at this presentation openly admitted they were running their businesses inefficiently because they made more money that way. To our minds, this is unethical. These representatives of the health care provider industry were evidently incapable of understanding that, at least as far as we are concerned, running a hospital efficiently and at reasonable cost is vitally linked with the provision of quality health care for all.

The Flaw in Proposed Reforms

Almost all of the proposed reforms to our health care system, including the many legislative packages introduced both nationally and at the state levels, simply add to the already high cost of health care for everybody. These proposals give the stamp of approval to the already overly expensive system presently in place, and seek to extract an additional pound of flesh from consumers and businesses. We believe consumers and employers have already been overburdened with the costs of a commodity that is without question too expensive.

For example, none of the proposals we have seen so far attempt to decrease the cost of our health care by reducing the cost of a hospital day. None of the proposals we have seen so far investigates what a hospital charges for an aspirin and compares that charge to the actual cost of the aspirin. Or what an outpatient clinic chalks up to expenses to arrive at its charge for the use of its operating rooms.

We have discussed many of the attempts to reduce our skyrocketing health care costs in previous chapters in this book. With the exception of the suggestion that we eliminate administrative waste by eliminating the 1,500 different insurance companies and substituting a single third-party payer system, all the suggested ways to reduce costs have simply been attempts to "adjust" an already too expensive system. We maintain that "adjustments" are doomed to failure. What our health care system needs is substantive reform. Genuine change.

The Oregon Plan

...officials here [Oregon] have publicly confronted a fact that many Americans understand viscerally but that few have been willing to address: Government does not have the money to pay for all the medical services that science has to offer. As a result, officials here have decided to discard the current federal Medicaid program, which provides eligible poor people with many costly services while denying even the most essential coverage to millions of others.

"The current Medicaid program will give a kid five liver transplants and let his mom die from preventable breast cancer," said state Senate President John Kitzhaber, the emergency room physician who first proposed this plan four years ago. "Most of the things that get people in trouble are not strange cancers or rare bone diseases. They are the routine problems of fundamental health care. We don't have an endless supply of money. It's time we were fair about how we use what we have...."

...Oregon explicitly rejected the nation's prevailing rationing strategy, which excludes entire classes of people—poor men, for example, or indigent couples without children—from the health-care system. Instead, officials here have attempted to ration by denying access to low-priority services.

Unlike any other state, Oregon has figured out how much money it can spend on health care for the poor and decided what services it ought to buy. A commission made up of doctors, social workers and health-care advocates listed 709 health services, which they priced and ranked in importance to society by applying a complicated mix of social values and actuarial statistics.

Michael Specter
p. A1, A12.

On May 2 [1990], state officials announced details of their plan—a 150-page list of more than 1,600 medical treatments. Each item on the list had a number that reflected its cost-benefit rating. Treatments such as antibiotics for meningitis had a very high cost-benefit ranking, while cosmetic surgery and end-stage treatments for AIDS had a very low ranking. When and if Oregon obtains federal approval to put the list into effect, the state will draw a line on the list based on how much Medicaid money is available. Medicaid recipients will have access to treatments that are above the line and will be denied treatments that fall below it.

Patrick G. Marshall
p. 668

The legislature will fund all services through line 587.

1. pneumonia
2. tuberculosis
3. peritonitis
4. foreign body in [throat].
5. appendicitis
50. heart attack
164. comfort care to the dying
357. sinus infection
533. minor burns

The following conditions will not be funded under the plan:

590. chronic cystitis
602. infertility services
668. infectious mononucleosis
690. alcoholic cirrhosis of liver [requiring transplant]
695. acute upper respiratory infections and common cold
702. end-stage HIV disease [comfort is provided]
708. extremely low birth weight [under 1.1 pounds] *and* under 23-week gestation

condensed from Michael Specter
p. A12

The Oregon Plan

The state of Oregon has come under considerable criticism recently because they faced reality and admitted that the state did not have the funds to provide every possible medical service to those eligible for medical assistance. A Health Services Commission involved the public in developing categories of care and assessing the value of treatments. Various health conditions were then assigned a level of importance by comparing the cost of the treatment to the ability of the treatment to prevent death, encourage full recovery, and extend lifespan and quality of life.

Is this rationing of health care? Yes. And some critics claim that this rationing is unacceptable because it is aimed at the poor rather than the population as a whole (Daniels, p. 2235). Defenders of the program point out that the care to the poor and elderly is already rationed, but arbitrarily, at the same time allowing policymakers to "avoid assuming any direct accountability for the consequences" (Rabchuk, p. 1). Some policymakers claim that what we call *rationing* would be better called *rationalizing* (Marshall, p. 668-669). We believe there are some hard decisions ahead of us as a nation in the allocation of basic health care. And that we as a nation can no longer continue to hide our heads in the sand and hurl prejudicial epithets at those proposing reform. And we believe that it is absolutely critical that consumers play an active role in developing the definition of basic health care, how it will be allocated, and how it will be paid for. Because insurance companies have shown little indication that they are willing to bring some rationality to the process. Only increased premiums and copayments.

Studies have shown that a centralized insurance system would save more than $100 billion a year that 1,500 different insurance companies spend on administration, marketing, claims processing, and coverage regulation (Rich, "Health Care Paperwork," p. A-1). We may find we can get along with only two or three insurance companies, as Hawaii does. But one thing is certain—we don't need 1,500.

The real problem here? What to do with the unemployed insurance workers who would

Care at the Margins vs. Basic Health Care

Alyssa Plum, the 9-year-old Coon Rapids girl who became the first in Minnesota and the fourth ever to receive a lung transplant from a living donor, died May 18 shortly after a second transplant at the University of Minnesota Hospital.

Alyssa had been healthy up to April 1, when she developed a cold that was later diagnosed as pneumonia.... Doctors were unable to determine the cause of infection, which destroyed almost all of her lungs' abilities. She was transferred to the University of Minnesota as a lung-transplant candidate.

A national search failed to find a donor lung. Fearing that Alyssa could die any day, physicians spoke to her parents about one of them possibly donating part of a lung. The girl's father, Roger Plum, was determined the best candidate.

In surgery, Edward Humphrey, M.D., removed the upper lobe of the father's right lung, and R. Morton Bolman III, M.D., assisted by Sara Shumway, M.D., removed the girl's right lung and replaced it with the father's. After surgery, Alyssa's condition seemed to improve, but she remained on a respirator and soon developed pneumonia in the transplanted lung.

Her condition rapidly deteriorated. In an effort to save her life, doctors replaced Alyssa's left lung with part of her mother's lung, but she died shortly after the surgery, apparently of heart failure.

News Clips
"Living/Related Lung Donor,"
p. 47

... a burst of Medicaid spending is contributing significantly to the budget crises of many states and localities, which pay almost half the program's costs. (The split is 57 to 43 percent between the federal government and states and localities.) Between 1988 and 1990, annual Medicaid spending rose one-third to $72 billion. By 1992, it's expected to jump another 46 percent to $105 billion.

The spending spiral might be more tolerable if Medicaid fulfilled its original mission—insuring most of the poor. It doesn't. When created in 1965, it was seen as the smallest part of a comprehensive health insurance system. Most Americans would get insurance from their employers, the elderly would get it from Medicare (also created in 1965) and the poor from Medicaid. The disabled and mothers on Aid to Family with Dependent Children were automatically eligible for Medicaid. States were urged to expand coverage to more of the poor, including low-income workers without private insurance. Thirty-eight states provide extra coverage.

It hasn't been enough. In 1990, about one in seven Americans (a total of 33 million) lacked health insurance.

Robert J. Samuelson
"Medicaid Monster,"
p. A19

There will be some tough choices about what should be included in the basic health care services we should all have free, easy access to and the kinds of health care which should be rationed according to who can pay for the services. Other choices will be less difficult.

be out of a job with the kind of reform required to achieve this saving. Notice that cost is not the problem. Nor the quality of health care. Rather, what would we do with all these unemployed people.

Welfare programs are often criticized because they pay people for not working, for not being productive. WE BELIEVE THERE ARE SOME COMPELLING PARALLELS BETWEEN A WELFARE SYSTEM AND A HEALTH CARE SYSTEM THAT PAYS PEOPLE TO BE INEFFICIENT.

Blaming the Consumers

Consumers, we are told, love walk-in clinics. Walk-in clinics offer basic health care to consumers who have the audacity to get sick outside the regular office hours. Or offer consumers the ability to get medical attention without taking time off from work. Or offer consumers the opportunity to get medical attention without a three-day wait. Neighborhood clinics are popular because they are "consumer friendly."

Do they cost a lot of money and raise your health care premiums. You bet they do. The administrators making money off these expensive clinics blame the consumer for demanding them. We suspect that consumers don't really demand these clinics, these clinics fill a health care need that consumers cannot meet in any other way.

Do consumers really need expensive, convenient care clinics that offer medical care outside the standard clinical setting? No, they don't need the expensive, fancy building. What they really need is some service, a way to reach a nurse or, if needed, a doctor, so they know whether they can wait to visit their doctor during regular office hours, what to do in the meantime, or whether they should see a doctor immediately. But our health care system, rather than provide some sort of access to physician advice after regular office hours, chooses at great expense, to erect lovely looking, well-advertised, designer clinics at excessive cost to the consumer. A rational health care system would provide for the need in a cost-effective, simple manner. A rational health care system would satisfy the need, even if there were no great profit for the provider in offering the service.

This is not the only situation in which consumers are blamed

Drugs and High Profits

If the U.S. health care system is in critical condition, one reason has to do with the drug market. On the average, drugs in the United States cost 62 percent more than they do in Canada. They also cost 54 percent more than in any country in the European Community.

Healthy Americans have as much stake in a solution as the sick. State and federal Medicaid agencies spend $5 billion a year on pharmaceutical drugs for the health needs of 27 million low-income citizens. A study by Health and Human Services Inspector General Richard P. Kusserow indicates that if the United States adopted Canada's drug-pricing system, Medicaid could save $474 million a year.

There is an army of profit-first drug manufacturers bent on making sure that never happens....Drug makers were reaping pre-tax profits of about 18 percent. Industry spokesmen say prices are pushed high by the expensive U.S. drug-approval system and research and development costs.

Sen. David Prior (D. Ark.), chairman of the Senate Special Committee on Aging, has led the crusade to stop soaring drug costs. He pushed though legislation last year that requires drug manufacturers to give Medicaid patients the same discounts they give their best customers—hospitals and health maintenance organizations—instead of the higher price Medicaid routinely reimbursed.

The drug lobbyists made sure Prior's victory was short-lived. The legislation was circumvented by hiking drug prices to their "best customers"—even to the Department of Veterans Affairs during a time of war.

The cost of a key painkiller went up 800 percent for the VA soon after the measure passed. In fact, the VA says hikes in its drug costs may lead to taxpayers footing an extra $150 million this year.

Jack Anderson and Dale Van Atta
"Battling Pharmaceutical Profiteers,"
p. E3

...In 1983, Congress passed the Orphan Drug Act to give pharmaceutical companies incentives to develop new treatments for diseases that afflict fewer than 200,000 people—often called "orphan" diseases. Drug companies had been reluctant to spend the average $231 million and 12 years required to take a drug from discovery to final approval because the potential market for such drugs is so limited.

To make orphan drugs more attractive commercially, Congress gave the drug makers a seven-year monopoly on a new medicine, eliminating competition and allowing companies to charge whatever they deem appropriate....

Adagen...was the first enzyme replacement therapy to win FDA approval. Adagen treats a rare inherited illness called severe combined immune deficiency, in which the children fail to develop a normal immune system and suffer serious, chronic infections. Before the drug became available, patients died by age 2. Children now survive with their weekly injection, but each vial of the drug costs $2,200, putting annual treatment costs somewhere between a quarter-million and a half-million dollars, depending on the patient's body weight.

Another orphan drug...erythropoetin... stimulates the production of red blood cells. Patients with kidney failure stop making this normal body hormone and need regular blood transfusions. Treatment with erythropoetin eliminates the need for transfusions for many patients, but it costs an average of $4,500 a year for each of the 50,600 people who need it for the rest of their lives. These patients receive treatment through Medicare, putting the annual government cost for the drug at $280 million...

Larry Thompson
"The High Cost of Rare Diseases,"
p. 10

for demanding expensive ser-vices when, we are told, they do not need them. Hospital ad-ministrators (Knutson, p. B-1) and insurance administrators (KFGO-AM, 28 May 1991) find it convenient to blame consumers for demanding expensive technology. There's been a lot publicity over the years about families or hospitals which would like to withdraw life support systems from patients who are comatose and have no chance of recovery. We have no health policy to address this problem, and whether the cord is or is not pulled varies from court district to court district. A rational health care system would develop policy to define when maintenance on life support equipment was appropriate and when it was not. If a family requested the continuation of such care beyond the point that doctors considered it to provide any benefit, each family would be free to bear the cost of the care. A rational health care system would not put stumbling blocks in the way of basic, preventive health care, which we know saves millions of dollars, while at the same time wasting billions of dollars on surgeries and in some instances life support systems which provide little change or improvement in a patient's health or quality of life.

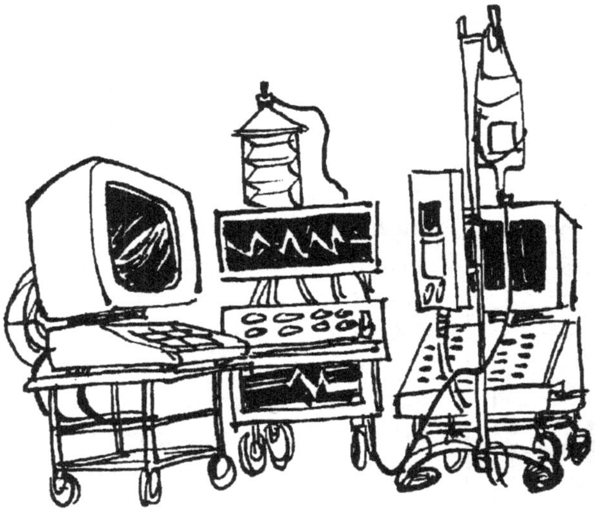

The changes we have seen come over our health care system during the past 20 to 30 years have not been for the benefit of the consumer, but for the benefit of big business profiteers. The consumer has not been given a choice between fancy window dressings and better quality, more cost-effective care. The consumer has been offered only expensive, glitzy care and then been blamed for demanding the expensive, glitzy care when that has been the only care available.

Let us explain.

No Real Consumer Choices: A Case Study

Twenty years ago, when one of our group moved to a new town of about 30,000 people, she had two small children, one only 10 weeks old. The infant, who had been born prematurely and weighed only about five pounds at the time of the move, caught a cold which developed into bronchitis. The mother had taken the trouble to ask her previous pediatrician for a recommendation (the move was within the same state, a mere 40 miles away), but the pediatrician chose not to recommend anyone. At this new location, there were only three pediatricians listed in the telephone book, and only the newest of the three, a group practice, was taking new patients.

Glitz

She took her sick infant to this new group practice office, and a fine office it was. Her baby did not have much of a fever, but was experiencing severe coughing fits which caused him to choke and throw up whatever milk he drank. Located in a new, modern medical complex, the office looked as inviting as an ad in any decorator magazine. The spacious waiting room was divided into a sick side and a well side. The sick side had a merry-go-round motif, with bright colors and seats like merry-go-round booths. There were lots of toys around. When she finally got to see the doctor, he summarily took the infant off breast milk and recommended watered down coke or tea. When the mother questioned him about this—this was a low birthweight baby and was still small—the pediatrician became defensive and downright rude. After all, why was she bothering to come see him at all if she was going to ignore his advice. She was given a prescription for a cough medicine for which the pediatrician readily admitted he had no idea how to figure out the dose for a baby this small.

On another occasion, her toddler was in the office with a fever of nearly 105 degrees. The doctor made no attempt to bring the child's fever down while the mother had the child in his office, sending her home without medicating the fever or any advice about what to do if the child convulsed, which had been a concern of her previous physician. This doctor advised the mother to bathe the child in cool water, even recommending that she get in the shower with the child, if necessary. Of course, the mother knew that when this child had a fever this high, he was unwilling to drink even water, much less take oral medication. Until the fever could be lowered—and bathing him in cool water, she knew from experience, did not work— he was essentially untreatable with home remedies. Needless to say, she was not pleased with the quality of care her children received here, despite the lavishly decorated waiting room.

The mother called a neighbor who was a nurse and asked who she took her children to. She then called this pediatrician's office, explained the situation, and asked if the pediatrician would see her children. He was very hesitant to take another pediatrician's patient, but when she asked him what her options were in this situation, a situation in which she considered the care clearly substandard, he finally agreed to see her.

Quality Care

His office was in an unrestored, less than quaint, downtown rowhouse rather than in a glitzy new medical center. Parking was a serious problem. The rubber tile floor had clearly seen better days, and while obviously clean, was probably twenty years old and showed signs of lots of wear. There was an old black and white television set with an expansive twelve-inch screen and a wooden rocking horse affair that would have brought good money at a flea market as a collectable. The only other adornments were a table full of the usual waiting-room books for children. The waiting room chairs looked like they came from a World War II temporary office building. The doctor had only two examination rooms, a larger one set up for physical exams with all kinds of eye-testing equipment, and a small room where he saw sick children.

He explained to this mother that the preparation for coughs that the other pediatrician had given her was extremely effective, but his experience was that most children vomited it up before it could do them any good. When he looked in her toddler's ears, he took the child on his lap. When he did a throat culture, he walked the vial over to the county lab during his lunch hour, where the test was done free, so there was no charge for this service. If he thought the mother and other children also needed throat cultures, he performed them himself in the office at no extra charge. When a child had a strep infection, he requested that the child be brought back ten days after the last antibiotic was taken so that he could be sure kidney function was normal. He did not charge for this recheck visit because he requested it. Even twenty years ago, this pediatrician knew that parents were not going to bring well children back for a recheck if they had to pay to do so. His office charge? $6.

Unfortunately, this doctor was near retirement age, and before these children were ready to move on to regular family practice physicians, he sold his practice to a young pediatrician. The office fees quickly tripled. Rechecks were no longer free. Nor were throat cultures. This young pediatrician soon moved into an office complex in the newest medical center. When the toddler had ear infections, the medication of choice was no longer PenVee 500, a very cheap form of penicillin, but amoxycillin (which made the child sick), and all manner of increasingly expensive antibiotics, all of which made the toddler sicker than the ear infection. On one occasion this mother had her toddler in the pediatrician's office with the

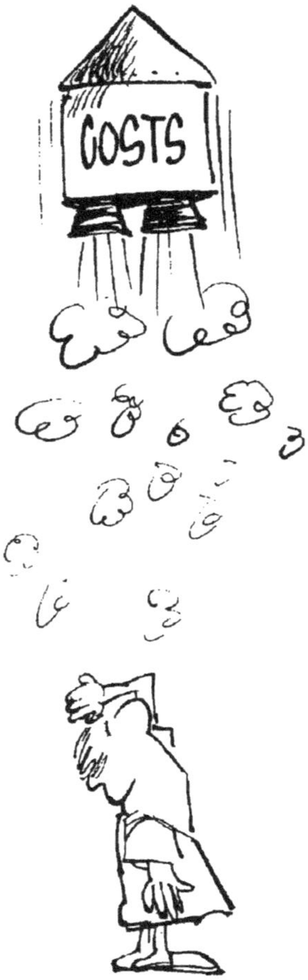

with significantly swollen lips, a clearly blue skin color, and shaking violently. For this ear infection the child had been given erythromycin. This mother questioned the doctor about why he simply couldn't give the toddler a prescription for PenVee, which had never made the child sick. This pediatrician insisted that these other medications were better for ear infections. Since the child only had one or at most two ear infections a year—these were not chronic ear infections that required continued maintenance on antibiotics—it seemed to this mother that the fancier drugs were hardly required. In fact, they obviously were doing more harm than good. (The toddler, now grown, still has to fight tooth and nail with doctors to get PenVee on the rare occasions he needs an antibiotic).

And of course, there came the day when this pediatrician decided that this toddler should really have tubes inserted in his ears to prevent these infections. The mother resisted. And resisted. She wanted to see some research articles which indicated that ear tubes were effective. She was told that she wouldn't understand them. Finally, when it became apparent that this mother was not going to allow the pediatrician to insert tubes in this child's ears, he admitted that there had been some research that indicated that a child with ear problems of this sort might be helped by blowing up balloons while holding his nostrils shut. If there was some indication that this was helpful, why did this pediatrician not suggest it long ago? It was certainly easy enough to try.

This child never did have tubes inserted in his ears, although he blew up a lot of balloons while holding his nose shut. Did the balloon therapy work? Perhaps not. But it also did not cost much, and it did not subject the toddler to unnecessary anesthesia. And his ear infections decreased without surgical intervention over the following few years.

The differences between the two kinds of practices—the glizty, showy, and unnecessarily expensive ones of the younger pediatricians and the low key, economical, concerned care offered by the older pediatrician illustrates well how greed and glitz have taken over the health care system in this country. And how consumers do not choose glitz, but as older doctors retire, have no real alternatives.

Given a choice, this member of our group would have chosen to remain with a pediatrician who actively sought to keep health care costs down, even if it meant a stodgy, old-fashioned, but nonetheless utilitarian waiting room for patients. And even if it meant treatment with old-fashioned, but nonetheless effective medications—medications the experienced pediatrician knew worked, despite the glossy ads in medical journals for the newer drugs.

This case study illustrates in a nutshell how the health care system we have allowed to develop has gotten too expensive, wasteful, and downright harmful to consumers. And how the system has encouraged an adversarial relationship between the doctor and the consumer. None of the proposals for reform—absolutely none of them—have addressed the deterioration in the quality of our medical care illustrated in this mundane narrative.

Crisis Care vs. Preventive Care

Dever (p. 7) tells us that in 1925 was a watershed year in health care. Before 1934, the "health care industry" spent more time and effort treating communicable diseases—smallpox, flu, measles, mumps, rubella—than in treating degenerative diseases such as stroke, arthritis, heart disease. He emphasizes that although the type of disease consuming most of our health care dollars is often generally no longer catching, but rather more likely to be a result of an individual's genes and lifestyle, our health care system has lumbered on in the old "catching mode." That is, presently the approach to treating disease is generally one of "let the person, whatever the cause, get sick enough to require crisis care, then treat the crisis." With catching diseases, this method of treatment was oftentimes useful. With diseases which are comprised largely of a genetic and lifestyle components, this approach is not only inappropriate, but also largely ineffective. Not to mention extraordinarily expensive.

First and foremost, crisis medical care is extremely expensive, especially in the case of chronic, degenerative diseases such as stroke. The model of letting a disease take its course can be useful with the kinds of catching diseases that come and go, generally leaving the individual with little residual damage. With these kinds of communicable diseases, the individual survives the peak of the disease (possibly even without the help of medication), and gets better in time, able to resume normal activities. Obviously there are exceptions: strep infections can lead to

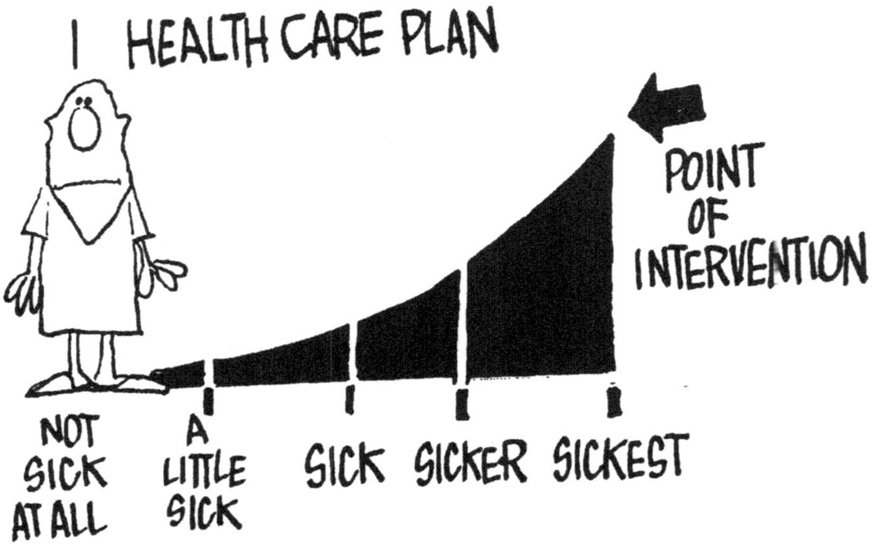

rheumatic fever; polio can paralyze; syphilis can kill. But the great majority of bodily infections, when left to run their course, or treated if they reach a crisis stage, result in full recovery with few complications.

Degenerative diseases follow a different pattern. Left untreated, these diseases continue to whittle away at abilities, health, and quality of life. Many of these types of diseases can be related to a hereditary component. The incidence of certain types of cancer, for example, can be higher in some families than others. Lifestyle can worsen the progress of the disease. If a family has a history of heart disease caused by clogged arteries, changing diet and exercise patterns can slow the progress of the artery clogging, and even cause some of the clogging to diminish.

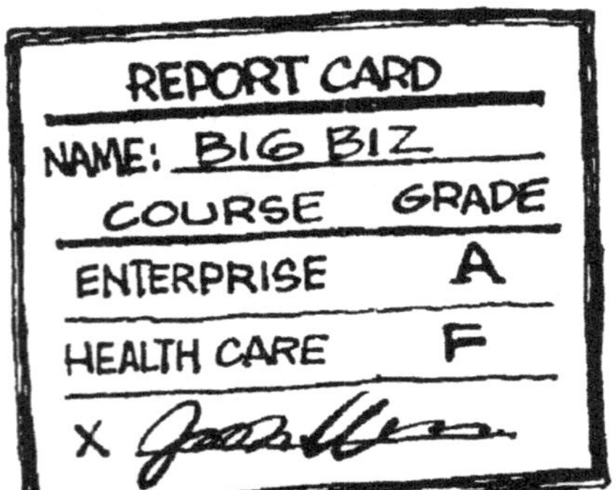

Dever's point, and it is a good one, is that our medical system presently operates in crisis mode. We have a health care system which treats what are largely degenerative diseases as if they were communicable ones.

The result? A health care crisis. We deny a lot of pregnant women access to prenatal care, only to finally treat their premature infants at a cost which can easily run as high as $150,000 per child, if the treatment is successful. Unsuccessful treatment can run into millions of dollars. We allow postpartum depression to go untreated, only to remove the abused child from the home at some later date, sometimes only after the child has been severely traumatized. We discourage people from getting routine screening tests by making them hard to get or too costly, only to spend thousands of dollars warehousing stroke victims in nursing homes. We drug the active kindergarten kids to make them sit quietly during story hour, only to wonder why

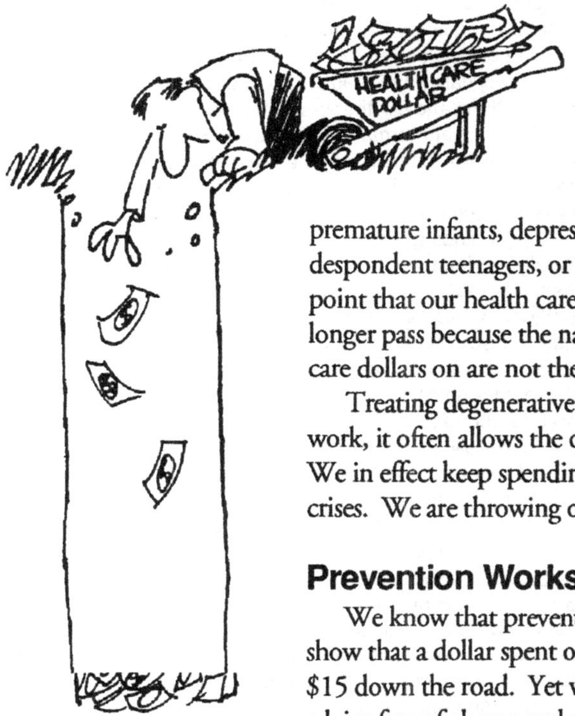

teenagers commit suicide. We anesthetize our senior citizens to keep them from getting mad about being strapped in wheel chairs, only to wonder why they don't recognize their own children.

Please do not misunderstand us. We do not mean to trivialize the extreme difficulties in handling premature infants, depressed new mothers, abused children, hyperactive students, despondent teenagers, or disoriented senior citizens. We simply want to make the point that our health care system still operates in crisis mode, only the crises no longer pass because the nature of the diseases we now spend most of our health care dollars on are not the kind that will respond to a shot in the arm.

Treating degenerative disease as if they were communicable not only does not work, it often allows the quality of life to ebb away and it is obscenely expensive. We in effect keep spending our health care dollars on crisis care for non-ending crises. We are throwing our money down the proverbial rathole.

Prevention Works

We know that prevention works. Time and time again we see studies that show that a dollar spent on preventive health care today can save as much as $15 down the road. Yet we continue to expect doctors to provide their preventive advice free of charge and make their money with diagnostic tests or procedures. We have no health care policy, but by default we have allowed a health care system to develop which is not only very expensive, but in many ways, counterproductive.

Prevention works. We know that immunizations keep kids healthy. But we make the shots to prevent childhood diseases expensive and at times hard to get. For example, many states used to provide some basic immunizations free to doctors and the immunizations were sometimes available free through public health clinics. States, pressured by decreasing federal support, have begun cutting out this practice. For example, we've been told by a representative from the insurance industry that the state of Minnesota stopped supplying free immunizations and at the same time mandated that insurance companies provide free childhood immunizations to policy-holders. This single budget cutting-measure has significantly increased the cost of every Minnesotan's health insurance. This is a fine example of lousy health care policy. The state of Minnesota has now made a fundamental, highly cost-effective health care measure more expensive than it needs to be, and at the same time, increasingly unavailable to all.

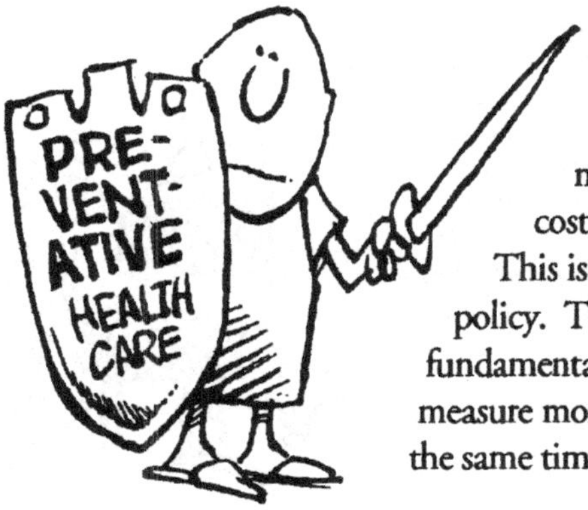

Researching Your Medical Conditions

We have tried to encourage consumers to discuss their medical problems with their doctors, have their doctors outline their treatment options, and encouraged consumers, with the doctor's guidance, to try the less expensive, more economical treatment first, unless there is some good reason not to. If every consumer would follow this guideline when seeking treatment, untold billions of dollars could be saved.

Some doctors will not like this. We suggest you find a doctor who encourages patients to participate in their health care decisions. We encourage consumers to go to another doctor and another if need be, to find a doctor they can work with.

But what do you do if you've tried several doctors and you are unsure that you are getting the best and latest advice? Your only alternative is to research your medical problem yourself.

Start with your library, and an encyclopedia. After you have learned a little basic information about your condition, see if there are any consumer books on the subject. The librarian can help you locate these. If your local library does not have the books you need, the librarian can help you borrow them from other libraries through interlibrary loans.

At the libary, use the Encyclopedia of Associations to locate any special interest organizations which might be able to help you gather information on your condition. There is a subdivision on medical organizations in this book. If your library does not have this reference, ask your librarian for help in locating this type of information.

Have your reference librarian help you search popular magazines for articles on your condition. There are many indexes to popular literature, and the librarian can direct you to the one that will be most helpful in your search. If your library does not have the magazines, you can usually get copies of articles through interlibrary loan services. Large libraries often have access to on-line databases of indexes and abstracts (short summaries of entries). If you cannot personally search the databases, such libraries sometimes offer a research service for a fee, or know of some organization that does.

Once you have researched the popular literature, you should be ready to locate medical journal articles on your condition. Many larger hospitals have medical libraries. You can visit them and ask the librarian to help you locate technical information on your condition. Many of these articles may be beyond your understanding, but journal articles almost always are prefaced by an abstract that tells you the major findings of the study. You can usually understand the conclusions of the research, even if you cannot understand the methodology of the study. You want to collect data. If you need help understanding the results, you can take copies of the the information to your doctors and have them help you interpret the results.

Obviously, this approach is not for everyone. Doctors develop their preferred treatments, and if you are satisfied with the preferred treatment of your doctor, that is fine. But if you are unsatisfied with the treatment options offered you, even from several doctors, then your only recourse is to start researching your condition yourself. You will find that for most conditions, there are probably several approaches to treatment. People respond differently to treatment. Only you, with the help of your doctor, can decide which options are best for you.

Are you playing doctor if you do this? Absolutely not. You are researching your condition so that you, with the advice of your doctor, can make more informed decisions. Once you have gathered your data, take your questions to your doctor.

Is this approach right for everyone? Certainly not. But in this information age, consumers have access to much more data than they ever had before. And if you need that data, we encourage you to use it.

The Health Resource

Consumers can research their medical problems themselves, but if they feel unsure of their abilities to do a thorough job of it, or if they do not have the time for such a task, consumers should know that The Health Resource will do a literature search on medical problems for them.

Why would anyone pay for such a service? One of our group has a family member with Parkinsons. There is considerable variation among doctors about the best time to begin drug therapy. The drugs given this family member caused confusion, but various doctors attributed the confusion to the disease. Not one doctor recommended physical therapy to keep muscle tone in good condition for as long as possible.

The family had written to the various Parkinson's associations for information, and discovered that at least these associations recognized the value of physical therapy. This information also explained that patients react very differently to the various Parkinsons drugs.

Still not totally satisfied with the information they had been able to gather about Parkinsons, they asked The Health Resource to do a search for them, with their particular concerns in mind:

- the complete story on deprenyl (most doctors they asked about side effects claimed it hasn't been used long enough to really know much about possible problems),
- whether the drugs given this family member were causing his confusion,
- what types of physical therapy were recommended with Parkinsons patients.

When they called to order their research report, their questions were carefully noted. They had the report in their hands in a little over a week—a bound volume over two inches thick containing photocopies of articles from both popular magazines and research journals, plus abstracts of other articles. There was a table of contents and a glossary.

Although The Health Resource may well have done Parkinsons reports for others, many of the articles included were clearly chosen in direct answer to this family's specific questions. There were sticky notes among the pages referencing some of their specific concerns.

They found out that deprenyl usually only works in preventing the progression of Parkinsons for about a year, and that it is usually the first drug given. This family member had been started out on other drugs besides deprenyl, and had already been taking deprenyl more than a year. They also found out that with deprenyl, there are many common foods that can cause spikes in blood pressure which can lead to strokes. Not one doctor—not one—had mentioned this.

There were several articles noting a definite difference between the type of eye-hand motor coordination problems that occur in Parkinsons (and makes it very difficult for these patients to do common IQ test tasks like puzzles) and senility or dementia. Confusion, per se, is not necessarily a result of the Parkinsons, and could well be caused by the medications.

When they reported that Sinemet prevented this family member from being able to read, the were told no patients had complained of this problem before. The pharmacological information provided by The Health Resource indicated that vestibular dysfunction (which can cause problems with reading) has been reported with the use of Sinemet.

The cost of this report? Less than the cost for a three-month's supply of deprenyl—which this family member, after consulting with his doctor, decided he should no longer be taking anyway, after reviewing this information.

Reading research reports is not for everyone. And we are not suggesting that patients treat themselves. We are suggesting that if consumers feel unsatisfied with available information, The Health Resource will help them find the information they need to talk about specific treatment issues and options with their doctors. This family member now had the information he needs to address his specific questions in working out the management of his disease with his doctors.

The Health Resource
209 Katherine Drive
Conway, Arkansas 72032

(501) 329-5272

We know prevention works. But our archaic health care system lumbers on like William James's tyrannical machine, throwing good money after bad, following the mesmerizing propaganda that "the market" will resolve all our health care system problems. We're here to tell you those reformers advocating a market solution to our health care system are out to lunch—a very expensive, three-martini lunch that you, the consumer, are paying for. While your health care needs go unmet.

Where Does the Money Come From?

Whenever the issue of universal health care comes up, the question of who pays for the services is not far behind. Hey and Carlson (p. 13) tell us that American's want health care reform, and they want a system that provides the same level and quality of care that they now enjoy, but they don't want to pay any additional taxes for such a system. The writers of these articles, and we have seen many like these, wring their hands and complain that consumers are unrealistic to think that they're going to get all this additional service without paying higher taxes.

We think these pollsters miss the point. We've talked about misleading statistics before (pages 80-84). For example, many pollsters report that consumers demand luxury health care facilities because after all, if you ask consumers if they like wall-to-wall carpeting better than yellowed rubber tile, they say yes. We maintain that if you asked consumers if they would accept yellowed rubber floor tile instead of designer waiting rooms if it meant their doctor bills would go down, they would almost universally tell those asking the questions that they'd rather have lower doctor bills. Many pollsters know which side of the bread to butter. They are capable of casting their questions in such a way that they get the kind of answer that those paying for the poll want to hear. Most of us have had the experience of being asked a yes-or-no question that required an answer somewhere in between black and white. But those collecting the data will often get quite grumpy if you suggest there is more to the answer than a simple yes or no.

Furthermore, we believe that many of the pollsters asking questions about better health care or higher taxes have missed the point. We suspect that when people say they want the same level of care with no new taxes, they may well be indicating that they know our health care system is terribly wasteful. What the

yes-or-no answers may really reflect is the suspicion on the part of consumers that they see no reason whatsoever why every single U.S. citizen couldn't enjoy a very high level of health care without substantially increasing the cost to individuals.

We believe the reform efforts offered to date simply cast in concrete an overly expensive health care system, one our elected representatives simply propose to pay for by increasing taxes. We would prefer to see reform efforts address the factors driving up the costs of health care: too many unused hospital beds, overly expensive outpatient care clinics which duplicate hospital services at a higher price, too many huge hospitals and clinics run expressly for the convenience and profit of owners, unfair inequalities in reimbursements between urban and rural health care facilities, too little readily accessible preventive care, too many expensive procedures and tests, too little effective means of dealing with substandard care either with hospitals or physicians, and understaffing of hands-on caregivers to save administrative positions.

We believe that only consumers can keep the real intent of reform on task. Consumers, we hope, will not feel intimidated by the complexity of the problem. We hope this book provides consumers the encouragement to take an active part in reform that is inevitable. Only consumers can guide the effort to put the *caring* back into our health care system.

The Information Explosion

Many consumers, because of the complexity of health care issues, think they have to leave the decisions to "experts." This is a serious mistake. As Alvin Toffler tells us in *PowerShift* (p. 41), the source of power has undergone two previous revolutions and is in the process of undergoing a third. From the dawn of civilization to feudal times, control was in the hands of whoever had physical power. The biggest military stick was the most powerful. With the industrial revolution, control shifted to those with money.

Toffler (p. 41) tells us that we are in the process of a third revolution, one in which the source of power is passing from those with money to those with information. In short, the personal computer has given individuals access to amounts and kinds of information never before possible, and with access to information, the barriers between, say, professionals such as doctors and their patients, are becoming more and more transparent.

Twenty years ago, consumers generally went to their doctor for a problem, picked up a prescription for some sort of medication, took it to the pharmacy, and had the prescription filled, took it home, downed the medication, and that was that. Chances are, the consumers asked no questions of their doctors about the medication. Chances are the doctor didn't say much about the medication either, except to possibly ask if the patient was allergic to anything.

But times have changed. Now, the doctor not only asks consumers if they are allergic to any medications, but also explains any possible side effects and gives consumers advice about whether to take the medication with meals or to avoid certain foods while on the medication. Consumers may well question doctors about the kinds of outcomes to expect. In other words, there's simply a lot more information available to consumers now. There are a lot more choices to make, and consumers should ask for information and become actively involved in choices about their health care.

Consumers have a vast amount of information

available to them about their medical problems. Popular magazines carry articles about health care. Those with personal computers have access to all kinds of information services. The pharmacist supplies consumers with the drug inserts which explain the chemistry of a prescription as well as all possible side effects. Some pharmacies even have computerized customer data bases where they keep track of consumer prescriptions so they can check for conflicting medications. Various medical schools and hospitals produce newsletters for consumers explaining procedures and health statistics. National organizations exist for many diseases which can supply consumers with specialized information about specific conditions or diseases, including networking for support groups.

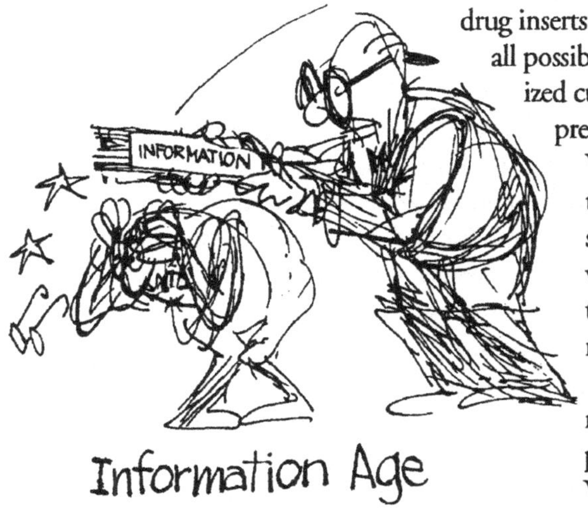

In short, consumers have an incredible wealth of material available to them to learn about their health problems. And with that information comes power. With the kinds of information available to consumers today, consumers have the *power* to take back their health care system. The critical question is, will they?

Consumers must look at these proposed reform bills carefully. It is no longer acceptable to turn important decisions like these over to the "experts." Consumers have the access to the information they need to make knowledgeable decisions about the quality, cost, and effectiveness of their health care and the system which provides it. Health care is not something that only the "experts" can understand. Consumers must monitor what is being proposed and make their wishes known to their elected representatives time and time again.

Consumers Must Take Back Their Health Care System

Consumers need to become actively involved in learning the real causes of our obscenely expensive health care system. Only consumers can bring back a health care system that puts affordable, quality health care above all other considerations. If state and federal legislatures were capable of bringing about meaningful reform, they would have done so long ago. If the medical profession were capable of bringing about meaningful reform, they too would have done so long ago. If consumers do not grasp the reins of reform, the reform measures offered will simply paper over the existing problems with a more

expensive solution. We've already seen that no one—absolutely no one—is addressing the real causes of our health care crisis. Care, even the simplest of care, is too damned expensive.

We don't need a new delivery system. We don't need new administrators. We don't need more health care workers. We don't need more "managed care" folk. We don't need more paperwork. We don't need more esoteric medical specialists. We need to draw the line at $300 a day for hospital beds and say, sorry, all you're going to get is $175 a day. If all the other developed countries can provide quality health care for that price, so can this country. Period.

Oh, spare us the threats that hospitals will close down because they can no longer afford to stay open. There are numerous small hospitals struggling to survive in a system that destines them to failure. Not because these hospitals are being managed poorly, although some of them are. Not because the care they provide is unneeded, because often these hospitals provide the only care for many hundreds of miles around. These hospitals are being driven out of existence by a health care system that does not value access to basic health care for everyone, a health care system that cannot realize any profit in providing such low-tech care, and hence a health care system that would apparently just as soon see this level of care disappear altogether.

Consumers must work for reforms that will bring fair compensation across the country to the caregivers who provide the basic health care we need, including Medicaid and Medicare. Even though every person covered by Medicare pays the same premium, what the government pays a doctor to treat the person covered by Medicare can vary as much as 300 percent. As far as we're concerned, treating bronchitis in Newark, New Jersey, shouldn't be worth more to a doctor than treating bronchitis in Rugby, North Dakota. But Medicare considers it so.

The cost of our health care should not be inflated with paper losses. Medicare pays a set fee to hospitals for treating Medicare patients. Medicare usually pays less for a procedure than hospitals can get from private insurers for the same care, or private insurers plus copayments from the patients. For example, Medicare may pay hospitals $5 for care that they can charge private insurers $10 for, with private insurers covering the full $10, or the patient paying $2 and the insurance company $8. The hospital, for accounting purposes, considers the $5 it does not get from Medicare as a loss, much in the manner it considers charity care. That $5 "loss" shows up later as a loss which many states allow the hospitals to tack on to operating expenses when hospitals go to the insurance companies and state insurance commissioners to ask for higher reimbursement rates. In other words, Medicare pays the hospital what it considers fair reimbursement, but many states allow hospitals to create a paper loss by considering Medicare payments underpayments. We think its time health care providers revealed what their actual costs are and based health care reimbursements on real costs, not paper losses. We believe consumers pay $2 for aspirin in hospitals because hospitals consider themselves underpaid, even when they are paid, and can turn those paper losses into justificataions for higher fees. The average cost of a day in a United States hospital is $360; in other developed countries, $175. We need to make public how hospitals arrive at what they purport to be the cost of their day, and how much of the $360 is based on paper losses.

We need a simple system that does not promote fraud. A simple system that gives consumers access to the real costs of their medical care in a form they can understand, where consumers have real choices about whether they'd like newer wallpaper or less costly care.

If more of the costs of our health care went into compensating the caregivers rather than managers of that care, if the quality of that care were assessed on the basis of patient outcome rather than on administrative process, if problems were corrected by the caregivers and consumers without adversarial wrangling, if administrators of that care were compensated much less grandiosely for buildings, unneeded remodelings, corporate art, real estate boondoggles, and board of director meetings in Acapulco, and if consumers had access to the information they needed to make informed decisions about their health care and took responsibility for those decisions, we suspect that the charlatans would drop out of the medical biz like flies. The field would then be left open for the consumers and the genuine caregivers to take back the business of providing reasonably priced, quality health care services to us all.

Chapter 6 Summary

PROBLEM #1:

We have no national health care policy which spells out what types of care should be available to everyone without restriction.

Issue:

Access to certain types of basic health care—the kinds that we know prevent costly problems later—should be free and accessible to everyone.

Action:

Develop national public policy, perhaps in the manner of Oregon, which spells out the level of care which should be available to everyone without restriction.

PROBLEM #2:

Reimbursement practices encourage health care providers to specialize and practice in urban areas.

Issue:

Rural and sparsely populated areas are short—sometimes critically short—of health care providers and services.

Action:

Do away with the largely artificial distinction between the cost of providing rural care as opposed to urban care.

PROBLEM #3:

Publicly scrutinize the accounting practices of health care providers and begin to disallow paper losses as justification for reimbursement increases.

Issue:

Develop the mechanism for making public knowledge what health care providers pays for items. For example, make public what a hospital pays for an aspirin for which it charges patients $2.00

Action:

Limit markup for health care supplies and services to a certain percentage of the actual cost—not the manufactured paper cost.

PROBLEM #4:

Simplify the heatlh care delivery system.

Issue:

The present system promotes fraud by its very complexity.

Action:

Remove complexity from our health care system, and remove much of the mechanism and motivation for fraud.

Epilogue

Relevant Health Care

Relevant: We need relevant health care. Health care that is a reasonable response to what people need. The sin of modern medicine is irrelevance. Our crisis-oriented health care model was fine 100 years ago, but it is now no longer appropriate. It is irrelevant. It is anachronistic. It is not what we need. And it is terribly wasteful, not only of our health, but also our money.

In order to decrease the cost of medical care, we have to change the way we deliver health care. We spend millions of dollars treating sick children—and letting some of them die—rather than be sure each and every child has the basic immunizations and checkups that they need. We would rather spend untold millions treating victims of stroke and heart disease rather than help these people learn how to change their lifestyles to alleviate their problems before they suffer disabilities or death.

A very large proportion of our health care dollars go to birth and death related expenses. It is generally accepted that half of what a person spends on health care over a lifetime goes to the high cost of dying. In order for the health care delivery system to become relevant, it must be changed from a sickness industry to a wellness industry. We need good prenatal care to prevent or decrease premature births. We need to address social issues—abuse, neglect, depression, learning problems, parenting, child development—all critical to keeping down the numbers of dysfunctional families.

The medical profession needs to start looking at a person as a whole. We have overspecialized and overcompartmentalized the delivery of health care. Depression can take the form of something as simple as an earache that doesn't respond to treatment. In our present system, the earache is treated, and when the standard treatment is unsuccessful, the patient is sent to a specialist in earaches. When the specialist can't stop the earache, the patient is sent to another kind of specialist. The depression often goes unrecognized and untreated. If I spot depression in a patient, the health care system presents me few options in getting my patient the kind of help needed. A relevant health care system would provide the mechanism for dealing with the social problems that cause dysfunction before they become exceedingly expensive, and essentially unsolvable, medical problems.

Relevant care doesn't hang its hopes on medical miracles.

References

Abramovitch, Michael. "8 GI's Last Skirmish in VA Hospital May Lead to Better Medical Care." *The Washington Post* (17 May 1991), A4.

A Guide to Hospital Charges by Diagnosis Related Group No. Bismarck: North Dakota Health Care Data Committee and the State Department of Health and Consolidated Laboratories, 1990, p. 30.

AHIA. See Association of Health Insurance Agents.

Aiken, L.A. and C.F. Mullinix. "The Nurse Shortage: Myth or Reality?" *New England Journal of Medicine 317*, 10, 641-646.

AMA. See American Medical Association.

American Medical Association (AMA). "The AMA Proposal to Improve Access to Affordable, Quality Health Care: A Minimum Benefits Package." *Health Access America.* Chicago, Illinois:The American Medical Association, (n.d.).

Anderson, Jack and Dale Van Atta. "Battling Pharmaceutical Profiteers." *The Washington Post* (17 May 1991), E3.

AP. See Associated Press.

Artz, William E. "Malpractice Problems Persist." *Washington Post Health* (23 July 1991), p. 4.

Associated Press (AP).
Minneapolis, MN. "Cities Hospital Agrees to Pay $750,000 in 7-Year-Old's Death." *The Forum* (1 January 1991), B1.
New York. "Health Care: Old Problem Needs New Solution." *The Forum* (26 January 1991), B3.
St. Paul, MN.
—"Minnesota HMOs Continue Rebound With $51 Million Profit." *The Forum* (31 March 1991), A10.
—"2300 Children Denied Health Care." *The Forum* (2 October 1991), A10.

Association of Health Insurance Agents (AHIA). "Legislative Report." (12 June 1991) p.1.

Atkinson, Carla. "A National Health Plan: Separating Fact From Fiction." *Public Citizen 11*, 4 (July/August 1991), 20-21.

Bazerman, Charles. "Scientific Writing as a Social Act: A Review of the Literature of the Sociology of Science." In *New Essays in Scientific and Technical Communication: Research, Theory, Practice*, ed. P.V. Anderson, J. Brockman, and C.R. Miller. Farmingdale, New York: Baywood Publishing Company, 1983.

Bok, Sissela. *Lying: Moral Choice in Public and Private Life.* New York: Vintage Books, 1979.

Booth, William. "When Medical High Tech Isn't Necessarily Better." *The Washington Post* (29 October 1991), A1, A14.

References

Boston Women's Health Book Collective. *The New Our Bodies, Ourselves.* New York: Simon and Schuster, 1984.

Broeker, Geer, Fletcher & La Fond. "What's Happening to Doctors Today is Enough to Make You Sick. Advertisement in *Minnesota Medicine 72,* 7 (July 1989), 382.

Burke, Edmund C. "Medicine Finds Itself on Solid Ground." *Minnesota Medicine 74,* 9 (September 1991), 5.

Burns, John A *For Profit Hospitals.* Editorial Research Reports (18 July 1986). Washington, D.C.: Congressional Quarterly, 1986.

Broder, David S. "Activist Government Works, Mr. President." *The Washington Post* (19 May 1991), D7.

Bruffee, Kenneth A. "Social Construction, Language, and the Authority of Knowledge: A Bibliographical Essay." *College English 48,* 8 (December 1986), 773-790.

Califano, Joseph. *America's Health Care Revolution: Who Lives? Who Dies? Who Pays?* New York: Random House, 1986.

Carlson, Elliot. "Readers Cry HELP!" *AARP Bulletin* (January 1992), p .1, 14.

Cheney, Lynne V. *Tyrannical Machines: A Report on Educational Practices Gone Wrong and Our Best Hopes for Setting Them Right.* Washington, DC: National Endowment for the Humanities, 1990.

Christensen, Robert D. "President's Letter." *Minnesota Medicine 72,* 10 (October 1989), 599.

Cohn, Victor. "HMOs and Other Managed Care." *Washington Post Family* (24 April 1991), p. 22.

Cooper, Mary H. "Liability Crisis: Is It over?" *Editorial Research Reports* (24 June 1988). Washignton, D.C.: Congressional Quarterly, Inc.

Cox News Service. "Poverty 'Worst' in U.S." *The Forum* (19 September 1991), A1.

Daniels, Norman. "Is the Oregon Rationing Plan Fair?" *Journal of the American Medical Association 265,* 17 (1 May 1991), 2232-2235.

Danovic, Claudia, ed. "Miracles Don't Come Cheap." *The Business of Health Care 1,* 1, (Fall 1991), 1, 4.

Davies, Nicholas E. and Louis H. Felder (1990). "Applying Brakes to the Runaway American Health Care System: A Proposed Agenda.æ" *Journal of the American Medical Association 263,* 1 (5 January 1990),. 73-76.

Day, Kathleen. "Medlantic's Ill-Planned Expansion: Growth Leaves Health Group with Debt, Anemic Ventures." *Washington Business* (10 June 1991), pp. 1, 22-24.

References

Dever, G.E. Alan. *Community Health Analysis.* 2nd ed. Gaithersburg, Maryland: Aspen Publishers, Inc., 1991.

DeVine, Terry . "Is Congress a Morally Bankrupt Body?" *The Forum* (7 October 1991), A4.

Digest, Editor, *The.* A Medical Liability and Risk Management Newsletter. "Case Study: 3 Nurses' Comments, Physician Insensitivity Cited in Lawsuit." *The Digest 19,* 3 (Fall 1991), 4.

Dreyfus, H.L. and S.E. Dreyfus. "Why Skills Cannot be Represented by Rules." In *Advances in Cognitive Psychology,* ed. N.E. Sharkey. Chichester, England: Ellis Horwood, 1986.

"Disciplinary Acts Against Physicians." *Washington Post Health* (18 June 1991), p. 5.

Editorial. "FlimFlam is Raised to Art Form" *The Forum* (18 June 1991), A4.

Economist, Editors, *The.* "Quantum Physics: The Power and Mystery of the Subatomic World," in Jacques Richardson, ed., *Models of Reality: Shaping Thought and Action.* Mt. Airy, Maryland: Lomond, 1984.

Ellwood, Paul M. "Special Report: Shattuck Lecture—Outcomes Management: A Technology of Patient Experience." *New England Journal of Medicine 318,* (9 June 1988) 1549-1556.

Enthoven, Alain C. *Health Plan: The Only Practical Solution to the Soaring Cost of Medical Care.* . Reading, Massachusetts: Addison Wesley, 1980.

Escobar, Gabriel. "Ex-Navy Doctor Practicing Medicine Again." *The Washington Post* (12 May 1991), A12.

"Face to Face."
—Robert H. Anderson, MD. *Minnesota Medicine 72,* 10 (October 1989), 565.
—Paul S. Sanders, MD. *Minnesota Medicine 73,* 12 (December 1990), 13.

Forum, The, Fargo, North Dakota.
—"Blue Cross Names 5 Vice Presidents," (24 August 1991), B3.
—"Blue Cross Promotes Three to Assistant Vice Presdient," (31 August 1991), B3.
—"Blue Cross Promotes 3," (7 September 1991), B8.
—"Blue Cross Names Carlilse to New Post (17 August 1991), B5.
—"Larson Takes Post with Health Insurer," (17 August 1991), A1.

Glazer, Sarah.
—"Policing the Professions." *Editorial Research Reports* (26 May 1989). Washignton, D.C.: Congressional Quarterly, Inc.
—"The Failure to Contain Medical Costs." *Editorial Research Reports* (14 October 1988). Washington, D.C.: Congressional Research Service.

Goleman, Daniel. "Holographic Memory." *Psychology Today* (February 1979), pp. 71-84.

References

Grumbach, Kevin, Thomas Bodenheimer, David Himmelstein, and Steffie Woolhandler. "Liberal Benefits, Conservative Spending: The Physicians for a National Health Program Proposal." *Journal of the American Medical Association* 265, 19 (15 May 1991), 2549-2554.

Harmer, Ruth Mulvey. *American Medical Avarice.* New York: Abelard-Schulman, 1974.

Hatlie, Martin J. "Professional Liability: The Case for Federal Reform." *Journal of the American Medical Association 263,* 4 (26 January 1990), 584, 586.

Health Insurance Association of America. *Source Book of Health Insurance Data: 1990* Washington, D.C.: Health Insurance Association of America, 1991.

Health Letter. "What You Can Do." April 1988, p. 11.

Herman, Robin. "Reducing Alabama's Infant Death Rate." *Washington Post Health* (6 August 1991), pp. 8-9.

Hey, Robert P. and Elliot Carlson. "Health Reform Gridlock?" *AARP Bulletin* (Jaunary 1992), pp. 1, 12-13.

Hofstadter, Douglas R. *Metamagical Themas: Questing for the Essence of Mind and Pattern.* New York: Basic Books, 1985.

Holister, Geoffrey S. "On Modeling, Limits and Understanding: Dennis Meadows Interviewed by Geoffrey S. Holister." In *Models of Reality: Shaping Thought and Action,* ed. Jacques Richardson. Mt. Airy, Maryland: Lomond Publications, 1984.

Inlander, Charles B. and Charles K. MacKay. Medicare Made Easy. Reading, Massachusetts: Addison-Wesley Publishing Co., 1989.

Jencks, Stephen F. "Quality Assurance." *Journal of the American Medical Association 263,* 19 (May 1990), 2679-2680.

Joint Economic Committee, Congress of the United States, Subcommittee on Education and Health. *Medical Alert: A Staff Report Summarizing the Hearings on "The Future of Health Care in America."* Washington, D.C.: U.S. Government Printing Office, 1989.

Kellie, Shirley E. and John T. Kelly. "Medicare Peer Review Organization Preprocedure Review Criteria: An Analysis of Criteria for Three Procedures." *Journal of the American Medical Association 265,* 10 (13 March 1991), 1265-1270.

KFGO-AM, Fargo, North Dakota. News broadcast, 28 May 1991.

Kinsley, Michael. "Quayle and the Lawyers." *The Washington Post* (22 August 1991), p. A23.

Kuhn, Thomas S. *The Structure of Scientific Revolutions.* 2nd ed. Chicago, Illinois: University of Chicago Press, 1970.

References

Kralewski, John E., Janet Shapiro, Hung-Ching Chan, Kevan Edwards, and Yuanli Lui. "Health Insurance Coverage of Minnesota Farm Families." *Minnesota Medicine 73*, 5 (May 1990). pp. 35-38.

Kunnes, Richard. *Your Money or Your Life: Rx for the Medical Market Place.* New York: Dodd, Mead & Company, 1971.

Lacter, Mark. "Nationalized Health Care on the Way." *The Forum* (14 December 1991), p. A4.

Landers, Robert K. *What is Causing the Nurse Shortage?* Editorial Research Report, (25 March 1988). Washington, D.C.: Congressional Quarterly, Inc.

Larson, Kristin. "The National Practitioner Data Bank: From the Physician"s Perspective." *Minnesota Medicine 73*, 9 (September 1990), 35-37.

LeFevre, K.B. *Invention as a Social Act.* Carbondale, Illinois: Southern Illinois University Press, 1987.

Lemish, Jesse. "She Will Die A Victim of Insurance Company's 'Managed Care' Mandate." *The Forum* (17 April 1992), A4.

Localio, A. Russell, Ann G. Lawthers, Troyen A. Brennan, Nan M. Laird, Liesi E. Herbert, Lynn M. Peterson, Joseph P. Newhouse, Paul C. Weiler, and Howard H. Hiatt (1991). "Relation Between Malpractice Claims and Adverse Events Due to Negligence: Results of the Harvard Medical Practice Study III." *The New England Journal of Medicine 325*, 4 (25 July 1991), 245-251.

Los Angeles Daily News. "Study: Uninsured Newborns Get Less Care." *The Forum* (8 March 1992), A9.

Malcolm, Robert (1990). "Little Battles." *The Journal of the American Medical Association 263*, 1 (5 January 1990), 90.

Mann, Judy.
—"The Abandoned U.S. Child." *The Washington Post* (12 July 1991), B3.
—"Trading Career for National Dialogue. *The Washington Post* (7 June 1991), BC.

Manthey, Marie
—1988. "Myths That Threaten." *Nursing Management 19*, 6, 54-55.
—1988. "Primary Practice Partners." *Nursing Management, 19*, 3, 58-59.
—1989. "An Expert Answers Common Questions About Primary Nursing. *Nursing Management 23*, 3, 22-24.

Marshall, Patrick G. "Setting Limits on Medical Care." *Editorial Research Reports.* Washington, D.C.: Congressional Quarterly, Inc., 1990.

McEwen, Craig. "Medical Group Head Seeks Rural Health Care Changes." *The Forum* (13 October 1991), C2.

References

McGinn, Paul R. "Doctor Discipline Actions Leveling Off." *American Medical News* (3 August 1990), p. 3, 25.

Melloni's Illustrated Medical Dictionary. Ida Dox, Biagio John Melloni, and Gilbert M. Eisner, eds. Baltimore, Maryland: The Williams & Wilkins Co, 1979.

Meyer, Charles. "A Crisis in Spirit." *Minnesota Medicine* 2, 8 (August 1989), 451.

Meyer, Harvey. "...With Liberty and Access to All: Minnesota's Quest for Guaranteed Affordable Health Insurance. *Minnesota Medicine 73*, 5 (May 1990), 27-33.

Minnesota House of Representatives. "HealthRight Bill Approved." *Session Weekly 9*, 12 (24 April 1992), 17-20.

Minnesota Medical Association. "The Health Care Quality Improvement Act." *Minnesota Medicine 72*, 10 (October 1989), 593-595.

Moriarity, Joe. "The Duluth-Petrozavodsk Connection: Doctors Exchange Knowledge, Culture." *Minnesota Medicine 74*, 9 (September 1991), 18-23.

Moseby Medical Encyclopedia, The. Walter D. Glanze, Kenneth N. Anderson, and Lois E. Anderson, eds. New York: New American Library, 1985.

Mullinix, C. F. "Research on Influences Affecting Availability of Resources for Patient Care Delivery." In proceedings of a conference at the National Institutes of Health, Bethesda, Maryland: U.S. Department of Health and Human Services, U.S. Public Health Service, National Institutes of Health, 1988, pp. 11-15.

News Clips.
—"Record HMO Profits." *Minnesota Medicine 73*, 5 (May 1990), 49.
—"Image Boosting." *Minnesota Medicine 74*, 10 (October 1991), 51.
—"Infant Mortality and the Uninsured." *Minnesota Medicine 73*, 5 (May 1990), 49.
—"Living/Related Lung Donor." *Minnesota Medicine 74*, 6 (June 1991), 47.
—"Misleading Statistics." *Minnesota Medicine 72*, 8 (August 1989), 449.
— " HMOs See Record Profits. " *Minnesota Medicine 74*, 5 (May 1991), 43.
—"Twin Cities Health Care Costs." *Minnesota Medicine 72*, 9 (September 1989), 531.
—"Uninsured Hospital Patients." *Minnesota Medicine 74*, 3 (March 1991), 45.

News Upfront. "Health Care Wasteland." *Public Citizen 11*, 4 (July/August 1991), 5.

New York Times. "Plan to Trim Medicare Costs Targets Outpatient Services." *The Forum* (9 June 1991), A6.

Oppenheim, M. "Can This Really Be Quality Control." *Minnesota Medicine 72*, 9 (September 1989), 507.

Pflaum, Douglas D. "Reaping the Rewards of Rural Practice." *Minnesota Medicine 74*, 5 (May 1991), 7-9.

References

Potts, Mark. "CEOs Get a Bigger Piece of the Pie." *Washington Business* (15 July 1991), pp. 1, 20-21.

Preston, Julia. "Brazil's Soaring Rate of Surgical Births." *Washington Post Health* (10 September 1991), p. 6.

Priest, Dana. "Health Care a Major Concern on Hill's Civil Service Agenda." *The Washington Post* (8 April 1991), A15.

Quam. Lois. "Universal Health Insurance Would Be Best Route to Medical Cost Efficiency." *St. Paul Pioneer Press* (16 May 1991), editorial page.

Rabchuk, Esther. Personnel communication, 8 November 1991.

Ralston, Jeannie. "Applachian Blues." *American Medical News* (10 August 1990), pp. 19-20.

Reece, Richard L.
—"A Look at Today's Hospital Board." *Minnesota Medicine 73*, 11 (November 1990), 9-12.
—"A New Breed of Physician and a New Brand of Cost Containment." *Minnesota Medicine 72*, 7 (July 1989), 387-390.
—"I Bid You Farewell." Minnesota Medicine 73, 12 (December 1990), p. 7
—"Editor's Notebook." *Minnesota Medicine 72*, 7 (July 1989), 383.

Rich, Spencer.
—"Employers Becoming Pharmacist, Physician." *The Washington Post* (6 March 1991), A1.
—"Health Care Paperwork Called Wasted." *The Washington Post* (2 May 1991), A-1, A-16.
—"Rich Got Richer, Poor Got Poorer, Study Says." *The Washington Post* (24 July1991),A4.
—"State Medicaid Payments Faulted as Too Low." *The Washington Post* (2 July 1991). A5.
—"Tracing Medical Costs to Social Problems." *The Washington Post* (28 August 1991) A21.

Rovner, Sandy. "Risk of Breast Cancer Rises to 1 in 9 American Women." *Washington Post Health* (5 February 1991), p. 5.

Rover, Sandy and David Streitfeld. "Insuring Good Health: A Bill to Protect VolunteerTreating the District's Poor." *The Washington Post* (3 June 1991), C5.

Rowen, Hobart. "Poor People in Rich America." *The Washington Post* (4 July 1991), A15.

Russo, Marty. "Health Care: There Is a Plan That Works." *The Washington Post* (9 October 1991), A19.

Samuelson, Robert J.
—"Medicaid Monster." *The Washington Post* (15 May 1991), A19.
—"The Numbskull Factor," *The Washington Post* (26 June 1991), A19.

Sandok, Mary. "Carlson Says Health Package Commits State to Access." *The Forum* (24 April 1992), B1.

References

Schmidt, Susan. "S&L Buyers Big Givers to Candidates." *The Washington Post* (10 July 1991), C1.

Sinclair, Molly. "Hill Hospital Closes Out 103-Year Era." *The Washington Post* (6 March 1991), D1, D2..

Sisk, Jane. *The Quality of Medical Care: Information for Consumers.* Washington, DC: Office of Technology Assessment, 1988.

Siwek, Jay. "What is a Family Physician?" *Washington Post Health* (24 September 1991), p. 15.

Solberg, Leif I. "What is CQI?" *Communicating Quality Initiatives 1*, 1 (Fall 1991), p. 2.

Specter, Michael. "Medicaid's Malady: New York's Poor Relegated to Storefront 'Mills'." *The Washington Post* (8 July 1991), A1, A8.

Springer, Patrick.
—"Fargo Clinic Sets Major Cutbacks." *The Forum* (16 January 1992), A1, A18.
—"Many Rural N.D., Minnesota Hospitals are on Critical List." *The Forum* (4 November 1991), A1.
—"New Medicare System is Bad News for N.D." *The Forum* (8 December 1991), D1,D12.
—"N.D. Care Group Questions Medicaid Screening Expenses." *The Forum* (2 February 1992), A1.

Squires, Sally.
—"New NIH Chief Backs Transplant Ban." *The Washington Post* (16 April 1991), A5.
—"U.S. Immunization Campaign Struggles." Washington Post Health (22 October 1991), pp. 6-7.

Stapen, Candyce H. "Rx for a Physician." *The Washington Post* (2 May 1991), D5.

Stiegler, Farrell S. "Private Quality Assurance Companies: Our Enemy from Within." *Minnesota Medicine 72*, 9 (September 1989), 505-506.

Taber's Cyclopedic Medical Dictionary. Ed. and rev. Clayton L. Thomas, MD. 12th ed. Philadelphia, Pennsylvania: F.A. Davis Company, 1968.

Taylor, Paul. "One Stop' Prenatal Care System Urged." *The Washington Post* (24 April 1991), A19.

Thompkins, Richard B.
—"Evaluating Technology's True Value." *Minnesota Medicine 74* , 7 (July 1991), p. 41.
—"MMA Could Ensure Educational Role for Peer Review." *Minnesota Medicine 74*, 9 (September 1991), 41.
—"Payment Reform Takes a Turn for the Worse." *Minnesota Medicine 74*, 8 (August 1991), 35.

Thompson, Larry. "The High Cost of Rare Diseases." *Washington Post Health* (25 June 1991), pp. 10, 12.

References

Toffler, Alvin. *Power Shift: Knowledge, Wealth, and Violence at the Edge of the 21st Century.* New York: Bantam Books, 1991.

Torry, Saundra. "Malpractice Settlement Sets Off Dispute Over Doctors' Databank." *Washington Business* (1 April 1991), p. 5.

Turner, Raymond W. "Desperate in D.C." *The Washington Post* (21 April 1991), B8.

U.S. Department of Health and Human Services. *Cesarean Childbirth.* Report of a Concensus Development Conference Sponsored by the National Institute of Child Health and Human Development in Conjunction with the National Center for Health for Health Care Technology and Assisted by the Office for Medical Applications Research. September 22-24, 1980. National Institutes of Health, Bethesda, MD. NIH Pub. No. 82-2067, October 1981.

Veres, Robert N. "Solving the Health Insurance Puzzle." *Your Company* (Fall 1990), pp. 32-37.

Wallach, Edward M. "When a Child is Brain Damaged." *Contemporary OB/GYN* (September 1990), pp. 11-12, 15-16.

Waxman, Henry A. "Research that Could Save Lives." *The Washington Post* (21 May 1991), A21.

Webster's Sevventh New Collegiate Dictionary. Springfield, Massachusetts: G.&C. Merrian Company, 1963.

Will, George. "How It Came to This." *The Washington Post* (10 October 1991), A24.

Wilmar, Harry A. "About the Men of Mettle: University of Minnesota Medical School 1936-1940." *Minnesota Medicine 73,* 12 (December 1990), 19-23.

Wohl, Stanley. *The Medical Industrial Complex.* New York: Harmony Books, 1984.

Woolhandler, S. and D.U. Himmelstein. "The Deteriorating Administrative Efficiency of the U.S. Health Care System." *The New England Journal of Medicine 324,* 18 (2 May 1991), 1253-1258.

World Almanac and Book of Facts: 1991, The. Hoffman, Mark S., ed. New York: World Almanac, 1991.

Wright, John W. *The American Almanac of Jobs and Salaries.* New York: Avon Books, 1987.

Young, Richard E., Alton L. Becker, and Kenneth L. Pike. *Rhetoric Discovery and Change.* San Diego, California: Harcourt Brace Jovanovich, 1970.

Chapter 3: Rationing Health Care the Insurance Way

A basic level of health care should be free and accessible to everybody.

Insurance companies should revise reimbursement practices, evaluating preventive procedures and scrutinizing the costs of health care relative to improved results.

Insurance companies need to develop ways to quickly identify those procedures which can be more economically performed in doctor's offices than in hospitals.

Involve the insurance industry in designing uniform claims forms that consumers can read and understand.

Chapter 4: The Nursing Shortage

Remove unreasonable barriers which prevent two- and three-year nurses from practicing their profession and upgrading their degrees.

Hospitals should hire persons with training appropriate to the task and let nurses devote their time to doing what they are trained—and paid—to do.

Require hospitals to use nurses appropriately and hire aides, orderlies, and ward clerks to do non-nursing tasks.

Chapter 5: Doctors, Lawyers, and Liability

The health problems of consumers need to be taken care of, and blame—and hence malpractice suits—are irrelevant to providing that care.

Health care reform needs to address how to efficiently identify harmful health care providers and correct the problems.

Health care reform needs to remove the issue of blame from the issue of compensation, providing consumers with whatever care they need to solve the health problem.

Data on outcomes for hospitals, clinics, and doctors should be available to consumers.

Chapter 6: Quality Health Care For All

Develop national public policy, perhaps in the manner of Oregon, which spells out the level of care which should be available to everyone without restriction.

Do away with the largely artificial distinction between the cost of providing rural care as opposed to urban care.

Limit markup for health care supplies and services to a certain percentage of the actual cost—not the manufactured paper cost.

Remove complexity from our health care system, and remove much of the mechanism and motivation for fraud.

(continued from inside front cover)

Find Out What's Wrong With Our Health Care System!

- why we have a health care crisis,
- when our health care system veered towards self-destruction,
- why efforts to reform our health care system have failed, and
- why consumers must take over the reins of health care reform.

ISBN 0-9632244-0-9
90000>
9 780963 224408

Made in the USA
Monee, IL
04 November 2026

67377576R00144